![Garda Síochána Retired Members Association]

"The Garda Síochána Retired Members Association
are delighted to support our member, Tim Doyle,
for undertaking the very important research in
*Changing of the Guard* outlining the struggles of
Jack Marrinan, who was a central and pivotal figure
in the modernisation of An Garda Síochána over a
considerable period."

Mick Lernihan, General Secretary GSRMA.

# CHANGING
## *of the*
# GUARD

——

Jack Marrinan's battle to modernise
An Garda Síochána

TIM DOYLE

CURRACH
BOOKS

First published in 2021 by

 CURRACHBOOKS

Block 3b, Bracken Business Park, Bracken Road Sandyford
Dublin 18, D18 K277
www.currachbooks.com

ISBN: 978-178218-929-9

Set in Adobe Garamond Pro 11/15 and Essones Display Light
Cover and book design by Alba Esteban | Currach Books
Cover picture by Julien Behal | Alamy Stock Photo
Printed by Hussar Books, Poland

This book took 10 years to write, 10 years I wouldn't have had were it not for three wonderful people at Dublin's Mater Hospital, Renal Consultant Nephrologist Dr Denise Sadlier, Clinic Supervisor Elaine Mannix and Ann Marie Mulligan who painstakingly coaxed me into learning how to live with Peritoneal Dialysis. And just before Christmas 2017, Mr Richard Power, Consultant Urologist and Transplant Surgeon and his team at Beaumont Hospital gave me – literally a new lease of life – a kidney transplant. I have no words to adequately express my gratitude to all who looked after me throughout, nor to the organ donor's family for their priceless gift. I dedicate this book to them all; to my wife Agnes, my rock throughout; and my amazing grandchildren, Barra, Béibhinn, Senan, Darragh, Tadhg, Fiachra and Michael.

# CONTENTS

# 1

## Jack Marrinan joins
## An Garda Síochána

Like all the best stories this one begins at the end, with Jack Marrinan's son John rummaging in the attic of his childhood home and discovering that there was much of his father's life he knew little about. The first clue lay in his clothes.

'For as long as I was aware, Dad dressed in either a suit or a pair of slacks, a shirt and nearly always some sort of sports jacket. He had his favourite jackets, but they all looked the same to me. He loved a pinstripe suit. I don't remember him ever having a head of anything other than snow-white hair, which was managed by a metal comb that he always kept in his breast pocket, two and a half prongs missing.

'I was the youngest child in the family, born in the 1970s and by then his garda uniform, his tunic, had long since been put away. I'd come across it though, when I was sent to the attic to bring something back to earth. Sent to locate the Christmas decorations or something else my mother needed, I'd look into a bag or an old suitcase and see the uniform there. To me it was a costume. I never gave it much attention, unlike the accompanying pair of truncheons - one brown and one black, both with leather straps to keep them tethered to the wrist. I can't imagine Dad ever had much call to use them because to me he was such a gentle man, someone who could talk rather than beat any situation into submission.

'The last time I came across his uniform was when my mother was moving house after he passed away in 2015. At this stage it was just dawning on me that it deserved a bit more attention. I had met many of his old colleagues and friends around the time of his funeral, all of whom had a story to tell about their time with Dad. There were also letters sent to my mother, expressing gratitude for something he helped them with during his time in the GRA. All stories from a part of his life that had more or less passed me by. Stories from a time in his life that I should know more about.

'After the funeral I met Tim Doyle [the author of this book]. He pulled me aside and told me of how Dad had helped him out during his time as a garda and how he was compelled many years later to contact him. I think it was during these meetings with my father that the idea of this book was born.

'I'm not sure how my Dad viewed the uniform he kept in the attic, but he never got rid of it. I realised that it represented the garda rank that he held for his entire career, a rank of which he was very proud. I had never noticed before that one of the pockets carried his old *Oifig an tSolathair* (State Stationery Office) notebook with details of his encounters on the beat when he worked out of Rathfarnham Garda Station, entries made around the time of the Macushla revolt. I'm not sure if he would have been aware when he put it in his pocket for the last time that he'd never be adding to it again.

'When I was young, Dad's job was probably a bit of a novelty to me. He seemed to be on the radio or the television a lot. We'd have the television on when he was due to appear and we'd all watch, but I'm not sure I ever listened to what he said. But whatever he was saying, he gave the impression that he knew what he was talking about. When he wasn't on the news, he was listening to the news, whether it was on the car radio or the tv.

'The job also took him away from the house, into the office and around the world. So he was away for a long time. The phone was always ringing at home and when I'd pick it up, I wouldn't know if he was upstairs, in the office or at a conference or something. I remember answering the phone to someone asking was he at home. I called to my mother, "Is Dad home?" And she replied: "No, he's in America".

'I know now that his job was done under great pressure, but at the time I never noticed him releasing it at home. He was always good humoured and funny. He got angry with me probably only a couple of times, so rare that I was slightly shocked when it happened. But maybe the fact that he had to have a heart bypass in his 50s suggested the job bore more heavily upon him than I had ever realised. I'm sure my mother knew.

'My other experiences of his work were going into his office in Phibsboro Tower, sometimes the Phoenix Park or Dublin Castle. There was a very impressive letter packing machine and a franking machine in Phibsboro Tower; machines he was not let near because he had a poor track record with technology, despite his fascination with it. I think the first time he used a Banklink machine he broke it as a frustrated queue grew behind him.

'His talents lay elsewhere. When I was in college I met another student whose father knew or worked with mine. He told me his father said Dad was "a tough bastard of a negotiator", meaning it in the most complimentary sense. I was kind of impressed. The man I knew at home was nothing like that. At home he seemed very conservative. He was very conservative. But his job was as a trade unionist.

'At the time too, I probably learned how hard he worked when he was in the job. He asked me once how many hours of lectures my course involved. "About 20", I said. This was a pitiful amount to him and he said to me, "Would you not do Arts as well?"

'His colleagues were also his great friends. I'd say it was no accident that he surrounded himself with such decent people, people who remained his friends right until the end.

'Tim Doyle says he hopes that this book fills in some of the blank pages in Dad's garda notebook which I found in his tunic pocket in the attic.'

\*       \*       \*

Jack Marrinan was born in Lisdoonvarna, Co. Clare in 1933. Both his parents came from Kilkee. His father Thomas was a builder, and his mother Mary Heaney's people were shoemakers. Thomas and Mary married when she was just 19, and they found a house to live in at Lisdoonvarna - just a house, no land. Their first son Tommy was born in 1925. Eight years later, Jack, the second son, was born on 10 June 1933. The gap came about because his father had to emigrate to Manchester to get work for some years after his first son was born. Jack's birth was soon followed by seven more siblings: Micheál, Nuala, Oliver, Rose, Dympna, Josephine and Mary.

Their mother Mary had trained as a dressmaker, and she knew that education mattered for her growing family. She enrolled Jack at the Christian Brothers school in Ennistymon, where he said the main lesson he learned was to be a good listener. He relished the seven-mile cycle to and from school. Maths and English were his favourite subjects. He got a good Leaving Certificate and became an auxiliary primary school teacher at schools in Doolin, Kilshanny and Carron in the heart of the Burren. He often covered 15 miles a day on his bike. His pal Mick Guthrie, who was working as a clerk of works with McNamara builders, was a noted Gaelic footballer on the look-out, like many young men, for a safe civil service job with a pension.

Secure jobs were as scarce as hen's teeth. One day Mick had exciting news: the Garda Síochána were recruiting. If a young man was tall enough and passed a none-too-difficult written examination, he would be sent to Dublin for a medical examination. Passing that he would get a free uniform and accommodation, be trained as a garda and after 30 years be entitled to a good pension. Like its predecessor the Royal Irish Constabulary, garda recruitment came mainly from the western seaboard. The presence of big strapping fellows at any disturbance is a useful means of calming inflamed situations, or so it was thought.

Both young men went to Limerick city for the written test in early 1953. The examination room was relaxed, and the subjects consisted of Irish, English, Mathematics and Geography. In the Irish section someone asked the Irish for soup. Jack answered – annrai.

Bill Ryan from Nenagh was also sitting the test that day – he later became a superintendent. Jack and Mick Guthrie returned to Clare on tenterhooks waiting to see what news the post might bring. Jack soon got a call to go to Lisdoonvarna station to be measured by Sergeant Bill Kelly. Being measured for the guards was a significant rite of passage. Mick Guthrie and Jack Marrinan were then called to the Garda Depot in the Phoenix Park in Dublin in November 1953.

At the depot Sergeant John Casserly called the daily roll. Each new recruit was assigned a number from the first day of joining. The very first member to join on 9 February 1922 was number 1 and other 'long numbers' followed in sequence from that. Jack's registered number was 10449. Clare men who joined at the same time as Jack are listed in Appendix 1.

Casserly had a typed list of surnames and numbers, but after a week he could call out the numbers from memory. Everyone answered smartly, except on Sunday morning when a few would be missing having been out late the previous night. He never made an issue of a nil response. In retirement, Jack recalled those days:

'The intake of recruits was divided into nine per room, with miserable outside toilets. My classmates included Paddy Faherty, an unusual man, who could mount several chairs on top of each other, grip the bottom one with one hand and raise the lot overhead. There were two other lads with me from Clare, Mick Hanrahan and my good friend Mick Guthrie.

'One young lad was from the Gaeltacht west of Ireland. His name was Padraig Breathnach, and his registered number was 10608. He was fluent in Irish but had very little English. He was let go; the rumour was that he was too slow on the uptake. The truth was he didn't have enough English. He was very upset at this, and rather than go home, he took the boat to England.'

Bernard King from Mayo also sat the 1953 examination. He still has the documents he received at the time. They tell us that of the 550 young men who sat the test that year, almost 100 failed, mainly because of poor Irish. The November intake took 240 from the top of the qualifying list. Both Jack and Bernard were in that group, and Jack was then known as Sean O Mearnain. Bernard claims that he never heard Jack using his Irish names. One day an instructor enquired if any of the class had experience of hairdressing. Instantly Jack's hand was up, and he became assistant to the depot barber. Jack did well in all subjects and not surprisingly came top of his class in debating.

After six months of training Jack passed out on 22 April 1954. He was the last member to be allocated a station. His posting was to Rathfarnham; a south Dublin station, even though it was part of the Dublin-Wicklow Division. Rathfarnham was seen as a 'good station', half Dublin suburb, half rural. The building was on Butterfield Avenue which linked the village with the rural hinterland. He had two capable skippers (sergeants), Molloy and Morris.

One would take an interest in this smart young recruit, while the other was more interested in discipline, a word to strike terror into young recruits.

On Jack's first day in Rathfarnham, he got a typical Tir Conaill welcome from Donegal Garda Brian Kelly. 'Bernard James Kelly, long number 9710. I've prepared a nest upstairs for you with warm blue blankets.' Sergeant Morris had told Kelly that there was a young recruit arriving. 'I was brushing and tidying up when he arrived. I came to attention and saluted the recruit, who answered to the name of Jack Marrinan.'

First impressions were good.

'Jack was an up-front individual, highly intelligent and saw [the big picture] outside the job as it was at the time. He had a streak of toughness and didn't back down in any debate, whether with colleagues or those of high rank. He was studious and always had a big book on his lap, and could recite off what he was reading. He was a generous comrade and would never pass a cake shop without buying a Swiss roll. At teatime he would produce the cáca milis and put it on the table for the lads.' (This is taken from a conversation with retired Superintendent Brian Kelly in 2004.)

Leo Maher, a Dubliner from Stoneybatter, was the superintendent in Rathfarnham. That made him a rare bird in the gardaí where almost all the members came from rural parts. Maher took a long hard look at the latest recruit.

'Have you pull?', he asked, meaning political influence.

'No sir'.

'Anyone belonging to you in The Job?', meaning did he have any relations who were guards.

'Not a soul, sir'.

Jack had fond memories of another colleague. Jim Quinn was a native of Co. Roscommon and a famous county Gaelic footballer. When serving in Rathfarnham he quit and emigrated to America. After being drafted into the American army he saw service in Fort Benning, Georgia. In 1950 he returned home as part of the New York Gaelic football team. They beat Cavan in the national league final, after which he re-joined the Gardaí and served until retirement.

Ger Connolly from Cork, who joined the force in 1955, was another station colleague. He recalled a telling incident:

'I had Jack Marrinan and John Paul McMahon as colleagues in Rathfarnham station. It was a Sunday evening in 1958 and Kerry and Derry were at it in the All-Ireland football semi-final. It was pre-television days, so the radio was tuned into Micheal O'Hehir's commentary on Radio Eireann. JP was probably the only Kerry man in history who had no interest in the game. He was ensconced in the station mess hall, devouring tracts of Sheehan's *Law of Evidence*, determined to pass the Garda inspectors' exam. Jack was seated across from him, fielding questions and drop-kicking them back. The action between them was every bit as heated as it was in Croke Park, with John Paul reading definitions aloud before handing the book to Jack and asking him to put the question to him. Over and over again, JP gave the answer, only for Jack to shake his head and say he'd got it wrong. Finally, Jack closed the book and JP went at it again.

'"Wrong again" shouted Jack.

'"How do you know?" roared JP.

'"I have it off by heart" replied the indefatigable Marrinan.'

McMahon was set on getting promotion and he did, eventually becoming a deputy Commissioner. Jack Marrinan could see the way his colleague was thinking and saw the sense in it. He tried to enrol to study law at Kings Inns, but the bureaucracy defeated him. Then an advertisement for part-time courses in Trinity College Dublin caught his eye, and with the encouragement of Sergeant Molloy he applied. There was an unexpected problem. The Catholic

Archbishop of Dublin, John Charles McQuaid, had forbidden the faithful in his diocese to attend Trinity College as it was a Protestant institution. Jack asked a local priest what he should do.

A short time later, Sergeant Molloy collared him.

'Do you go to Mass?'

'Of course'.

Jack asked why the sergeant wanted to know.

'The parish priest was enquiring'.

The enquiring Rathfarnham parish priest, Canon Thomas O'Donnell, was a religious conservative who, despite frowning on dances in his parish, was a decent and thoughtful man. He carefully examined his archbishop's ruling on Catholics attending Trinity. The ban was not an outright one. A Catholic could seek permission to attend Trinity. O'Donnell was anxious to do right by a keen young parishioner with a good attitude. He recommended to McQuaid that as Marrinan was a mature adult, a member of the police and a practising Catholic, he should be given permission to attend the university. McQuaid agreed. The archbishop, who forgot nothing, would have good reason to remember this young Clareman the next time they met.

With the blessing of two conservative Catholic clerics, Marrinan found himself sitting in a lecture hall in a bastion of Protestantism beside another Catholic. Andy O'Mahony had got a similar dispensation – as the procedure was known – from his bishop in Waterford. He went on to be a prominent writer and broadcaster who worked for RTE and the BBC.

Meanwhile the *Clare Champion* was keeping an eye on the progress of the young man from Lisdoonvarna.[1] Under a headline reading 'Talented Garda', it reported that John Marrinan had recently passed his final interview for promotion to the rank of sergeant. While attending night lectures (the Protestant university was not

---

1    Photo of cutting available from Tim Doyle.

mentioned) this talented young garda had secured BA, B Comm and Dip PA (Bachelor of Arts and of Commerce and Diploma in Public Administration) qualifications.

There were other developments. From early on in his posting to Rathfarnham, Jack had spotted a girl in Washington Park near the station. She had plenty of admirers and was not in any hurry to get married. One night in the mid 1950s, Mary Dempsey, then an 18-year-old who had just completed her Leaving Certificate examination, attended a dance in the Crystal Ballroom on Dublin's South Anne Street. A young man asked her to dance. He introduced himself as Jack Marrinan; later she gave him her phone number.

Mary worked in her mother's bakery shop in Crumlin. 'They were very innocent days' she recalls. 'We were aware of each other for a long time. Jack knew where I was – and I knew where he was.' And there it stayed for a while.

'In Rathfarnham, I worked away in uniform and occasionally as a buckshee crime detective' Jack later recalled. 'One day I discovered a cache of stolen property hidden in bushes near Milltown golf club. A great sack of teapots and silverware. The crime lads had a prisoner charged before the sack was emptied. I didn't get a mention on the information route, nor was there a sign of form A26, which was a commendation for good police duty'.

That was one lesson learned. Others would follow. When Jack Marrinan passed the sergeants' examination there was no immediate prospect of promotion. On paper he was well qualified but when he sought promotion he was refused. He felt that his superintendent was blocking him on the grounds that he was more interested in books and book learning than becoming an effective policeman. A rank-and-file policeman with degrees from Trinity College and a diploma in public administration looked like a square peg in a round hole. Surely, he would shortly be moving on to a position more suited to one with his qualifications, a desk job in the Garda

Depot perhaps. The answer to that question was a partial yes, but not in the way the superintendent who asked it expected.

The expanding suburbs around Rathfarnham were home to two important figures in Irish life, both founding fathers of the new state, and they were both provided with garda protection. One had been Taoiseach, the other would become one. Strictly speaking, William T Cosgrave was the first president of the Irish Executive Council from 1922 to 1932. That title was later changed to Taoiseach. Now retired, and living quietly in Scholarstown Road, he was provided with an official driver, and Jack became one of his two drivers. The one-day on/one day off rota left plenty of time for attendance at college and the study that went with it. Jack was occasionally posted to stand guard outside Taoiseach Sean Lemass's modest bungalow in Churchtown, close to the newly opened Landscape Cinema, and Mary Dempsey sometimes found herself in the neighbourhood and stopped to chat to Jack.

After de Valera, Lemass was the most significant member of Fianna Fáil. He became Taoiseach in 1959 when Eamon de Valera was elected president. Both Cosgrave and Lemass had been vulnerable to attack in earlier years. They been on opposing sides in the Civil War and Noel Lemass, brother of Sean, had been murdered in 1923 by pro-Treaty forces. From the anti-Treaty side, the IRA had murdered Cosgrave's deputy Kevin O'Higgins in 1927.

But passions cooled over the years and driving Cosgrave to yet another funeral of an old comrade, or helping Kathleen Lemass, wife of Sean, to unpack her shopping from the basket of the upstairs model bicycle she used to ride around Churchtown was about the height of the excitement these duties provided. It was ideal for a studious and ambitious young guard.

In the station Jack Marrinan was beginning to make his presence felt, even though with the promotion route blocked, there were not many opportunities. His Rathfarnham colleagues already knew that he could argue his case. In many jobs at the time trade union representation provided an outlet for talent like his. However, the Garda Síochána was a disciplined force, so there were no trade unions. Admittedly there was an institution called the Joint Garda Joint Representative Body (JGRB) which was supposed to represent all ranks. Gardaí elected representatives who could make submissions on matters of concern. In practice the process was lethargic and dominated by senior officers. As far as the younger members were concerned, the JGRB proved to be useless when it came to dealing with serious matters like pay and discipline.

When Marrinan joined in 1953, new recruits were paid less, in spending terms, than the first recruits joining in 1922 who were now retiring and needed to be replaced. And the harsh rules of discipline belonged to the RIC era, having been formulated in the 19th century. Chief Superintendent Tom Collins who ran the JGRB was the link between the men and women in the force and the Garda Commissioner. He had been an army cadet and it was said that in his young days he taught French in St Flannan's, Ennis. If gardaí wished to make a pay claim it passed through Collins to the Garda Commissioner, with no guarantee it would reach the Minister for Justice.

There was a story doing the rounds about JGRB representatives meeting in the Garda Depot library. The door burst open, and a senior officer demanded to know what they were at.

'Looking for a pay increase', was the answer.

'Get back to your stations', were the last words on that claim.

Jack was aware that there could be opportunities outside the force. One day he spotted an advertisement looking for an assistant inspector in the Rhodesian police. He had completed the application form when his cousin Marty called and asked how he was getting on.

When he relayed his plans, Marty responded, 'That's the lowest job for a white man in the Rhodesian police'.

Back in Rathfarnham Jack Marrinan and Mary Dempsey had been growing closer. 'He was a very captivating man' Mary said, 'things happened when you were with him.' But they didn't happen between them until after they had known each other for a few years. A step at a time, their lives became enmeshed. When he became involved in the Irish language debating society in Trinity College, she went along to support him.

In the meantime, a distinctly unmusical – one might say discordant – interlude in another Dublin dancehall one wintry night in 1961 was to change the pattern of their lives in a way neither could possibly have imagined. And this was to rock the Garda Síochána and the administration of justice in Ireland to its very foundations.

To understand what happened at a run-of-the-mill Dublin dancehall off Amiens Street, one must go back to 1922 when the Garda Síochána was formed. The majority of those who joined in 1922 and afterwards were young men, some as young as 19. After training, the new guard was expected to live in single quarters at the allocated police station, which usually had one suite of married quarters for married sergeants. The force had adopted the RIC practice of a life spent in barracks unless permission had been granted to 'live out'. Even up to 1952, many guards worked in barracks that were uncomfortable and unsuitable. By then most of the force lived in rented accommodation, with a rent allowance to soften the blow.

By the 1950s most of that first intake had their 30-year stint done, and they were retired or were about to. In the 1950s major recruitment occurred and these young men – joined by young women – who replaced the pioneers had greater expectations of what a decent standard of living involved. It was only a matter of time before an explosion occurred. Following the second world war, the world had changed and Ireland – belatedly – was changing with it.

The police force that Jack Marrinan had joined in 1953 was falling short on four main fronts and the younger intake took the brunt of them. Living quarters were a big problem for a force which was largely staffed by people who had to leave their home places to join. Pay, already mentioned, was another crucial one, and representation – the need for a representative association recognised in a meaningful way by the command structure in the Garda Síochána and Department of Justice – was the third front. The fourth was the cruel way in which an antiquated code of discipline was being imposed by some officers. This will be dealt with later in this account.

In the 1950s there was one big difference, and it would prove crucial. The average age of members was dropping fast. Whereas in 1926, more than 90% of guards were below the age of 30 and most of them were under 25, by 1950 the majority were between 45 and 57. More than 3,500 retired in the 1950s and when they did, the trouble began.

The 'second generation' simply could not live away from home on the low pay the job brought. Nor would they tolerate the Dickensian barracks which their predecessors had endured. Their lot compared unfavourably with other jobs where trade unions could serve claims and obtain improvements, going on strike if necessary. Gardaí were not allowed to strike, and this meant that in seeking improvements in pay and conditions, they were fighting with their hands tied.

Now the Departments of Finance and Justice, which had overall responsibility for the force, were about to be confronted by a new problem: the rank-and-file were about to find among its ranks a new voice, a new articulate leader to confront that of the establishment.

For most workers, and the guards were no exception, there had been little improvement in the standard of living since the 1930s and little prospect of any. It was a cruel time to try to house and feed a young family in a country with underdeveloped social services. In increasing numbers trade unions were winning pay increases and the great battle for what were known as 'relativities' began. If you couldn't win a cost-of-living increase on its merits, say increased productivity, you could try to get one on the basis that someone else doing the same or similar work was being paid more.

The Civil Service had developed an internal 'conciliation and arbitration' scheme to handle pay claims in an orderly fashion. Some said that it was merely a stalling device. Either way, the Garda Síochána had been excluded until 1959, and thus a useful negotiating mechanism/safety valve was not available. Relativities were not much use as a bargaining tool either in a state with one police force. In the 1950s, with no plan B, tax revenues stagnant at best, governments of differing political stripes fought public service pay claims. The 6,000 members of the Garda Síochána were left seething in barracks large and small throughout the country in a period of noisy industrial relations unrest. More than half a million people had left Ireland looking for work in the years between 1946 and 1960. 'Most countries send out oil or iron, steel or gold, or some other crop, but Ireland has had only one export and that is its people' President John F Kennedy noted on his trip to Ireland in 1963.

For the gardaí of Jack Marrinan's generation, pay was the most obvious flashpoint. The pay of first-time joiners in 1922 was £3.10 shillings per week. In 1924 it was reduced to £3. In 1952 it was £5. The nominal sum had changed, but 30 years had elapsed and the spending power was no greater. Between 1953 and 1963, a total of 456 members resigned, two thirds of whom were in the first five years of service.

In 1959 Harold Macmillan had won a British general election by telling people 'You've never had it so good'. At home, Taoiseach Sean Lemass expressed himself more laconically. 'A rising tide lifts all boats'. But some boats remained beached on the arid shores of the economic austerity which had been a feature of Irish life since independence. The six thousand strong Garda Síochána was on the sharp end of this. On 21 December 1960, arising from an agreed recommendation of the Conciliation Council, garda rent allowance, which varied from £17 to £62 per annum, was abolished and replaced by a flat yearly payment of £65; with a caveat that £52 would be deducted at the rate of £1 per week for official accommodation. The *Garda Review* welcomed the award, but younger members of the force were not pleased to discover that the balance of £13 would be wiped out by the tax due on the £65.

A year later, on 1 November 1961, the internal conciliation council increased the salary of gardaí with six years' service to £11.2.0, rising to £14 for members on maximum salary. Members with five years or less service, those recently recruited to replace the early joiners, got nothing. They had their hopes pinned on a basic starting pay of £10 per week.

Michael Murphy, then a garda and later a superintendent, explained how that had happened: 'At that time all ranks in the force were represented by one body presided over by a chief superintendent. In 1961 a pay increase was awarded. Chiefs and supers got £4.50 and £3.50 respectively. Inspectors and sergeants benefitted by £2.50 and £1.75. A garda on maximum pay got £1.50, while members with over five years' service got 20 pence, and those with five years or less got nothing. There was even a suggestion that there should be a reduction in salary for the latter group'.

And this was the last straw. There had been warning signals, but they were ignored. The Garda Joint Representation Board (JGRB), then in existence, sought to be included in the public service conciliation and arbitration scheme, and put its case to Minister for Justice Oscar Traynor, who in 1957 accepted the claim should be conceded. The Department of Justice took up the cudgels in 1958, telling the Department of Finance that there was a problem with gardaí morale that needed to be addressed. The mandarins in Merrion Street, who were fighting against conciliation and arbitration being extended to higher ranks in the civil service, were having none of it, and delivered a telling off to their colleagues in the Department of Justice, the JGRB and by implication, the Garda Commissioner Daniel Costigan.

A letter from the JGRB to the Department of Justice had given great offence. According to Garda historian Gregory Allen[2], the letter recalled Minister for Justice Oscar Traynor's acceptance of the case, expressed outrage at the exclusion of officers and the use of threats against the other representative bodies.

This prompted the Department of Justice to send a stinker of a note. Not a reply, because the impertinent letter did not merit such. Accusing the gardaí of 'want of propriety' in addressing the Minister in such terms, the departmental note accused the JGRB of including false accusations 'made in a deliberately disrespectful way'. The original offending letter was probably drafted by Chief Superintendent Tom Collins and the indignant note of rejection by Peter Berry who would shortly become secretary of the Department of Justice, according to Allen's account of this episode. The JGRB had fought and lost. The war would continue by other means, and the opening shot would be fired in a dancehall near Amiens Street station, under a banner held aloft by 800 angry young men. It is hard to believe that industrial relations could be conducted in such a primitive way in recent times, and the obduracy of the higher echelons of the civil service – independent Ireland's 'brightest and best' – was truly worrying.

While Jack Marrinan enjoyed the cut and thrust of his daily job and the company of the band of brothers in Rathfarnham station in particular, he was becoming more and more conscious that they were not being fairly paid. From his half-in/half-out vantage point of almost a decade as a rank and file policeman with the

---

2    The Garda Síochána, Policing Independent Ireland 1922-82, Gregory Allen, Gill & Macmillan Dublin, 1999, pp.155-60.

added perspective of university education, Marrinan could sense the unrest building up. He didn't know then that he would become the voice of the second wave of gardaí. But he did take his pen in hand and compose a letter to the editor of the Dublin *Evening Mail* which triggered off a sequence of events that was to heavily influence policing in Ireland for three decades to come. Signed by a 'Concerned Member', it told of the appalling pay rates and working conditions being endured by gardaí as they operated under harsh disciplinary rules and regulations from the 19th century Royal Irish Constabulary rulebook.

The vivid language employed by the anonymous letter-writer provoked strong feelings within the garda force, mainly among younger members. Many were convinced that it was time for action. For their part senior officers were shocked by this impertinence and wanted to know the identity of the agitator.

The traditional singer Joe Heaney from Connemara was a popular performer at the time. One of his most popular songs went 'What would you do when the kettle boils over?' The question of what was to be done about discontent in the police was about to be answered. The kettle finally boiled over on a rainy night in Dublin in November 1961, in the dingy back streets around Amiens Street station, now known as Connolly station.

# 2

## Mayhem at the
## Macushla Ballroom

Ireland was beginning to change in 1961. A visit from Prince Rainier of Monaco. and his Irish-American bride Grace Kelly gave a much-needed lift to national prestige. Photographs of the young royal couple with the ageing president Eamon de Valera and his wife Sinéad were proof that a small, recently independent country had taken its place on the world stage.

An Irish officer Sean Mac Eoin, was appointed commander of UN peace-keeping forces in the Congo. In June 1961, a Patrician Congress was held in Ireland to mark the 1,500th anniversary of the arrival of St. Patrick in Ireland. Some 90,000 faithful attended an open-air Mass in the Phoenix Park in Dublin, with the wonderfully exotic bearded Papal Legate Cardinal Peter Gregory Agagianian from Armenia presiding, and red robed cardinals Doepfner, Castro, Giobbe, and Marella, in support.

The domestic economy was at last beginning to show signs of growth. Although the 1961 census would show the population at its very lowest figure since the famine, 2.8 million, the population may already have begun to climb. By the end of the year, Ireland would have its own television service. Many homes would soon have a flickering screen in the corner, bringing the world in black-and-white to ordinary citizens' firesides. Brand names like Bush, Phillips and Pye were on everyone's lips. Change was in the air as the first post-war generation approached adulthood. Nothing was spared. In Rome Pope John XXIII had already announced that the second Vatican Council would shortly meet to consider how the Catholic Church could achieve spiritual renewal and reach out to others in a joint quest for Christian unity.

For another view, let's see how it was for one young garda. Gerry Denn had joined the force in 1955, part of an influx of young men replacing the first joiners, now reaching retirement age. Come 1961, garda pay was low, and his cohort reckoned they had been promised a rise. He described the furore when the young guards realised that for them the so-called pay rise was in fact a pay cut.

'In late 1961 I was a patrol car driver covering Store Street and Fitzgibbon Street stations. The previous decade had seen thousands of young men joining. About 60 of us single members lived in the top three floors of Fitzgibbon Street station, near Croke Park, which were given over to garda accommodation, and we had a mess hall cum canteen there. It was a hive of activity with members on the three-relief 24-hour duty roster coming and going.[3]

'Due to the strictness and rigid enforcement of the discipline we hardly had a thought of our own and did what we were told. Money was fierce scarce and if a garment of uniform or a pair of shoes went missing the first place to check was the pawn.

'As most of us had under five years' service we were excluded from the November 1961 pay award, and that raised hackles.

3    Members of the station included: John Collins, Paddy and Eamon Moriarty, Michael Murphy, Donie and Ned Slattery, Tom Bennett, Joe Dunleavy and Bill Kavanagh, Paddy Moore, Joe O'Connell, Mick Guthrie (Jack Marrinan's friend from Clare), John Joe Reilly, Mick McDermott, Mick Moran, Joe Power, Tim Hurley Jim Cleary, Jim Liston, Mick Coyle, Tom Langan and Paddy Irwin.

However, it was when the authorities began to charge £1 per week for our beds, that the melting pot of rebellion began to simmer.'

If the senior ranks had given the matter any thought, they would have realised that allowing Dublin superintendents to vet the recruits during training and allowing them to 'cherry-pick' the tallest young men was going to lead to stations like Fitzgibbon Street bursting at the seams with big volatile and underpaid young men whose energies could prove difficult to contain.

'The mess hall (canteen) was our haven where we drew a long breath in the wake of duty and a brief exhale prior to heading out. Dan Hanrahan was the messman, in charge of the canteen. He was armed with a bread knife instead of a baton, the best of grub with a full kettle constantly on the boil for fresh tea. He was also the fountain of all the news, and gossip.'[4]

Denn couldn't remember the exact moment when the grumbling turned to revolt.

'But in a short space of time the upper floors of Fitz Street became a ventilation forum for young members, including lads from nearby stations who trooped in the back entrance via Charles Lane. Dan Hanrahan had the key of the canteen door and when the clamour got deafening, he locked the door.

'The public offices on the first floor were manned by senior gardaí, and a station sergeant by the name of Barney Clinton. One late October evening Barney appeared in the mess. His manner was affable, and having called for quiet, he spoke.

---

4    Joe Dunleavy had been the messman prior to Dan's appointment and he had a list of those who lived in at the time. They included: Tom Reilly, John Dwyer, Jim and Paddy Daly, Patrick Tansey, Patrick Kennedy, John O'Connor, John Conroy, Tony O'Donoghue, Tom Mooney, Gerry Courtney, Mick Hanrahan, Paddy Farrell, Brian Sheehan, Con Hearty, Jarlath Lee, Michael McDermott, Dan Sullivan, Martin O'Hora, Vincent Boyle, Dick Fitzgerald, Tom Forde, Hugh Byrne, Barney Mullen, Mell McGarry, John O'Keeffe, Tom Byrne, Michael McKeown, John Flaherty, P J Cullen, Leo Plunkett, Patrick Reynolds, Andy Moran, Liam Scannell, Aiden Forde, Gerry Denn, Dan McHale and Colm Mellett.

'"Gentlemen. Could I enquire as to what's going on?"

'Mick Harlowe from Kevin Street said, "We're having a chat".

'"I can hear that from my public office. But I must inform you all that this meeting is both illegal and unauthorised and as the member in charge of this Garda station I cannot allow it to continue." With a half about turn the station sergeant added, "However, should ye wish to meet outside the precincts I'll not interfere."

'At the time, any rank above ours was swathed with authority. You did what you were told, full stop. If Barney had not added that rider our protest would probably have disintegrated. With 'meet outside the precincts' ringing in our ears we left the station and re-assembled at Croke Park's canal end.'

Gerry Denn believed that moving the meeting away from Fitzgibbon Street station was a watershed. Now they were 'on their own turf' at Croke Park, free to say and do what they wished. The notion of the Macushla meeting was born there and then. The sergeant probably never realised the effect of his words.

'Croke Park was a familiar haunt where we often gathered for crowd control duty at GAA matches. Indeed, Mayo's Tom Langan – who could bend a long ball long before David Beckham was born – and Paddy Irwin had won All-Ireland medals there in the 1950s. All present were consumed with fervour and the chat back and forth rose to a crescendo. Except for the fact that we were policemen we would be guilty of disorderly conduct.

'There was no great order or plan, but the lads I've already mentioned, along with Dick Keating from Pearse Street, the Bridewell's Dave Walsh, Donie Murphy and Tom Bennett, between us all we came up with the idea of an indoor open meeting and the Macushla ballroom seemed an ideal venue.

'Virtually all of us had danced in the Macushla. Located at the intersection of Foley Street, Buckingham and Amiens Street, I knew the proprietor, a decent Belfast man, Eric Lavery. He taught dancing and used to run dances at weekends. He had great time for the lads and would ring the station inviting us to his dance hall. It was all free gratis and for nothing. I don't believe much money changed hands for our use of the hall on the night of the Macushla. Perhaps it was the first and only time that he had a full house.'

For the young guards the Macushla hall was ideal, large and centrally located, near Amiens Street (Connolly) railway station and close to Store Street and Fitzgibbon street stations. It didn't much matter to them that the surroundings were not very salubrious.

Notices began to appear in Garda stations about a meeting in the Macushla dance hall on Saturday 4 November 1961. Jack Marrinan, whose name does not figure in any of the pre-Macushla excitements, recalled those notices. Speaking in retirement[5], he described the reaction in Rathfarnham: 'There was talk of a garda meeting the following evening in the Macushla dance hall, Foley street, in the Dublin north inner city. I told my sergeant I was attending. He pretended not to hear.' Marrinan had heard that a Store Street detective named Dick Keating and some colleagues had booked the hall and gotten some circulars printed.

In the days preceding the Macushla meeting in Dublin 1961, there had been some worries about a chilling precedent in Britain. In 1919 a committee had been appointed under the chairmanship of Lord Desborough to report on the pay and conditions of service of the English, Welsh and Scottish police. The forces called a strike for trade union status. More than 2,000 police went on the picket line. They were sacked and never reinstated. For a garda with long service it would be a career death sentence to be sacked: no job, no pension, no prospects.

That could happen here. Section 14 of the Garda Síochána Act 1924 stated that if any person causes dissatisfaction among members of the garda force, or induces or attempts to induce, or does

5    To Tim Doyle.

any act calculated to induce any member of An Garda Síochána to withhold his services, or to commit a breach of discipline, they shall be guilty of a misdemeanour. Section 6 of the 1924/1942 disciplinary regulations directed that it is a disciplinary breach of the garda code for any member to call or attend any unauthorised meeting to discuss any matter concerning the force.

On Saturday morning 4 November 1961, a young Store Street garda, Paddy Garvey, was approached by Inspector Dawson who said that there was an unauthorised garda meeting in the Macushla hall that evening and asked him if he knew of any way it could be prevented. Paddy simply replied that he didn't. Dawson had been reading newspaper reports saying that the Macushla meeting was taking place that day, mentioning the unrest among younger gardaí. During the week gone by in central Dublin, there had been a go-slow, the reports said, gardaí on point duty were not making the usual efforts to keep the traffic flowing, and motorists were not best pleased. Another aspect of the protest was more welcome to the public. Parking restrictions were not being enforced. On the morning of the Macushla meeting, *The Irish Times* published a cartoon of a car being parked illegally under the nose of a garda who took no notice. The driver is asking the policeman: 'Is it true that you aren't happy in your work?'

Here's Jack Marrinan's own account of going to the meeting on Saturday night:

'Approaching the Macushla entrance I fell under the gaze of a line-up of light blue [uniform] garda inspectors. It was a strange feeling walking past them. They reeked of authority and infallibility. For the most part they ruled in fear holding a pen and a half sheet[6] in one hand and the code of conduct in the other. However, none of them expressed or demonstrated any intent to halt my progress.

6    A half sheet was a single foolscap page which directed individual gardaí to explain any matter relating to their behaviour or attention to duty.

'The hall was bedlam. Gardaí fill a lot of space and I estimated their number to be in the late hundreds. I had never seen so many huge specimens of manhood clumped together, almost bursting the walls. My initial thoughts were that these men had been sworn in to uphold law and order; here they were creating massive disorder.'

Many of those present appeared to have tried to conceal their identity, with caps and scarves deployed to ensure maximum anonymity. Jack put this down to genuine fears about the security of their jobs, their families and pensions.

John Collins recalled the excitement.

'Prior to and during the Macushla I was in Fitzgibbon Street, a hotbed of agitation. Dan Hanrahan, Gerry Denn, and Donie Murphy had a few bun boards plastered with notices of the Macushla meeting. Donie had a big printing machine for making placards in his home. We sent a local youngster to put them on the walls around the Macushla. An inspector spotted him and told him to display them nearer the hall!'

As Jack Marrinan and others were converging on Foley Street, Bill Herlihy began his shift as a section sergeant in Store Street.

'There was talk of members of garda rank holding an unauthorised meeting in a nearby dance hall later that evening. This was contrary to the disciplinary regulations, which were strictly enforced at the time. Prior to going on outdoor duty Inspector Albert Dawson directed me to accompany him to the hall. He was a popular officer of Church of Ireland persuasion and as we walked towards the Macushla, gardaí were gathering from all directions. There was no outward sign of their intention and as they walked casually past us, they saluted and didn't appear to be in any way furtive. Under the Amiens Street railway bridge Albert stopped and said to me, "My eyesight is failing a good bit, and you still have 30 years to serve in this job, so it might be more beneficial to your career if you made yourself useful somewhere else."'

Herlihy took the hint kindly and vamoosed.

John Relihan from Knockanure, Co. Kerry, had joined the gardaí in July of that year. Just before noon on 4 November Larry Wren, then a training instructor – later Garda Commissioner, strode into their classroom in the Garda Depot and said that an unauthorised meeting was being held that evening in Dublin's north inner city. He stressed that if any recruit attended, they may as well not come back to training.

Later, Relihan's classmate Mick Clifford from Killarney nudged him and said, 'Are you going to that meeting?'

'Sure, we're barred'.

'That's it so. Let other lads put their heads on the chopper on your behalf. I'm going no matter what'.

That night both young recruits made their way to the Macushla ballroom. John Relihan later recalled that the place was jammed with gardaí, all of whom seemed to be shouting abuse at an invisible protagonist. When Dublin Metropolitan Area representatives went on stage, and especially when one young garda clambered up and spoke, things cooled down, Relihan recalled. The lad who spoke was slight for a garda, many of the others dwarfed him. Marrinan was his name, and he was from Clare, and he had an air of authority that the noisy speakers lacked.

On 5 July 1961 Sligo-born Aidan Byrne began training at the Garda Depot. Next to him in the roll was Kerry native Jim Clifford. On Friday of the first week of November, word of the Macushla meeting swept through the depot. Byrne recalled:

'Leaders are bred in a crisis and I had one of the best beside me, so when Jim whispered that he was attending, I gave him the nod. We agreed that if we were sacked, we would head for London.

'The approach to the Macushla hall was lined with Sam Brownes [senior officers wore a special type of belt with an extra diagonal leather strip] staring hard-faced at each of us. Every one of them was a stranger, so we figured they didn't know us either. We got in and went upstairs to the balcony, as the main hall was not a safe place for recruits. It was an amazing sight, all those huge, agitated men packed in like sardines.

'There were gardaí on the stage. They were trying to get the house in order. They would be there yet only for a young garda, Jack Marrinan, who spoke words that caused the agitation to abate. Inspector Tim O'Brien, a well-respected officer, came in and was greeted by a storm of boos. Marrinan's calm words caused the rumpus to subside. O'Brien said his piece and left, after which Marrinan formed a committee which he chaired.'

The level of excitement and indeed fury was mounting. One garda present remembered it – and what had brought him to attend – vividly.

'I joined the job in the early 1950s when there was no other option but the emigrant boat. When news came to my home place [a West of Ireland fishing community] that I was to become a garda I was treated like a celebrity. The night before I left for training neighbours had a ceili.

'I got through the training and because of my height I was sent to Dublin's city centre. At first parade my sergeant sized me up and commented that my long arms would be useful for keeping city traffic moving. Each day I would be on a traffic point keeping the population of Dublin on the move. I loved it. Imagine being paid for having a smile, saluting people, swivelling on the balls of my feet, and swinging my arms. Things I inherited from back home; the fishing, the strokehaulin' and the gaffin', the haulin' of the currach … they were all hard labour. Garda duty I could do in my sleep.

'Off duty was a different reality. All the shops, but not enough money to post a letter home, buy a pair of socks or a hanky. Living-in with a station full of grousers. Money meant a few notes rolled up around a few coins, minus a quid for a shakedown [rent], rooming with a football team of the biggest men that ever snored.

'The Macushla was a dangerous place to be if one wasn't in control of their faculties. Gardaí are armed with loud voices and expect people to listen when they talk. Packed into the ballroom, the exchanges became a shouting match. I had a mind to make my escape when a young garda was called onto the stage. "That's Jack Marrinan", someone whispered. I had never heard of him, but the next few seconds will live as long as my memory. He stood silently in a dignified, and non-threatening, un-police-like manner. The clamour dribbled away.

'A knock on the door. The hall quietened, like a light switch. The voice of authority spoke demanding entry. Mayhem erupted worse than ever. Chants of "No. No. Out. Out." Marrinan raised his hands. The bedlam subsided. Marrinan spoke calmly, "If we refuse entry we are playing into their hands and our cause will be lost forever. Open the door." Immediately the door was opened, and inspectors Tim O'Brien and Albert Dawson entered. After saying a few words they left, and Marrinan took over.'

Jack Marrinan recalled:

'The meeting was out of control, and there appeared to be no agenda. Dave Walsh, a staunch supporter from the Bridewell, had a broken leg in plaster. He kept banging it against the floor and shouting, "The Commissioner is worse than Hitler". Another member present remarked that Dave Walsh would need winkers with a double bit to keep him quiet.'

Most of the men present were completely overtaken by the excitement of the moment. 'Huge men swelled to twice their normal size. I didn't know how the walls of the Macushla withstood them', said Mick Connaughton, a garda photographer who attended. 'Hundreds of the biggest men in the state were shouting and roaring as one. For the first and only time in my garda service I was afraid, he said. Perhaps because of his photographic background, he saw the assembly in visual terms. It was a cauldron, he said. As a garda he had experience of having to break up street disorder. 'This was different', he said, 'members were consumed with fury.'

'There was a call for representatives from the Dublin Metropolitan Area to go on stage. Bray-based garda Acton pushed up a Rathcoole-based member named McSweeney. He went up all right but wasn't long coming down. In the excitement he forgot he was on the sergeants' list [for promotion]. Jack Marrinan was called up on stage by John Acton.'

In Marrinan's own words:

'I had no sooner faced the crowd than I heard and saw someone down the back roaring about government authority. Having noted that the loud-mouth individual was too small to be a garda I went down. He was still shouting out against Charles Haughey, the Minister for Justice. He got a mighty cheer. He was Councillor Sean Loftus.[7] I explained to him that it was a garda meeting, and he had not been invited. He was slow about carrying out my command to leave, and I had to use as much force as was necessary to remove him. I got booed for my trouble.'

That was when the two inspectors came to the door. Marrinan insisted they be admitted. A slight lull followed. Inspector Tim O'Brien said he was checking on the dance hall licence. Small Tim Twomey, a Kevin Street member, roared: "There'll be no one effin' dancing here tonight". Marrinan recalled that, 'O'Brien spoke calmly, saying that while he accepted that we were trying to solve our grievances, we were going about it in the wrong way.

'During their visit I don't recall seeing the inspectors taking out a book or noting names. I felt that feelings were running so high that if a notebook was produced it would not have gone back in the pocket.

7    Loftus was an independent member of Dublin Corporation, with a penchant for self-publicity. He had a tactic of changing his name by deed poll to publicise campaigns he pursued. Later he called himself Sean Dublin Bay Rockall Loftus.

'A Special Branch member produced his notebook to record my personal phone number for future contact. Suddenly, my closest ally Dick Keating swooped and whipped the book from his grasp. Later, Dick explained that he thought the man was making notes of those attending, or other furtive activities. Feelings were running that high.

'Again, a call went up for district representatives to assemble on stage. One member from each Dublin garda district was invited up. I was again nominated by Garda John Acton[8] and seconded. There was a heated objection – "he's from the country". At the time Rathfarnham was regarded as a country station rather than a city one. However, my colleagues from Bray held tough and I remained on stage. I believe when the gathering saw their own local members on stage, they cooled down a little.'

According to Joe Dunleavy from Fitzgibbon Street, 'There wasn't a squeak when a square blocky Clare man, Jack Marrinan, was called on to the stage. His presence filled every pair of eyes. I didn't know what I expected but I was astounded how he put words on our thoughts. Like a light switch the gloom doom evaporated.'

Jack recalled that stage of the meeting:

'It was all very disorganised with no chairman, or agenda. I suppose I helped to bring order and guidance to the proceedings. Addressing the gathering, I said that it was critical to spread the word throughout the force and get the backing of members countrywide. A few members from Cork invited me to travel and address their local members, and I agreed to chair their meetings.'

Eamonn O Fiachain was one of those present who spoke from the platform. He represented members in the Technical Bureau. He recalled speakers giving loud speeches, against the government, against senior garda officers and even against the Special Branch, though what it had to do with garda pay was not clear.

'I felt we were going nowhere until Garda Jack Marrinan stood

8    From Glin, Co. Limerick and stationed in Bray Co. Wicklow.

up. He was so calm and authoritative. Deliberate and thoughtful, he put words on most of the moderates and cooled the hotheads. I was hugely impressed with him and would follow him to hell.'

In fact, O Fiachain thought that by speaking out in public he had contravened garda regulations, so he never turned up for work the following day. It came as a surprise to him that he was not disciplined and could resume duty as if nothing had happened.

Michael Cecil Cawley was the station beat man in Store Street that night, dealing with personal callers, phone calls and prisoners and keeping the station sergeant in the picture on what was going on. After the Macushla ended, 'a cavalcade of high ranks took the front door off its hinges' he recalled. 'They charged in, commandeered all the phones, whipped out notebooks and began ringing their stations.' Some were shouting so loudly they didn't really need phones, Cawley said. 'They called out the names of all their gardaí and demanded to know if they had attended the meeting.' All this was done in the sight and hearing of Cawley and his sergeant, 'That despicable act will never leave my memory', he said, adding that if the officers deployed such fervour fighting criminals instead of their colleagues, Dublin would have been crime free that weekend.

Ger (Jeremiah) Connolly had joined the force in 1955. Following training he was allocated to Rathfarnham station. He had a vivid recollection of the immediate aftermath of the Macushla.

'I didn't attend as I was on the 2 pm to 10 pm shift that evening. In my opinion it happened with no great plan or design. It got legs, took off and nearly lost them. I know one thing for certain – Jack Marrinan and Dick Keating ran the show. Marrinan served in my station; he was educated, and more especially intelligent. He had an amazing control of his thoughts and expressions, as well as leadership qualities. In a profession accustomed to obeying rigid 'do this, do that' directives, he spoke passionately, yet reasonably, and in my opinion he out-thought, out-talked and out-lasted the great thick men of the job. Dick Keating was cool; he would give a wink, slant his head sideways, curl his lip, and communicate with short pertinent bursts.'

Marrinan, having guided the meeting from chaos to a kind of consensus, was now at the centre of a storm. The next day, Sunday, was like no previous Sabbath, with non-stop phone calls. 'The talk was of mayhem in the gardaí. An awful lot of loose talk. Policemen are the ultimate rumourmongers, and every member had a question, an answer, or an opinion, so much that it's almost impossible to hammer out a coherent plan', Ger Connolly said.

Back in Fitzgibbon Street Gerry Denn clearly recalls the aftermath.

'The next day was Sunday, a day of rest; in my case neither the mind nor body could come to terms with the previous evening's unreal episode. Monday dawned like they all do. The Macushla mayhem was like sulphur. The name of a young west Clare garda Jack Marrinan was in our thoughts as we waited breathlessly for the hammer of discipline to fall. Officers were falling over one another clutching half sheets. They had been empowered to stamp out the embers of the Macushla blaze with the harshest discipline. The split between young gardaí and higher authority became a chasm.

'Post-Macushla was an unreal and fearful time. All the goings-on shook me to the core of my being, almost an out of body experience during which I felt so nervous or unsure of my future as a garda. The usual banter had vanished. It was every man for himself.'

In short order Joe Dunleavy and Gerry Denn were served with D1 disciplinary forms. This was a very serious sanction, involving a summons to appear before senior officers at a hearing which could lead to a recommendation to dismissal from the force. It stated, 'That you Garda [name] … on 4th November 1961 did attend an unauthorised meeting at Macushla Hall, contrary to regulations.'

They felt like criminals, not gardaí sworn to uphold the law, they said. Joe Dunleavy recalled he had been asleep in the dormitory in Fitzgibbon Street when his deep slumber was invaded by a growling station sergeant, McManus. 'He shouted me to attention and read the dreaded disciplinary form that was the D1 [form] accusing me of attending an unauthorised meeting.'

The word was that Store Street and Fitzgibbon Street stations were 'confettied' with D1s, the ultimate disciplinary action and a certain prelude to sacking. 'Senior officers were all over the place', Denn said.

'We had a new inspector Albert Dawson. He was a Protestant, and I didn't know what to make of him. The week after the Macushla I met him on duty. He whispered, "How's it going?" I shrugged. He responded, "Keep it up. Ye have them."'

On Monday superintendents in many Dublin stations handed out D1 forms to 116 guards thought to have been present at the Macushla ballroom the previous Saturday. Each man was required to sign the form saying that he had not attended an unauthorised meeting, nor would he do so in the future.

Marrinan and his colleagues consulted an eminent lawyer and former Taoiseach, John A Costello, who advised the men who received the D1 forms to sign them saying that they had not attended an unauthorised meeting – as they understood the term unauthorised. This advice was hand delivered to garda stations. When it appeared on the Fitzgibbon Street notice board, Gerry Denn and the others were mightily relieved, and signed the form with the suggested disclaimer.

On Monday, Jack Marrinan had been about to travel south to meet like-minded gardaí in Cork and Limerick, when a phone call from the Department of Justice asked him if he would be available to meet the Minister. He agreed to defer his trip, but nothing came of the suggested meeting. Ger Connolly recalled that postponement. 'On Monday a meeting was arranged for Cork. It was cancelled as Jack was called to the justice department. Jack, Dick, Donie Murphy and myself went to Cork the following day. I drove a big Ford Consul car. I remarked to Jack:

'"This thing will die on its feet."

'"Not if we keep hold of it and control it", he replied.'

'The weekend and early into the following week was unreal', Marrinan said later. 'District representatives, who had been appointed during the Macushla, met several times. Donie Murphy used his Clontarf home to hold meetings. A Department of Posts and Telegraph official tipped him off that his phone was being tapped. Jack recalled that time:

'I was on call all over the country. I had to defer the Limerick meeting as we had got another call from the secretary of the Department of Justice requesting another meeting. Again, there was no developments.

'Mid-week we held a meeting in Pearse Street detective office. Dick Keating was attached to that unit. We were very close. An SDU (Special Detective Unit) member arrived, and when Dick spotted him, they had words. The conversation ceased with Dick giving him a belt and knocking him into the fireplace. SDU men were suspected of collaboration with higher authority, though they collected a lot of money for the cause.'

Pearse Street detective Dick Keating was Marrinan's right-hand-man throughout this period. He was a native of Nicholastown Castle, Grange, Clonmel, Co. Tipperary, and attended Clonmel High School. His father Thomas was a well-known bloodstock breeder, and Dick and his two brothers John and Michael represented their county in hurling and football. He had four years' Garda service and would later serve as a detective sergeant in Whitehall station until retirement.

'It was decided to hold another rally in Bray on Sunday 12 November. Bray in Co. Wicklow was close to Dublin and coincidentally the Assistant Commissioner in charge of the DMA, William P. Quinn lived just around the corner from the garda station.'

Michael McNamara, a native of Killaloe, Co. Clare, had joined the force in 1959. Apart from a short stint in Togher, Cork City, he spent his service in Cobh, Co. Cork. A few days after the Dublin Macushla he attended a garda meeting in Cork city, which was held in the CYMS hall. There were four 'Sam Brownes' on duty outside, but they didn't interfere. Later when they were directed to identify those who attended, they responded that they didn't recognise anyone, or so the story went.

At the Cork meeting there was a full turnout of gardaí from Togher, which was McNamara's station, and the hall raised a mighty cheer when the Dublin members arrived. They spoke well; especially Jack Marrinan, he said, and the gathering was very receptive to what was said about money and hours of duty. McNamara recalled a colleague saying that even if they got half the shillings they were looking for, he might be able to get a loan for a car.

'On Wednesday Dick, Jack, Tom and myself headed for a meeting in Limerick. Michael Murphy, a young member stationed in Fitzgibbon street, had a sister nursing in that city, and got a lift down to see her. The meeting was in the Mechanics' Institute and an officer spotted the bold Mick. He must have put him on paper [reported him] as Mick was sacked with the Macushlaites', Ger Connolly recalled.

The Minister for Justice, Charles Haughey, on Tuesday had said that once discipline had been restored, he would undertake an examination of the existing negotiating machinery available to the gardaí and if it proved wanting, improvements would be made. This was a major concession. Reading Haughey's statement, it appeared that the young guards had won. The issues they had been protesting about were at last going to be dealt with. The Minister had blinked first. But the problem was the genie of revolt was out of the bottle.

Back in Dublin the tension in the stations was building. On that Wednesday gardaí were making a public protest. Members on point duty stopping traffic were allowing only a small number of vehicles to move on. As most major junctions had guards on point duty controlling the traffic, this caused mayhem at rush-hour. It was also a very public display of defiance. Trivial offences such as illegal parking and illegal street trading continued to be ignored. The guards were not on strike, but this was definitely industrial action of a sort. Was discipline about to break down completely? In the stations some of the older hands were stirring the pot, goading the younger members saying they'd never get anywhere through protest and they'd just thrown away their careers.

Garda Marrinan was on duty in Rathfarnham that Wednesday evening. His notebook shows that at 8.50pm on 8 November 1961 at Grange Road, he stopped and cautioned a 16-year-old girl riding a bicycle without a front lamp or a rear reflector. Her excuse was that she had a hand torch, but it was defective. Lighting up time that evening was at 5.11pm.

At 10.10pm he responded to a complaint of youths causing annoyance to a night watchman at Whitehall road near the Hughes Brothers dairy. Having searched the area, he located the individuals responsible, noted their names and addresses and cautioned them. Shortly thereafter at 10.30pm, at Nutgrove Avenue while on checkpoint duty, he stopped and noted the particulars of two cyclists for offences under the lighting regulations.

On Thursday morning *The Irish Times*, under the guise of an analysis by an unnamed political correspondent, advised the garda rebels to respond positively to what it called a relaxing of the official position. It advised gardaí to state that they had not attended any unauthorised meeting, nor would they do so. The unofficial committee should disband itself and desist from collecting funds for its cause. It said that it was the view of 'many experts' that the civic guards have nothing to lose by the disbandment of the committee, 'now that the threat of discipline seemed to have been withdrawn'. The alternative, the political correspondent warned, was, 'a dirty prolonged conflict with nasty results.'

The uneasy intermission continued. For Jack Marrinan and most other gardaí, day-to-day police work continued. On that fateful Thursday he went to work as usual in Rathfarnham station. At 10.30am he stopped a large Bedford lorry on Nutgrove Avenue for tax offences and not having its unladen weight on display. Back at the station Sergeant Morris kept avoiding him but followed his movements until they got to a quiet place, when he whispered that the superintendent was looking for him. Eamonn Doherty (The Doc), who afterwards became Garda Commissioner, was that superintendent. At 4pm, he handed Jack a dismissal notice. It said that the Commissioner was exercising his powers under Article 24 of the Garda Síochána (Discipline) regulations 1926.

So what the Minister for Justice Charles Haughey had given on Tuesday, Garda Commissioner Daniel Costigan had taken away on Thursday in a very brutal way. What had happened in the meantime? Two things: the go-slow in traffic controls in Dublin had inflamed fears of a full-scale mutiny, and the return of the D1 charge forms with what were regarded as unsatisfactory answers to the question attending unauthorised meetings.

This was now very serious, as serious as it gets. Marrinan, Keating and Connolly immediately convened a meeting of the sacked men, attended by John A. Costello. In addition to being a former Taoiseach, Costello was a highly respected member of the Irish Bar, much in demand for high-profile disputes. The meeting lasted four hours and issued a statement in time for Friday's newspapers. It set out four criticisms of the existing garda representative body which purported to represent all ranks.

1. It was not independent.
2. Senior officers take part in and dominate its discussions.
3. The system of electing representatives was undemocratic.
4. There was no effective communication between the members of the force and those representing them on the GJRB.

Costello also gave his clients another piece of advice which they chose not to make public. 'As we were no longer gardaí if we sought to assemble, call, or attend any further garda meetings, or in any way attempt to promote dissatisfaction within the force, our activities would be considered a breach of the Offences against the State Act 1939, and we would be liable for detention under Section 30 of that Act.'

Aidan Byrne recalled:

'I was at the back of the clock in the Garda Depot when about a dozen of the Macushla committee came marching around the corner. I don't think Jack Marrinan was in the group, but later the news broke that they had been summoned by the Dublin Metropolitan Chief Superintendent William Quinn to be sacked'.

When the news of Jack Marrinan's sacking spread, his staunch Rathfarnham station ally Ger Connolly stormed into Doherty's office and said, 'If Jack Marrinan is being sacked, I deserve it as well'. Doherty was taken aback but responded that if he wanted to, he could apply to resign. Connolly, beside himself with rage, repeated his ultimatum.

The Doc handed him a half sheet [of paper] and said, 'There now; put your resignation on that if you feel you deserve it.' A sergeant was detailed to shadow Jack and ensure that he left Rathfarnham station. Some 10 other members from the DMA districts were also sacked. They were young men, junior in service, who had joined during the mid to late 1950s. Along with Jack Marrinan they were:

- Donie Murphy Regd. No. 13193. Born Clontarf, Dublin on the 2 March 1936. Joined 9 May 1957.
- David J. Walsh. Regd. No. 13298. Born Westport, Co. Mayo on the 20 Nov 1936. Joined 12 Dec 1957.
- Dick Keating. Regd. No. 13302. Born Ardfinnan, Co. Tipperary on the 23 Feb 1936. Joined 12 December 1957.
- William T. Corcoran. Regd. No. 13570. Born Thurles. Co. Tipperary on the 2 Nov 1937. Joined 21 August 1958.
- Patrick J. G. Muldoon. Regd. No 13575. Born Dundalk, Co. Louth on the 30 April 1937. Joined 21 August 1958.
- J.A. Staunton. Regd. No 13577. Born Tuam. Co. Galway 27 Oct 1935. Joined 21 August 1958.
- Mick Harlowe. Regd. No 13626. Born Co. Galway 25 August 1935. Joined 1 December 1958.
- Thomas Hegarty. Regd. No. 10466. Born Limerick in 1930. Joined 1953.
- Michael Murphy, Regd No.13575. Born Newmarket. Co. Cork. Joined July 1959.
- Tom Bennett. Regd. No. 14382. Born Croom. Co. Limerick on 7 July 1940. Joined 13 July 1960. (Bennett had less than a year's service.)

Most of those 11 sacked joined between 1957 and 1958. Tom Hegarty had been in the 1953 intake with Jack Marrinan. Michael Murphy would be the only one to later reach senior rank. He was promoted to superintendent in January 1992.

Ger Connolly recalled being in a pub near Rathfarnham station when news of the sackings broke. In Delaney's public house at Firhouse, Mrs Delaney burst into tears when she heard that her favourite local guard Jack Marrinan had been sacked.

Garda Jim Walsh, who served at the Bridwell, had a vivid memory of another sacking. 'A few days after the Macushla, Dave

Walsh was sacked and turfed out of his room, with a sergeant detailed to make sure he left with all his belongings, except his uniform. The skipper followed him around like he was the worst criminal. I remember Dave gathering up his few bits and leaving'.

The situation was now very dangerous. Everything had changed, and not for the better. Tempers were running high, nerves were fraying and all eyes were focused on the upcoming meeting in Bray. Loyalties to the job, to friends and colleagues who had taken huge risks, loyalties to the welfare of their young families- all were coming under unbearable strain. The sackings had caused many young guards to reconsider – their jobs, their careers, their families, were now at stake. 'After the sackings the void was not filled by members as forceful and passionate. Support was slipping away, fellas not turning up, not answering phones and generally hiding', Connolly recalled.

'On Friday we heard that the president of the Dublin Council of Trade Unions, a fella called [Paddy] Donegan, spoke out strongly that the dismissals were over the top. Also, an ITGWU leader named Michael Mullen threatened to hold a march unless the gardaí were looked after. At the same time a circular issued from Commissioner Costigan directing that no more meetings should be held, and that those who attended unauthorised gatherings would be disciplined. For most members this meant only one sanction: sacking.'

These trade union interventions were more significant than most gardaí recognised at the time. Mullen was a very influential figure, leader of the largest trade union in Ireland, the ITGWU, and a powerful voice in the Irish Labour Party. Donegan, in addition to being a union official, was also a visionary figure in vocational education, and was respected in industrial circles as well as by the workers he represented.[9] Two significant figures in the trade union

---

9    What eventually became the Technological University of Dublin owed much to
     Donegan's influence and that of his colleague Mick Gannon on the City of Dublin
     Vocational Education Committee.

movement had clearly signalled to the political establishment that organised labour was very unhappy with the way the young gardaí had been treated, and the problem needed to be dealt with. However it had come about, and however little his own members understood it, Marrinan had recruited another influential line of defence for the protesting young gardaí.

Peter Berry, a Cork man, who would soon become secretary of the Department of Justice, had already twice tried to set up a line of communication between the Minister's office and the Marrinan group. He saw where the trade union interventions came from and understood their significance.

Despite the widespread gloom Jack Marrinan was not throwing in the towel. 'While support from within the force was waning, the public and the media kept stirring the pot. Some termed the Macushla 11 as martyrs. Despite all the warnings and threat, the 11 of us, along with Ger Connolly, and a few more, continued to meet', he said. Gerry Denn had similar memories. 'As we knew our movements were being monitored, we had a few safe havens for meetings. The Tower Bar, almost opposite the GPO Henry Street, was one such. A Tipp man called Ryan was the owner and he had family serving in Mountjoy Garda station. Dan (Hanrahan), Donie (Murphy) and myself met there.'

According to Ger Connolly, Dublin city centre meetings were also being held in Phil Reilly's pub in Hawkins Street. There was talk of more disciplinary action and it was said that if members were disciplined, they would not resign. In any event the appetite for a second Macushla was dissipating. 'Things looked bleak. Thankfully, the media kept stirring the pot of public opinion. That was crucial. A few of us, Jack and Dick mainly, talked about calling off the Bray Macushla, but we knew if we did the gardaí would never again stand upright', Connolly said.

In those mad days of comings and goings, of addressing meetings up and down the country, of being invited twice to meet the Minister but not seeing him, and of being summarily sacked, Jack Marrinan made time to talk to Joe Groome, who had a hotel in Cavendish Row, almost in the shadow of the Parnell monument. Groome was not just a hotelier, he was a man with connections. He had at various times been honorary secretary and treasurer of the Fianna Fail party. He had been a Taca (temporary wartime guard) for a while and his father-in-law was a famous garda drill instructor Johnny Beale. And Groome's Hotel was not just any Dublin hotel; the bar was where the Fianna Fáil 'young Turks' gathered and plotted. Men like Charles Haughey, now Minister for Justice, Brian Lenihan senior who would succeed Haughey as Minister for Justice, and Donagh O'Malley from Limerick who would later have a big impact as Minister for Education, were about to replace the de Valera regime in Fianna Fáil. In talking to Joe Groome, Marrinan had a direct line of communication to the Justice Minister Haughey, who also happened to be a son-in-law of the Taoiseach Sean Lemass, who was known to Jack from duty, guarding his home in Churchtown.

The immediate problem was what to do about the 'Bray Macushla' meeting on Sunday. Time was running out. Thursday's sackings had achieved what the Department of Justice and Daniel Costigan, the Garda Commissioner, had intended 'put the fear of God' into the unruly younger members and those who might have been tempted to support them. Few were likely to attend, and those who did would be clearly identified as troublemakers and could easily be picked off. There was also the worry that Jack and the other 10 already sacked members would be open to prosecution for fomenting rebellion in the ranks, as John A. Costello had warned. And, of course, a poor turnout would clearly mean that 11 young men would have sacrificed their livelihoods and careers for nothing. They would probably have to emigrate. Marrinan and his supporters were in a very danger-ous 'damned if you do, damned if you don't' position.

Fate then intervened in a most cruel way. On Saturday evening, Assistant Commissioner William P Quinn, the senior officer for Dublin, was meeting other senior officers to discuss how to handle the Bray meeting on the following day. What action they were planning, we don't know. While Quinn's meeting was taking place in Dublin Castle, his wife Helen died in a car accident. The car she was travelling in struck a taxi in the south Dublin city suburb of Blackrock.

Jack Marrinan took up the story. 'Immediately when we heard the news of her death, the Bray meeting was cancelled. The gesture came from a genuine feeling of respect for a colleague and his fami-ly. Mr. Quinn was one of our own, and the gardaí always supported each other in tough times.' Ger Connolly agreed. 'Like the rest of us, Billy Quinn had a family and a tragic accident had taken his wife. Gardaí couldn't but stand with him.'

In Dublin word of the cancellation spread. Though the re-volt had begun in Dublin's northside stations, it had lit a torch throughout the country. Though the second meeting was intended for Bray, there was a worry that out of town members would make their way to the Macushla. Donie Murphy and Dan Hanrahan swung into action making placards saying the meeting had been called off. 'I remember Dan had breadboards from the mess and a member's wife was great with the chalk and crayon', Denn said. 'She adorned the trays with notices of the cancellation. I think she was relieved that it was over.

'Now, all we had to do was get the posters up outside the Macushla without being arrested. We knew it was being watched and our movements monitored, so we got a local lad Tommy Watson to place them for us. Later we drove down to discover that he had placed the placards outside a bed and breakfast hostel in Buckingham Street. We quickly did the needful. We were accosted by two fellow members who had travelled from Cork and were mighty upset that the meeting had been cancelled.'

Over the winter of 1961 Noel Kevane served in Letterfrack and Lettermore, before moving to Glenfarne, Co. Leitrim. In November word of the Macushla revolt in Dublin spread through like wildfire.

'At the time every thought we had, and every word spoken were of huge admiration for the men of the Dublin Metropolitan. When the Bray meeting was announced five members from in and around Glenfarne downed tools and headed south east. Sean Linehan, Joe Walsh, Eamon Crosse, Pat Barrett and Sean Forde and myself hired transport. On arrival in Dublin we discovered that the meeting had been called off. We stayed overnight, and I remember we thumbed lifts back down to the west.'

Jim O'Shea, a native of Ballymore, Dingle, Co. Kerry, had finished training in 1961 and was posted to Cahir, Co. Tipperary. The second Macushla was a hot topic in the station, and he and two colleagues John Rowland and John Bennett, both from Limerick, were planning to attend. A bus had been organised to criss-cross local stations and pick up gardaí to attend the meeting in Bray. The superintendent John Nolan was a decent man', Jim O'Shea recalled. 'He spoke to us and said that orders had come from Dublin that any member who attended the meeting would be in breach of the disciplinary regulations and could be sacked.'

Serving in Mayo, Pat Tierney has a vivid account of that time[10]: He had joined the force in July 1958. From Nenagh in Co. Tipperary, he was one of an intake of 50 recruits. After training he was sent to Mayo, Belmullet at first, and was serving in Crossmolina in November 1961 when the station heard of an amazing turn of events in Dublin.

'The Macushla incident hit the country gardaí like a thunderbolt, bringing the job to a standstill. When word came that almost

10    In an interview with Tim Doyle, 2019.

a dozen of the members of my vintage had been sacked, every second was like an hour, waiting for the latest news.

"Then word came that the Galway guards– the most numerous group of members in the west – were holding a meeting of support that weekend. Parades and duty inspections became a daily exercise, and every word that was ever invented was used to warn us not to get involved. However, when the Galway colleagues named the day, date, time and place, we did a swift about turn and headed east. As we approached the hall, we were given a guard of honour by every officer in the west. In fairness they didn't interfere. We all talked in small groups, until someone said we needed a chairman. I'll never know why I was picked, maybe I had the loudest voice.

'Just as we settled down word came that Archbishop McQuaid had intervened, and the Dublin lads were being reinstated. In the immediate aftermath all thoughts focused on the Dublin members. This Jack Marrinan had been elevated to the rank of a garda god. Rumours abounded of a "pull" of money and better conditions. At the time we were existing on a monthly wage and the last week was like living every day with a toothache.

'At Crossmolina station, discipline was still on the menu morning, noon and night. At one inspection I made a remark about pay. The Super came to attention and barked at us, "Would any of ye be man enough to give your last increase to junior members?" Quick as a flash our senior man Frank Johnston replied that we all would. The Super snorted, picked up his papers and stormed out.'

The following day the newly-unemployed Jack Marrinan was getting ready to do what courting couples in Dublin did on Sundays – he was taking his girlfriend to the pictures. It was a welcome break from eight tumultuous days in which Jack had been sacked from a safe job for life. Soon after they were comfortably settled in their seats and the film had begun, the bulky figure of a uniformed garda could be seen making his way through the dark to where they were sitting. A short, whispered conversation ensued. Jack said that Archbishop McQuaid wanted to see him. So off he went. 'I knew then', Mary Dempsey said, 'that our life together would be different.' She was just 21 and she was right.

# 3

## Sacked Gardaí and the Archbishop

At 2pm on that same Sunday, Charles Haughey's ministerial car was seen turning into the driveway of Archbishop McQuaid's private house on Military Road, Killiney. (Connolly believed that it was a sharp-eyed garda who spotted the Minister's car. It is more likely that the tip-off came from Haughey's garda driver.) Be that as it may, Haughey and McQuaid had a brief conversation. They were both realists and they knew what they had to do. Haughey and McQuaid had a good understanding of each other, as McQuaid's private papers show.

Now the 'Bray Macushla' had been called off, the deal was there to be done. Haughey's statement earlier in the week had sketched out the staging points, a return to discipline and normal working matched by conceding in parallel a means of addressing the underlying grievances. McQuaid would publicly offer to mediate in the dispute, Marrinan and his colleagues would accept the archbishop's intervention, and the 11 sacked men would be reinstated. This would be followed by steps to reform the garda representative body and bring the force's industrial relations into the modern world.

Fr Tom Fehily a priest of the Dublin diocese, a man who had been at the fore while organising the Patrician Congress in Ireland earlier in the year, would act as the archbishop's intermediary. From Cork, Fr Fehily's official position was as director of the Catholic Social Service Conference in Dublin's Eccles Street, and he was his superior's trouble-shooter on various fronts. In fact, he had been involved in a failed attempt to head off the first Macushla meeting before it happened, an indication that Archbishop McQuaid was, at an early stage, worried about what was about to happen. Tom Fehily later became a parish priest and a monsignor, and many thought he would become a bishop.

Jack Marrinan found himself meeting his fellow rebels at the GPO in Dublin to share the good news of the breakthrough. He surprised them twice that Sunday, once with good news, once with bad. They had won the battle, but he had been having second thoughts about staying in the force. There had been a couple of job offers, one from an insurance company, another from Hallmark Cards, an American multinational with a plant in Rathfarnham. In the eight days it had taken to shake up the closed world of the Garda Síochána, eight days in which he had crossed a line from being a garda to handling a fast-moving and complex dispute and dealing with people way about his pay grade, it crossed his mind that there might be other and better opportunities for a young man with a Trinity College education.

'When the offer of reinstatement came, I was undecided on whether to re-join. I had other prospects and employments to explore. Immediately after the Macushla there was talk, a lot of talk, about changes, including the transfer of training to Templemore, a reorganisation of the Dublin metropolitan districts, and the government was considering drafting new representative regulations. I was suspicious of these rumours as the official side were adept at rumour mongering aimed at side-lining public opinion. As a result,

I considered my options carefully. During my eight years of service I had rubbed shoulders with the finest and most honourable garda comrades. Indeed, an overpowering bond had grown with garda colleagues in Dublin and in my trips around the country.'

There's an element of false modesty here. In eight action-packed days, the Garda Síochána had been rocked to its very core. The young guards whose patience had finally exploded at a makeshift meeting in a Dublin ballroom had a cause but no idea how to advance it. A young Clare man, admittedly one with third-level education, had emerged as a leader and channelled that frustration through to wringing a binding undertaking from the Minister for Justice of reform in the way in which the police force treated its most valuable asset, the skills and loyalty of its members. Jack Marrinan and Dick Keating had taken hold of an unruly and unstructured protest and reshaped it into a successful campaign.

Along the way, the evolving *ad hoc* leadership of the Macushla rebellion had drawn into its support network senior politicians of the main parties, including a former Taoiseach, and the highly influential figure of Dr. John Charles McQuaid and public figures. Jack would not be human if he didn't realise that more than just the gardaí had been changed by the Macushla revolt. Garda Jack Marrinan was now looking at much wider horizons. A quiet and watchful man, he had seen the good, the bad and the ugly in the Garda Síochána in his eight years of service. He had seen first-hand and treasured the good, the comradeship, the discipline and sense of public service. Much of what was needed for an effective police service was in place. The immediate problem was how to set about liberating the good from the bad. He was now about to begin a new phase in his journey.

'When I told the lads that I wasn't too concerned about going back, they were upset, especially Michael Murphy', Jack said later. Murphy was not alone; the lads were all horrified. Ger Connolly spoke for them: 'We were all shocked when we discovered that Jack was in no hurry to re-join. He was our leader, and while his makeup was combative it was no way antagonistic. He possessed a unique sense of right and wrong and was a strong believer in and used a lot of discretion. He liked people, helping them if possible, and was not heavy-handed or authoritarian with the public. He was constantly looking for the humanity and reason behind people's actions.'

On Monday 13 November 1961, Charles Haughey announced that the dispute was over. Following the intervention of the Archbishop of Dublin, the Minister for Justice had agreed to reinstate any suspended garda who applied for his job back. Steps would be taken to address the grievances raised by improvements in the arrangements for the representation of garda views. Elections for a new Garda Representative Body would shortly take place and when the group met, the matters raised by the Macushla revolt could be addressed.

So, had the rebels won? Yes, the man in the street would say, but the Old Lady of Westmoreland Street, having misjudged the situation only six days earlier, was in search of a fig leaf to cover her embarrassment. On Tuesday 14 November *The Irish Times'* anonymous political correspondent, who had told readers the day before the men were sacked that the dispute was over now, needed to do some fact-fixing. He told readers that Haughey had indeed solved matters last week, but the intervention of the Archbishop of Dublin had been needed to bring things to a conclusion. There was no mention of the tragic death of Mrs. Helen Quinn, nor the aborted Bray meeting. In future years, *The Irish Times* under Conor Brady would take an informed interest in the Garda Síochána but for now it remained blinkered.

Marrinan wasn't just looking at his own future. There were lessons to be learned from the past.

'A vital dimension [of the Garda Síochána in 1961] was the recruiting of several thousand young men in the 1950s. These had proved themselves less likely to take the bullying which had been the lot of the previous generations. During the Macushla they had not been afraid to stand up for themselves or each other and were determined not to accept without question bad pay, inherited work practices, as well as rigid authoritarian duties and harsh disciplinary systems. Deep down I felt we had won a little battle, and if we harnessed the momentum, changes and improvements would follow.'

After some days of consideration, he decided to stay. 'My parents were the real reason I re-joined. I had originally become a member with their blessing and encouragement, and they took it badly when I was sacked. Their sentiments were "If you want to leave the gardaí don't do it this way. Sign on again. Give it a while and then, if you wish, resign. We don't want a garda sacking in the family."' The advice was sound and he took it.

Some unhelpful observers said that the guards who were sacked would have to start over again in training as if they were new recruits. Wiser counsel prevailed. Jack was sworn in by a peace Commissioner in Cabra and returned to duty in Rathfarnham; the others were reinstated a few days earlier by a senior officer called Willie Halloran.

Archbishop John Charles McQuaid's correspondence file shows how closely he was involved in getting the 11 guards reinstated and his insistence that the men's concerns be taken seriously. A note from McQuaid's private secretary dated 14 November 1961 says, 'Fr Fehily telephoned at 12.50pm to say that the guards concerned have sent in their applications for reinstatement in accordance with the formula suggested by Dr. McQuaid. Their legal advisers have suggested the following addition: "'I have been advised that I was not lawfully dismissed from the force, and this application is not to be taken as admitting that I was lawfully dismissed."' The note went on to say that the men had chosen not to act on this. 'In deference to Your Grace they refused to make the addition, as they preferred to [leave the matter] in the Archbishop's hands.'

Later that day, Haughey called to the Archbishop's House. A note in McQuaid's handwriting says, 'Gave the men's' assurance. Very touched and grateful. Assured me that no officer would be on the commission [what would be known as the Fehily Inquiry which was part of the settlement]. No man, I asked, should be charged or prejudiced in regard to promotion.'

Another note the same day, timed at 8.15pm said, 'Saw gardaí with Fr Fehily. Reassured them. One by one each man made his little speech of gratitude. I warned them not to be worried by inevitable jolts, remarks etc. after such a settlement.' McQuaid instanced a 'very inaccurate report in the *Irish Independent*' which had upset them.

Marrinan knew that going to the top man worked, but he also knew that you needed to say thank you in writing. A letter in McQuaid's file dated 15 November shows he did just that.

> My dear Lord Archbishop
>
> Some of us have already had the privilege of thanking Your Grace in person for your kindness in intervening on our behalf in the recent Garda dispute. We are very conscious of the honour you did us, and indeed the entire force in your thus interesting yourself so personally and so effectively in our problems. We now, through this letter, all join together in expressing to Your Grace our united thanks and appreciation for your goodness to us.

The letter goes on to assure the Archbishop that the men will keep their side of the bargain. And is signed with a flourish:

> With sentiments of deep esteem and gratitude
> We remain, My dear Lord Archbishop,
> Your Grace's obedient sons,

The letter was signed by: John Marrinan garda , Jeremiah Connolly garda, Michael M. Harlowe garda ,Thomas Bennett garda, Thomas F Hegarty garda, David J Walsh garda, Richard J Keating garda and Francis M. Mullen garda. The address is given as Rathfarnham Garda Station, Marrinan and Connolly's station.

Elsewhere McQuaid notes that he spoke to Commissioner Daniel Costigan and assured that none of the men had said a word against him. 'On the contrary – all were loyal'. On 16 November McQuaid again met the men. He mentions that all 11 were present, also Sean O Colmain and Eamonn Gunn, members of the previous ineffective representative body. They were afraid that talk in the stations and some press meant that Haughey had gone back on his word. 'Spent three-quarters of an hour reassuring them'. Of the men, 'only one was really difficult but that is his type, and he has an offer of another job'. [McQuaid has as good as identified Marrinan here.] 'Eventually one and all declared themselves quite satisfied.'

Because McQuaid was in direct contact with the men, he could tell Haughey about the intimidation happening around the country in garda stations which was making a settlement more difficult. Senior officers were making threats. 'A sergeant in Fitzgibbon Street had spoken on 16 November about the Minister wiping the floor with the rebels. An inspector in Portlaoise had ordered three gardaí to explain their illegal assembly. These are the things that upset young gardaí at such a delicate moment as the present', McQuaid told Charles Haughey on the evening of 17 November. Haughey gave an undertaking to put a stop to this behaviour.

Unwelcome interventions persisted. Gerry Denn recalled two. 'Fr Joe Gill was a Jesuit in St Francis Xavier's church in Upper Gardiner Street, famous for hellfire sermons at the annual retreats. He often came into Fitz street for a chat, and we used to have a collection for him. A week or so after the Macushla he appeared, and the conversation got a bit hot. I remember him saying, "The Macushla was worse than the Curragh mutiny." Popular and all as he had been, he was politely told to be off with himself. He left.' And a Special Branch man who had been hanging around Fitzgibbon Street was sent on his way, according to Denn.

McQuaid's file also records an interesting exchange. 'Father F (Fehily) said that on 4 November, before the Macushla ballroom meeting he had phoned Assistant Commissioner Quinn and asked him to hear Garda Gunn who proposed to go and induce the young men to desist as they already had made their protest. Gunn could not attend without the implicit consent of the assistant Commissioner.' Gunn had attempted to play the role of peacemaker. Quinn asked for time to consider. An hour later he refused permission for Gunn to attend the Macushla meeting. McQuaid's note concludes: 'And Gunn is the secretary [representative] answering for 400 men.'

Eamonn Gunn played an interesting supporting role in the events which led up to the Macushla assembly, which feature in his memoir *Sit Down Guard*. He joined the force in December 1943 and following training was assigned to Dublin's Irishtown Station. In April 1945 he moved to Dalkey and in 1954 to Dun Laoghaire. In 1956 he was elected secretary of the Dublin committee of the Joint Garda Representative Body. In that capacity he was invited to the opening of the Dominic Savio youth club in Finglas. There he met Archbishop McQuaid who told him that gardaí should have a greater role in the social life of their communities. Gunn became involved with the Dublin Catholic Social Services Conference, a lay organisation of which Fr Tom Fehily was director. And, of course, Gunn had been in the patrol car called to the scene of Helen Quinn's fatal accident.

And on the Sunday evening of his intervention, Archbishop McQuaid summoned Gunn –fellow guards Sean O Colmain and Frank Mullen came with him. Over tea and cakes provided by the nuns in the adjoining Cenacle convent, McQuaid said that he was anxious to resolve the disciplinary crisis which had resulted in the dismissal of 11 gardaí. The Archbishop told Gunn that he had been in contact with the Justice Minister Charles Haughey, and he had offered to persuade the men to refrain from all undisciplined action, including militant meetings. According to Gunn, 'the archbishop wanted us to leave things to him, and the problem would be overcome'.

Here McQuaid was protecting the deal he had earlier that day brokered with Haughey by making sure that Gunn and those previously elected to represent the Dublin gardaí did not at this very sensitive stage intervene and torpedo his initiative. Mc Quaid concluded his chat with Gunn and the others saying, 'Your guardian angel will look after you all'. The time was 1 am.

Gunn and O Colmain also attended the 16 November meeting in Fr Fehily's office in Eccles Street with Archbishop McQuaid along with Marrinan and the other men who were about to be reinstated. Gunn said that almost four decades later that Fr Fehily told him that the Taoiseach Sean Lemass and the Justice Minister Charles Haughey were waiting in the next room for confirmation that the deal had gone through. This is possible but unlikely. Lemass was out of the country in much of November 1961 dealing with Ireland's first application to join the EEC.

The Macushla revolt occurred on 4 November and there is a gap in Jack Marrinan's garda notebook until Monday 27 November 1961 when he was back on active duty. On that day at Meehan's butcher shop in Mount Merrion he arrested a 16-year-old youth for burglary. This individual admitted to several similar crimes in the area. On the same evening at the Apollo Cinema Dundrum, he arrested two other 16-and-a-half-year olds for similar crimes. His notebook records that this entry was initialled and dated by Supt Eamonn J. Doherty, the officer who had served his dismissal notice two and a half weeks previously.

At 11.30pm on the same date he investigated the assault and robbery of a milkman. The victim had been badly beaten and had face cuts and swollen, blood-shot eyes and had difficulty walking. Jack had him taken into care and routed the crime. At 7.30pm the following Sunday he discovered the culprits for a previous crime in a motor car at Ballycullen. The record showed that two males were taken to Tallaght Garda station. On the same date he responded to a station call that two 15 and 16-year-old girls, originally from Drogheda and Clonmel, had absconded from St Anne's Orphanage in Kilmacud. His notebook records that he found them safe and asleep in the back of a car near Christy Lawlor's pub at Ballycullen.

Two months later in January 1962 Charles Haughey set up the Fehily committee to inquire into the conditions of garda service. While the findings were never published it was widely believed that the members were shocked with what they learned about garda working and living conditions.

In 1962 Jack applied for promotion to the rank of sergeant. Doherty must have given him a fair commendation as the promotion board placed him at number 20 on the promotion list. While initially delighted, as his number for appointment approached, he had a change of heart. He had become secretary of the new GRB and was getting stuck into the negotiations on improvements in pay, hours of duty, and conditions. In accordance with regulations he applied for an extension, which meant that the promotion list moved on to the next name, with Jack remaining as the senior member. When that list ran out, his name topped the next promotion list. Jack kept applying for extensions until he eventually informed his authorities that he no longer wished to be considered for promotion.

'I got a phone call from Peter Berry who was a senior secretary in the Department of Justice, saying that he would fix me up as a sergeant in charge of Tallaght, a plum job.' Jack declined.

Later Berry offered him a plain clothes job as a detective sergeant in headquarters. Again, his answer was thanks, but no thanks.

'Around that time, I met Commissioner Costigan on a number of occasions. I always considered him a decent man, but during one meeting the conversation got a bit hot, and he remarked, "You know, Garda Marrinan, you were sacked once and got back; if it happens again there's no second chance." I responded, "Commissioner, with weekly pay of £10 and change I don't think I'd be interested in coming back"', Marrinan recalled.

On 13 April 1962, under Section 14 of the Police Forces Amalgamation Act 1925, Charles J Haughey signed a statutory instrument which created the Garda Representative Body Regulations 1962. Section 15(1) stated that a member of garda rank shall be assigned to act as full time general secretary of the new body. According to his official garda notebook, Jack Marrinan's last day of uniform duty was 5 June 1962.

In the meantime, while the official wheels turned to reflect the Macushla changes, the old Joint Garda Representation Body which included all ranks met for the last time. A committee was formed. Jack nominated Supt Eamonn Doherty as chairman. Gregory Allen, a future Garda historian, was upset. Tradition said that a chief superintendent held the chair, Tom Collins having been the most recent. Marrinan got his way. The GRB nominated its most junior delegate, garda Patrick Lally and he was elected to take the chair.

The first committee of the new Garda Representative Body, when it met a few months later, were a new breed, most of whom had been active in the Macushla and included three of the sacked men. Jack Marrinan was unanimously elected as general secretary and Eamonn Gunn as chairman.[11]

---

11   The other committee members were: Pat Nolan, Mallow, Chris Ryan, Kiltyclogher, Jim Fitzgerald, Naas, Patrick Courtney, William Street, Limerick, Niall Scott, Tralee, Patrick Lally, Oldcastle, James Scott, Claremorris and John Lee, Dungloe. Mick Harlowe and Dick Keating represented the Dublin Metropolitan Area

Marrinan remembered those early days clearly. 'The first meeting of the new GRB was held in garda headquarters. We refused to use the office in the Garda Depot insisting it was too close to management and after considerable argument we accepted offices in Dublin Castle. A short time later we retained the services of barrister Michael O' Kennedy as our legal advisor. He later become a senior counsel, Fianna Fáil Minister for Foreign Affairs and an EEC Commissioner.'

Another appointment made at the time was that of a young Fine Gael economics adviser and future Taoiseach Garret FitzGerald. He had just been appointed as arbitrator to the Electricity Supply Board where industrial relations appeared to be a blood sport, the disputes were so bitter. Erskine Childers, the Energy Minister who had appointed FitzGerald to the ESB position, began to worry about a possible conflict of interest. What if the ESB unions presented a claim along lines previously formulated for gardaí by FitzGerald- how could he be independent? So, FitzGerald told Jack Marrinan he was withdrawing.

Jack contacted Sean Lemass, whom he knew from guarding his bungalow in Churchtown. Lemass swiftly reversed Childers' decision and Marrinan had a future Taoiseach on his team of advisors, thanks to the incumbent Taoiseach. He knew the pay claim he made had to be economically watertight, otherwise the Department of Finance would make mincemeat of it. A major plank of the claim was the unfairness of expecting a garda to carry out a wide range of duties for the same pay as an entry-level clerk in the public service or private enterprise. This was vigorously resisted by the official side, led by Peter Berry, a formidable assistant secretary of the Department of Justice, who would soon get the top job.

Marrinan submitted a claim for a pay increase of 25% pay for gardaí and 14% for ban gardaí. After six months' consideration by the official side, the claim was rejected, but Marrinan's immediate reaction was to re-lodge the claim with the board of arbitration. In effect that was District Court Judge Frederick Mangan. Marrinan's file on this claim still exists and it merits consideration because of the mind set it illustrates.

The garda claim consisted of a 70-page submission document, bound in a striking red cover, and is still in pristine condition. It included 16 appendices, listing the government departments for whom Gardaí performed duties. These included: Justice, Finance, Industry and Commerce, Agriculture, Lands, Posts and Telegraphs, Social Welfare, Defence and An Taoiseach. Another appendix revealed that since 1960, gardaí had become guardians of 27 new pieces of legislation, as well as complying with 125 new statutory orders. It took over a half-dozen pages to tabulate the variability of hours worked by members countrywide, and to elucidate comparisons between salaries of gardaí and similarly graded workers.

Marrinan's presentation was laid out like an official investigation file, with each segment supported by factual evidence. The backbone of the claim was the ever-increasing workload of gardaí, along with the extra responsibilities placed on the force. These assertions were further developed to include the high standards demanded of members, their social and economic contribution to the State, the adverse conditions of garda employment, the excessive hours of duty, the ever-increasing demand for their services, the importance of ensuring that the status of gardaí remained high in the community and the need for a contented force.

Marrinan claimed that a members' working week was between 45 and 74 hours, often supplemented by stand-by duty. He stressed that there was no limit to the weekly hours of such duties, and that the 'exigencies of the service' meant that the job always had first call on an individual member's time.

'Additionally, periods of duty were often irregular, split shifts, and included long periods of night work. In smaller stations some members worked as much as 120 hours per week, and when a station closed a garda had to keep himself in readiness at his home or within three miles of his workplace to answer calls and deal with complaints. Many members were rostered at weekends for sporting and other events which meant their home life was disrupted, with meals taken at awkward times of the day or night.'

He pointed out that during 1960 and 1961 there had been a major upward movement in clerical pay, and an appendix showed that those sectors had received increases averaging 25% over the period. In addition, his index of industrial wages revealed that pay in that sector had risen by a similar amount between March 1960 and December 1962. Marrinan wrote trenchantly on the unique and special qualities of the force, highlighting such features as; adaptability, integrity, physicality, initiative, discretion and responsibility, arguing that as garda work involved a much higher degree of initiative and responsibility than any entry grade clerks, their salaries should rise to at least a similar level as the private and public sectors.

He quoted from a 1969 report on the pay of British police. The Willink Report had laid down that a starting point for police pay should be the same rate as that of a skilled worker. To this, Willink added a 45% increase as compensation for shift work, night duty, weekends and bank holidays. Another percentage should be added in recognition of the policeman's value to the community, as well as their special duties, responsibilities and most crucially the drawbacks of a policeman's life, such as exposure to danger, subjection to discipline and a degree of social segregation. Marrinan stated that the current rate of pay for an English constable had outstripped garda pay by £200 per annum at appointment stage, and almost £250 per annum after ten years of increments.

In his penultimate paragraph Marrinan wrote on the issue of morale and discontent manifested by young gardaí prior to the Macushla. Events in the past few years have provided disturbing evidence of discontent. This had arisen from the growing disparity between the work conditions, the remuneration of the force, and that of workers in other occupations, he argued. This dissatisfaction has been made worse by the failure to have any regard for the legitimate claims of young gardaí in the 1961 pay review, refusing any increase to members with less than five years' service; apart from a rent allowance adjustment, which left some worse off after the deduction of income tax.

'Morale in the police is of paramount importance, and if pay levels fall substantially below what either members of the service or the public regard as fair, and as providing a reasonable standard of living, garda morale will suffer. Younger men, lacking traditions of service, and an immature sense of loyalty will drift away, while those who remain will tend to become dissatisfied and disillusioned, resulting in the tasks of older men becoming increasingly more difficult and frustrating. The damage can be done before anyone realises what is happening.'

In contrast to the GRB's professionally presented submission, the official response consisted of a 64-page uncovered file, loosely held together with what appeared to be brass staples and a treasury tag. At the hearings chaired by Judge Mangan, Peter Berry on behalf of the Departments of Justice and Finance, spoke emphatically rejecting each one of Marrinan's assertions. He used such terms as, 'lower quality and nondescript duties'; 'routine and calling for no special qualities' and 'normal intelligence and adaptability is established at recruitment stage. The following extracts from Marrinan's files give the flavour of the encounter. Marrinan was responding off the cuff to Berry's considered response to aspects of the claim.

Berry: 'The garda association alleges that the failure of younger gardaí to get any pay rise in 1961 was inexplicable. These members are already well paid, compared with young entry grade clerks in the public service or outside it. Even today the garda recruits are extraordinarily well paid compared with clerical employees, and there has been no radical change in their circumstances since 1961.'

Marrinan: 'Would the clerical officers [Berry mentioned] do a garda's work under garda conditions?'

Berry: 'The standard of clerical work performed by gardaí is not up to that of clerks, with whom comparison is made. Clerical work forms only a minor part of the duties of the average garda, and at best consists of a mixture of clerical and lower quality duties. The Ministers [of Finance and Justice on whose behalf Berry appeared] do not accept the contention that the responsibilities of the gardaí involve a much higher degree of initiative than that required at entry grade clerks, nor that they have clerical duties like those of clerical workers. The duties of gardaí are largely routine, and the standard of their clerical duties is well below that expected of a clerical officer in the Civil Service.'

Marrinan: 'This is degradation, and not in accord with ministerial pronouncements. Should this view be published the confidence of the public in the gardaí would certainly be undermined. It appears that the views of the Ministers as represented in this statement are irresponsible and contrary to the public interest.'

Berry: 'Integrity. Gardaí highlight the need for a high standard of integrity. A high standard of integrity is required of all occupations and the scope for bribery and corruption is not limited to any walk of life. Integrity is a moral quality, the absence of which can be exploited by the unscrupulous in all levels of society. Serious moral weakness in an individual cannot be eliminated.'

'Adaptability. It is evident that the duties of gardaí are many and varied, but a great deal of it is of nondescript character calling for no special qualities.'

Marrinan: 'Public officials never have to arrest and prosecute. Gardaí must also keep people on their side.'

Berry: (On the topics of initiative and discretion, raised by Marrinan. )'The duties of gardaí are defined in circulars, routine orders, as well as the *Garda Síochána Guide, Manual of Criminal Investigation* and *Police Duty* Handbooks. Gardaí are trained to deal with the problems they normally confront, for example: road traffic offences, breaches of the licensing laws, rowdy scenes, suspicious behaviour etc. When in difficulties they can obtain direction from their sergeants. Normal intelligence and adaptability which is established at recruitment stage, coupled with their experience, produces the degree of discretion which is adequate for the needs of the force.'

Marrinan's: 'Yes! Hundreds of laws and duties. You mean drunk in charge, and drunken rows in public houses. Arrests, varied powers, reasonable belief, reasonable grounds, good cause to suspect, or the person is known to the gardaí?'

Berry: 'Contented force? We agree that this is important as in other walks of life. However, it is doubtful whether contentment could be secured by the grant of the pay scales sought or even double those scales. It is difficult to understand why it should be alleged that discontent is prevalent in the force in the matter of remuneration.'

Marrinan: 'It would be remiss of the Minister to refuse to acknowledge the existence of discontent.'

The claim went to arbitration on 25 April 1963. In the meantime Marrinan kept up the pressure by introducing a direct, almost confrontational tone to his *Garda Review* editorials. 'The disappointment of gardaí at the progressively long delay in the settlement of pay claims had grown to serious proportions. This is felt most by the younger members, who must be wondering if the promise which their profession held for them when they joined will ever materialise. They have become frustrated and in despair following years of standing still and even occasionally going backwards, in an ever-progressing society', he wrote.

Judge Frederick J. Mangan, chairman of the arbitration board, held sessions during June and July 1963. With both parties remaining dead-locked, the chairman ruled in favour of the gardaí. This decision yielded an increase of 25 shillings for recruits on appointment and during training, bringing their total pay to £10 per week. An increase of 45 shillings for all other gardaí through the 10 yearly increments to £16.5 shillings. Ban garda pay started at £8.15 shillings, increasing in nine yearly increments by 12 shillings to £14.4 shillings after 10 years. These increases amounted to 14% on the minimum and 16% on the maximum, as well as increases on every point of the pay scale. The £10 increase for recruits was the exact amount claimed and made up somewhat for their nil return in the 1961 pay award.

And for Jack Marrinan there was an unexpected bonus. A confidential message[12] relayed to him from Peter Berry admitted that Marrinan had been correct on two points on which they had disagreed, the unfair comparison with Civil Service clerical grades, and the hours of duty that gardaí had to put in. Berry, a very tough cookie as his subsequent career showed, was showing his respect for a worthy adversary. There was also an excited call from Finglas station. Garda Brian Prendergast had just got £180 in back money in his pay packet and realised he could now put down a deposit on a family home and simply had to share the good news with the man responsible.

Daniel Costigan was proving to be an innovative Commissioner. On his watch, he got to introduce the Juvenile Liaison Scheme, an initiative in which youngsters under 16 who had become involved in crime could be cautioned, rather than appearing in court and being saddled with a criminal record. He was also due credit for the introduction of women to the police force in 1959, a move intended to change the face of the force, but which achieved much more. In 1964 Costigan was also responsible for shifting garda training to Templemore. Marrinan, conscious that many young recruits from

12  Photocopy of original document with Tim Doyle.

the country had little experience of city life, had thought training in the capital city was a useful experience for them, but the move went ahead and proved successful.

In 1965 as his term of office was coming to an end and as his health began to deteriorate, Costigan returned to a desk job in the Department of Justice from whence he had come. He was replaced by William P Quinn, the first Commissioner to have come up through the ranks since Eamonn Broy succeeded Eoin O'Duffy, and many saw in that appointment yet another consequence of the shenanigans in the Macushla ballroom. That the Commissioner was once again a serving guard was an unexpected by-product of the Macushla revolt, most observers felt, and the force was encouraged by it. Jack was moved to write a lengthy tribute to Daniel Costigan in the *Garda Review*. 'He was the first Commissioner to decree that while gardaí were responsible for the safety, peace and orderliness of their communities on a 24-hour basis, they did not have to be locked up in their stations at midnight to do so. When he took over, our members were badly paid, badly housed, not allowed to vote, and wore a uniform reminiscent of a previous force. During his reign for the first time our members were treated as individual adults, and as capable and responsible human beings.'[13]

This editorial also wished the new Commissioner William P. Quinn well. 'He is a kindly, family man widely-known and has many friends of all ranks in the force', Marrinan wrote, adding that Quinn's Commissionership was a fitting recognition of a career to which he has contributed so much of his talents and energies. What is important in this is Marrinan's tone. He gives credit to those he clashed with in the past. In this, he is clearly trying to lead his own people and those with whom he engages away from the surly unproductive exchanges of the past. And what is clear from Jack Marrinan's first years in office is how he goes at things. Muster

13  *Garda Review*, January-February 1965.

your supporters, work hard, use careful research to build a case, tap into the expertise of the best people in the field – John A Costello, Garret FitzGerald and others- network to broaden an asset base, listen carefully to what is said. Then when all the evidence is in, deploy it in forceful advocacy. Use the *Garda Review* to make a case and answer critics. Marrinan had already made a mark on the development of the Garda Síochána; more was undoubtedly to come.

# 4

---

# Battles with the Department of Justice

For Jack Marrinan the latter half of 1962 was devoted to building a solid foundation for the future of garda representation. The arrangements for setting up the new Garda Representative Body (GRB), signing up members, arranging elections of representatives and staffing the office took him all over the country, spreading the GRB gospel to more than 700 city and country stations. As general secretary Marrinan also had responsibility for the *Garda Review,* and with that came the wider responsibility of keeping members up to date on what was happening. 'I was determined to ensure the success of the *Garda Review* and knew that its popularity depended on the members countrywide rowing in with support. I was impressed by an exceptionally talented young writer, Conor Brady. His father had been a garda superintendent in Co. Offaly and Conor knew much more about the force than most policemen', Marrinan said later about the young man he had hired to help with the publication, and the two became lifelong friends.[14]

---

14    A native of Tullamore, Conor Brady went on to become editor of *The Irish Times,* wrote two books about the Garda Síochána and was a founding member of the Garda Síochána Ombudsman Commission.

'We encouraged members countrywide to report on aspects of their duties, movement of personnel, domestic and social events, as well as sporting achievements and a plethora of photographs. We also urged members to contribute articles and letters relative to garda topics. We also sought advertising to subsidise printing costs. Each issue had a fairly hard-hitting editorial, and within a short time it began to have an impact on the national media.' Another initiative was to introduce an information circular known as the *Broadsheet Bulletin*, as well as a bi-yearly *GRB Newsletter* which guaranteed that all members were updated on emerging developments.

Some progress was being made in modernising the force. New York-born Tom Casey was a powerful specimen of manhood, and he was a sight to behold as he swivelled and stopped and waved on traffic on point duty at the junction of Dublin's Dame and South Great George's Streets in the late 1950s.

In mid-1963 the force was introducing a Juvenile Liaison Scheme. This was an initiative in which youngsters under 16 who had become involved in crime could be cautioned rather than appearing in court and being saddled with a criminal record, and Commissioner Daniel Costigan was keen to promote it.

Supt Leo Maher was sent to Liverpool to observe the scheme in action there. Following his recommendation, it was decided to appoint a number of sergeants as Juvenile Liaison Officers; known as JLO men. Tom was duly selected and sent to Liverpool for training. On submitting a claim for subsistence, he was told that when he left Dublin's North Wall quay on the Liverpool boat he was outside his jurisdiction, and no longer qualified for the allowance.

On his return he was to appear on TV to publicise the liaison scheme. A few days beforehand he was directed to present himself before Peter Berry in the Department of Justice. He recalled that Berry's reaction was no more than a brief glance at him, as if to confirm that he didn't have two heads or four arms and that his mouth opened when he was asked a question. As for the tv journalist Brian Farrell who interviewed him, he was a thorough gentleman, said Tom.

The JLO scheme was first introduced in Dublin then extended to other cities and major towns in September 1963. Tom Casey's career trajectory, from being the big guy on city-centre point duty about to be replaced by traffic lights to getting young offenders back on track, showed that the force was reacting to change in a considered way.

Another innovation was the appearance of *Garda Patrol*, a weekly six-minute TV broadcast seeking the help of the public in solving crime in which the names and faces of serving guards were introduced into people's homes. Yet for every gain it seems there was a backlash. When one-way streets became part of Dublin's traffic management plan in 1964, there was widespread confusion for a few weeks as motorists came to terms with the changes and gardaí were blamed, not the local authority which planned the new street network. When the improved traffic flow became obvious to all, nobody thought to apologise to the force for the abuse heaped on it, as Jack ruefully noted in the first edition of the *Garda Review* of 1965, asking journalists to think for a moment before heaping abuse on the guards for problems not of their making.

At this time the GRB was beginning to find its feet. A party of guards went to New York to take part in a pageant in Madison Square Garden in 1964. A Clare man and friend of Marrinan's, John Collins who had joined in 1956, was one. In a New York dance hall run by Irish-born impresario Bill Fuller, Collins met up with his childhood sweetheart Bridget Crotty – they had lost touch when her family emigrated. Now he had found her again. 'She was a dote and I lost my heart'. Reunited, they were guests at Jack Marrinan and Mary Dempsey's wedding in Dublin on 2 April 1964. The Collins-Crotty wedding took place three years later. The

Marrinan's son David was born in 1965, daughter Clare, named for her father's birthplace in 1968, and John in 1971.

So what was it like for a young person joining the force in the aftermath of the Macushla? Roscommon-born John Smith gave a good flavour of the time speaking to me in his retirement. He began training in October 1962, just a year after the force had been 'marrinated', as Smith described it.

'On 14 February 1963 having completed 18 weeks training I was posted to Bray Garda station, the seaside capital town of county Wicklow[15], where every ebb and flow of tide needed garda monitoring', or so he was led to believe. There was another important local rule. Assistant Commissioner William P. Quinn lived just around the corner from the station, as did his five beautiful daughters. No recruit garda was ever to make eye contact with any of the five young women. And that was an order.

The new recruit had been working on building sites in England when the call came to training in the Phoenix Park, so the physical side of the job held no fears for him. Psychologically there were greater challenges. 'In and around the station my attitude, deportment and conversations were conscientiously analysed, as if an underlying meaning was sought. It came to me that the station party was cocooned in an atmosphere of nervous uncertainty, and I sensed that this emanated from the Macushla garda meeting, the second anniversary of which occurred in November 1963.'

While the fire was initially lit in Fitz Street, Bray had played a considerable supporting role fanning the flames of revolt. It was a Bray member who had called on Jack Marrinan to take control of the chaotic meeting, and Bray was the intended venue for the second Macushla which never took place. Jack had been stationed in nearby Rathfarnham and the tale of his sacking and that of the

---

15  Not really. Wicklow town is the administrative capital, but the people of Bray in the north of the county regard their town as the real capital.

other 10 members, and their reinstatement at the instigation of Archbishop McQuaid, was told and retold, hashed and rehashed in the station building on Convent Avenue, close to the seafront with its candyfloss and donkey rides and children playing with buckets and spades on the beach. Senior officers became agitated by any mention of Marrinan or the infamous dance hall, but the subject simply wouldn't go away. Already the man and the event had reached legendary status within the force.

'In early 1965, the inaugural members of the first Garda Representative Body had completed their three years' tenure and new representatives needed to be elected. Again, that meant the skeletons of the Macushla sackings were being rattled', John Smith told me. And it was made quite clear to Bray members that they would be best advised not to nominate anyone for the forthcoming election.

Was that the end of it? Not exactly. Jim Grace, a veteran garda who had won three hurling titles with his native Kilkenny, took Smith aside. Having made sure nobody else could hear, he began to whisper, 'We're too old and set in our ways to be any use in the coming struggle. Your generation will be the making or breaking of this job, so on behalf of all of us, I'd like if you put your name forward for that GRB.'

Therefore, despite his youth and inexperience, John Smith's name went forward and he was elected. Not long afterwards Jack Marrinan spoke to him after an executive meeting. He mentioned a young garda serving in Kilmainham. 'He was very young, very poor and very married', Jack said. 'Himself, his wife and their infant lived in a Bray flat and the distance to and from work was impossible: especially 6am mornings and the month of nights. Both him and his lassie were at breaking point. What they needed was some respite and a transfer nearer home would be a God send/garda send.'

So as area representative John Smith made an appointment to see the officer in charge, Eamonn Doherty.

'The Doc was a blocky, low-sized individual who sat forward on two elbows, arms and hands extended on his paper-filled desk. I'd been warned that he was both brusque and quick on the uptake. I had my submission rehearsed and let rip. His shoulders shuffled and lips gurgled. Senior officers didn't relish being out-talked.

'However, I had spotted a chink in his armour: he liked solutions. I came with a solution. At the time, during summer Bray station party was supplemented with a garda from an outside station. I placed that on the Doc's lap and his upper body leaned backwards. There was a silence eventually broken by a long *hmmm*. The young garda and his bride and baby came to Bray to stay.

'A while later Jack took the time to call in and thank me personally. That was his great strength. He kept his finger on the pulse of every garda. He must have thought about the job even when asleep.'

Jack had also become close to Michael Conway, who had been making his presence felt in garda circles. A fellow Clare man, Conway had an aptitude for figures which he put to work in the Garda Depot. His description of his workplace paints a picture of the force headquarters in the Phoenix Park.

'The pay office was located at the right of the depot clock as one enters the main gate. The pay book was a huge, hard-covered ledger type volume, and when it was fully open it stretched about two feet. It was columned off starting with basic pay, then there was a rake of allowances. Boot, cycling, clerical, detective, dog handler, Gaeltacht, immigration, training instructors, juvenile liaison, locomotion, official drivers, plain clothes; including a variety of technical bureau experts, as well as private secretary to the Commissioner, substitution allowance, subsistence allowance, and transport, public service vehicles inspectors, wireless and uniform allowances. In total they numbered about thirty.' This knowledge Conway would put to good use in the years to come.

As wages clerk he also knew how difficult it was to get money from members no matter how good the cause.

'The welfare of gardaí and their families had been talked about for decades, but money was a garda's god, and on payday when I lobbed the cash into their hand, the big paw closed around it so tightly one would need a crowbar to prise a penny from their fist.

'In 1968 I helped organise the Garda Group Assurance Scheme, which was of critical importance as widows and orphans of deceased gardaí were destitute. Some were depending on hand-outs from the Saint Vincent de Paul society. Members under age 50 who died in service would get £5,000; if over age 50 they got £4,000. But they needed to have paid £10 per year for insurance. Gardai were notoriously reluctant to sign anything that took money from their pay. Nothing stirred members into contrariness as money; the lack of it and especially deductions. I used to get upset when a member died in a city or country station and hadn't joined up.'

Jack Marrinan spotted Conway's talent and wanted him as his full time assistant. The Department of Justice refused. Marrinan then ran into Brian Lenihan in Groome's hotel. Lenihan had taken over as Minister for Justice from Haughey in November 1964. Lenihan gave Jack his standard 'no problem' response. However, Peter Berry blocked the appointment once more. Eventually Berry gave way after Marrinan's persistent efforts.

In all but name Conway was operating a one-stop welfare shop for the force. He also encouraged members to join the Garda Benevolent Society, a charity registered in 1936. In the event of the death of a serving or retired member or a member of their family, subvention grants were paid to survivors according to rank. In addition, annual grants were paid to the orphaned children of deceased members.

From the late 1950s Conway ran the Garda Medical Aid fund. 'All I had was a table, a chair and a typewriter. Head office was a room in Dublin Castle. Claim forms were available locally and posted to me. I wrote the cheques and recorded the amounts in a ledger for audit. Everything was done by hand. No payments for hospitalisation. I used to bring home bundles of claims and try and sort them out. Money was fierce scarce.'

Conway became Boswell to Marrinan's Dr. Johnston. 'During my time as Jack's assistant I sat, mostly quietly, making notes and listening in awe to the never-ending litany of queries and aggravations that issued from the four corners of An Garda Síochána.' He began to understand Marrinan's modus operandi. 'His great strength lay in the way he surrounded himself with a variety of talents from all over the force.

'Marrinan's committee had their fingers on the pulse of the force long before the term became fashionable. Those who sat around Jack's negotiating table were the most responsible and committed members who ever took the oath. When a serious matter came up, Jack's first act was to open his arms wide and go around the table. Moving his head from side to side, leaning back in his chair, he milked the discussion. Jack wouldn't utter a word until they all had their say. I saw reticent members blossom. They became confident in formulating and presenting their own proposals and arguing them forcefully. Sometimes I felt they got up from their seats several inches taller.

'I also recall his discussions with Tom O'Reilly, who later became an Assistant Commissioner. In the early days Tom was active in the Representative Body for Inspectors, Station Sergeants and Sergeants (RBISS). I understand he studied for the priesthood before he joined up. He was very bright, and Jack Marrinan and he used to have mighty one-to-one verbal tussles. O'Reilly was a liberal, – Jack was conservative. Listening to them debating was thought-and-talk at 100 miles an hour.'

The question was: where to focus next? While pay was the traditional fuse-blower in garda conversations, the oppressive hours of duty were a close second. The ink on the 1963 pay award was hardly dry when Marrinan began to build up a head of steam to deliver a shorter working week. There had been a claim for shorter hours at conciliation and arbitration since 1961, but no progress had been made. That now had to be changed.

The 1967 claim for a 48-hour week with designated free days came at a time when the management side was divided. Patrick Carroll, then Commissioner, had appointed an all-ranks working party under Chief Superintendent John Coakley. The Department of Justice, in the form of Peter Berry, decided that Coakley's job was to find ways in which costs could be contained without additional expenditure on increased manpower and without detriment to adequate policing. Coakley's view was he had been told to work out how to implement the shorter working week, as if the claim had been conceded. This conflict originated in a 1950s study by management consultants Urwick Orr. The Coakley group had the wrong message, Berry fumed. Their function was to close smaller stations and demolish the case for more money, not call for greater spending. He demanded greater ruthlessness in reallocating resources. In plain English that meant shutting down garda stations and employing civilian staff.

This meant that the management side was at odds with each other, and the representative bodies weren't singing from the same hymn sheet either. In 1967 a pay claim for middle ranks failed and Berry's attempt to bring about a united front on pay between the three representative bodies proved counterproductive. Berry thought he had played a clever hand by encouraging the various garda representative organisations to agree a common approach. This meant he wouldn't have to contend with 'leapfrog' pay claims, where each group sought more than the previous group got. Berry thought he could convince both the Department of Finance and the guards that his middle way was best. But Jack Marrinan wasn't going to have his hands tied in advance. The phrase micro-management was not in use then, but Berry was an early practitioner; he had a Machiavellian streak.

For the men and women led by Jack Marrinan, the 1963 Mangan award had been a down payment, not an over-generous final settlement as Berry wanted them to believe. As we shall see, there was more than money on the garda mind. The disciplinary code was very harsh, putting young members at risk of victimisation by senior members, some of whom were resentful of the spring in their step in the post-Macushla era. Bullying was endemic and it went right to the top. What Berry did not see, or chose not to see, was the new vigour in garda ranks, a willingness to engage and a need to be heard which had not been present before the Macushla meeting. The younger generation was impatient for change.

There was another petty tyranny exercised at local levels. From one day to the next a garda did not know what hours he would work, nor where he would be sent. Some of it just went with the job. I myself was serving as a garda in Dublin's Whitehall station and was just about to leave for a Christmas trip home to Co. Kerry in December 1967 when my leave was cancelled and I was sent north to the Border, as foot-and-mouth disease had broken out in England close to the Welsh border. That was tough but understandable. Foot-and-mouth could destroy the economy and put thousands on the breadline.

In contrast, sending members to stand guard all day on approach roads to predictable events like race meetings without notice, food, back up or relief was not reasonable, yet it was the lot of many. In October 1966 the National Farmers' Association staged an 11-day mass march from Bantry to Dublin, ending in a rally attended by 30,000 outside the Department of Agriculture. It was a very sore point that gardaí were on duty throughout this protest for lengthy periods without relief, food, or water. Hungry tired and demoralised gardaí are little use to anyone.

Improvements in working conditions were becoming part of the late 1960s employment scene, but in allocating daily duty the Garda Síochána was still in 1930s mode, and that hurt. There were other sticking points. A half-yearly GRB meeting early in 1966 passed a motion demanding that the morning parade for police duty classes, which required off duty members to turn up in full uniform for inspection, be dropped. It was an outrageous intrusion into private time and private lives. Deputy Commissioner O Maonaigh flatly refused this request when it was presented, but the practise was quietly dropped a few years later. A worrying matter was raised by Leinster GRB representatives in 1966. They accused 'elements within the Department of Justice' of a campaign to degrade members of garda rank. This was being accomplished, they said, by removing amenities, concessions and privileges which had been enjoyed by members almost since the force's foundation. They instanced the disbanding of the Garda Band without consultation, a very sore point indeed, the transfer of an efficient housing officer, Supt Ned Garvey who had been doing a great job, reducing staff of the Medical Aid and Benevolent Fund and the closing of garda canteens. They further alleged that many legitimate claims lodged at conciliation were being consistently stymied by official side delaying tactics so much so that GRB participation in negotiations was a waste of time. The Leinster committee made it clear that it was not blaming the general secretary for this, but thanking him for his sterling work. Whether the authors of this motion were correct in their assessment or not was largely irrelevant. The point was that they believed it.

The brutal application of the disciplinary code was another problem. On 29 December 1966, a young man from Co. Laois, James McCarthy, joined the force. After 18 weeks first phase training James passed out from Templemore in May 1967 and was assigned to Edward Street station in Limerick city. His arrival in Limerick coincided with that of Supt Laurence 'Larry' Wren. During those early months in Limerick, McCarthy was commended for excellent police work, while also being assigned to assist in an important case, the investigation of the rape and murder of a young girl found in a shed at the rear of a pub near to Edward Street garda station.

Fate dictated that the recruit garda and the superintendent were to have an unhappy relationship. Their first encounter gives flavour of the arbitrary and haphazard discipline and management culture which permeated the garda internal disciplinary system. James, returning to Edward Street station after a tour of night duty and scheduled to complete his patrol at 6am, entered the station at 5.50am. Gardaí were required to write up details of their patrol and associated occurrences during their tour of duty. On entering the station day room, the young recruit garda encountered Wren who was in plain clothes. Without introduction or other such courtesy Supt Wren confronted McCarthy, demanding to know why he was returning to the station, 10 minutes prior to completing his tour of duty.

The young recruit replied that his tour of duty concluded at 6am and that regulations required that he write up his patrol and other incidences before signing off at 6am. Wren dismissed this, saying that McCarthy could be under surveillance by criminal elements, who at this moment might, in his absence from the street, avail of the opportunity to commit crime. Saying that McCarthy was in breach of garda disciplinary regulations, Wren ordered him out of the station, and directed him not to return until after his tour of duty finished at 6am. Wren further intimated that he would regard any future return to the station by Recruit Garda McCarthy before the 6am deadline as direct disobedience of his orders. Wren intimated that he would view such a transgression as a breach of discipline, and the recruit garda would be punished accordingly.

Some weeks later, on a sparkling September morning, shortly after 11am, James McCarthy stepped through the front door of Edward Street station, returning from a few days' leave in Dublin. At that time single members were obliged to live-in on station premises. On his way upstairs, James passed the day room where the station party of gardaí were lined up for Supt Wren's monthly inspection. Shortly after going up to his quarters James heard the sergeant in charge calling from the stairwell directing him to dress in uniform and present himself in the day room for inspection. James, now standing in the stairwell, initially declined on the grounds that he was still technically on leave and not scheduled to take-up duty until 2pm later in the afternoon. The sergeant told James that on Supt Wren's instructions, he was directing him to kit-up in uniform and to parade for inspection with the other station party members.

Under protest, James kitted out in uniform and trudged downstairs to the day room, where Wren was waiting with the other station party members. Wren ordered James McCarthy to attention for inspection. He then walked around the recruit garda and directed the sergeant to note the fact that McCarthy had paraded for duty in an unkempt manner in that he needed a haircut.

Then, speaking directly to James, Supt Wren pronounced, 'That haircut will cost you one pound, McCarthy.' James pleaded that he had not been scheduled for duty until 2pm, but this fell on deaf ears. Then the most senior member of the station party with 35 years' service stepped forward and directly addressed the superintendent. In a solid clear voice, Garda Dennehy pointed out that over his long service in An Garda Síochána, he had never witnessed such discriminatory and, in his view, unfair treatment of a recruit garda. He felt that this was a mistake. In an era of iron discipline and total obedience to authority, Garda Dennehy's action was unprecedented. Wren made no direct response, merely repeating that the haircut would cost McCarthy the sum of one pound. The parade then ended, and the station party was dismissed.

Four weeks following this event, Supt Wren issued a disciplinary form (a D1) to recruit garda James McCarthy. The order cited a breach of discipline for bringing the force into disrepute, by parading for duty in uniform with an unkempt appearance, not having a regulation haircut.

James told the station sergeant that he would contest the decision based on the rules of natural justice and because he believed the superintendent had 'set him up'. The sergeant showed James an obscure section of the garda disciplinary code which stated that where a member of the force contested a disciplinary charge, that automatically exacerbated the charge. This meant – in plain language – that entering a plea of not guilty was in itself committing a further offence. James sought the advice of another sergeant sympathetic to his case. Sergeant James Dwyer advised that in the circumstances, as Wren had a reputation for vindictiveness, and as the young guard was still on probation, it would be better to say nothing and pay the fine of £1, even though it was a considerable sum in those days. Sergeant Dwyer also pointed out that Wren would not hesitate to use the 'exacerbate' clause to increase the fine. McCarthy knew the advice was sound and he paid up.

After six months' service James McCarthy was due a probationary evaluation meeting with Chief Supt John S. Flynn. McCarthy raised the issue of Supt Wren's treatment of him, and the chief superintendent said he would note his complaint.

In the meantime, Wren was involved in bringing a spate of disciplinary complaints against other gardaí in the city. This included eight members who were training in a garda rowing boat for an event on the Shannon and who had failed to seek the permission of the superintendent to compete. Anger among Limerick gardaí was mounting and culminated on the arrival of GRB general secretary Jack Marrinan to the city. Jack's temporary base was a room in Cruise's Hotel and members were encouraged to call to him in his office and describe individual complaints. Many aggrieved members visited Jack in his office on that day. To see Marrinan they had to 'run the gauntlet' of an inspector and a sergeant standing at the entrance, noting the names of all members entering the hotel.

In James's case Jack was sympathetic but cautioned that as he was still on probation the matter needed to be handled diplomatically. The upshot was that in February 1968, James McCarthy was transferred to a small rural station at Ballylanders, Co. Limerick. Soon afterwards, Wren was transferred from Limerick on promotion to chief superintendent.

Another indication that the problems went deeper than pay was a revolt at Dublin's Crumlin and Sundrive Road stations against heavy-handed discipline imposed by a recently appointed superintendent of the old school, Michael Fitzgerald. He was well-known to many in the force, having worked at Templemore as an instructor. Fitzgerald was a stickler for discipline. His inspections struck fear into the hearts of very experienced officers. On the morning of a general election in June 1969, the early shift in both stations threatened to report sick. Assistant Commissioner James McDonagh was sent to investigate the complaints. What Gregory Allen described as an uneasy peace reigned until a further row over the transfer of a young guard flared up, and 70 gardaí rostered for morning duty failed to appear. Fitzgerald was transferred, and Dan Devitt, a superintendent with a surer touch when it came to city policing, replaced him. There had been two angry meetings in the Garda Club with more than a thousand members present before matters settled down under Devitt.

The establishment of St Raphael's Credit Union in 1964 was a major contribution to garda welfare. The brainchild of a group of Dublin-based detectives with Brian Sheehan at the fore, it was a life saver for many members, especially when hit by unexpected expenses. The first loan was approved in November 1964 and the financial statement for 1964 had member's shares at £798.11 shillings and 10 pence. Outstanding loans were £653.16 shillings three pence, and cash deposits in bank amounted to £48.13 shillings and 11 pence. Today the garda credit union's assets are measured in multiple millions. In 1967 Chief Superintendent Patrick Power set up another garda credit union in Cork. His creation, St Paul's Credit Union, also continues to be a success today.

Pat Nolan, a founding member of the GRB executive committee, recalled a mid-60's meeting with officials to resolve a minor matter. It was an example of how high the hill was that they were trying to climb. 'Jack and I met O Buachalla, an assistant secretary at the Department of Justice. We were after an increase in the subsistence rate for guards away from home.'

A flat no was the response.

'Those people were little gods', Nolan recalled. 'I got angry and stood up. One thing we had over them was physicality. They loved to have us sitting down.' One of the official side made a smart remark about the Macushla.

'You know your department has an unhappy knack for letting the garda pot boil over', Nolan replied.

'It will not be tolerated ever again.' O Buachalla snorted.

'How wrong he was.'

There had been a claim for reduced hours of duty at conciliation since 1961, but the authorities had refused to act on it. Help was at hand from an unexpected source. Early in 1965 the inspector general (chief constable) of the RUC, Sir Albert Kennedy, a man who sought good relations between the two police forces in Ireland, set up a special committee to investigate the hours of duty performed by his force. Jack immediately pounced. In April 1965 he addressed gardaí working excessive hours. 'There is grave dissatisfaction at the continuous failure of conciliation to agree a reduced working week. Other workers are progressing inexorably towards a basic working week of 40 or even less hours.' He went on to say that he was certain that shorter hours of work were inevitable, but a weakness in the garda negotiating machinery meant that while conciliation dealt with all claims, arbitration for matters unresolved by conciliation was confined to pay and allowances, as well as claims for annual and sick leave.[16]

The three-year term of the first GRB executive committee had elapsed, and a new committee was in place for the half-yearly meeting at Dublin Castle from 10 to 14 August 1965. Naas's Jim Fitzgerald was elected chairman replacing Eamonn Gunn. The following members attended: Tom O'Leary and Brian Sheehan (credit union founder) representing Dublin, Pat Kearney and Bill Greer, Connaught-Ulster, Munster was represented by Jim Hughes, a Gaelic footballer from Portlaoise, stationed in Nenagh. (He was in the wrong place, Jack said. 'Hughes was 'some sight in a hurling mad town with a football on the carrier of his bike.') Ted Roche, a patrol car driver in Kanturk, and Andy Hallissey represented Munster, Michael Conway and Pat Tierney represented Leinster.

All would become part of the GRB story. Jim Fitzgerald, a garda clerk, would play a leadership role for many years to come. Pat Tierney was originally from Nenagh. He served in Co. Mayo and transferred to Kildare after he married in the hope of getting a house- which he did. In the west he had been getting ready to travel to the Bray Macushla when it was called off. Like Fitzgerald, he became a garda clerk with a detailed knowledge of the Road Traffic Act of 1961- an important and complex piece of recent legislation- and his admiration for Jack Marrinan and the original Macushla men knew no bounds.

At the August 1965 executive meeting, Jack Marrinan spoke about the upcoming pay claim for eight per cent which would do no more than re-establish parity with certain clerical, industrial and agricultural workers. He also raised a very delicate matter. Deliberately avoiding the words bullying or Templemore, he said: 'It's a pity that we find it necessary to mention that the treatment

16    Editorial *Garda Review* April 1965.

of our members in certain places leaves a great deal to be desired. We still have in our supervisory and administrative ranks a small number of persons who do not appear to have any conception of how dignified human beings under their control should be treated. Public criticism, barracking and abuse on parade or inspection are not yet unknown in our force and requires urgent investigation.' Marrinan's message to the top brass was coded, but the intent was clear. Bullying is happening in Templemore, do something about it or I shall have to spell it out in a more public forum.

Jack Marrinan was in a reflective mood about the nature of police service when he wrote the following editorial for the October 1965 *Garda Review*:

'Recently a young member called to the office and the chat came around to service and work conditions. It was then he made a spontaneous statement that warmed our hearts. "I love the job. On no account would I leave it for any other." Some might say he was a born policeman. In a sense he is, but he is more than that; he is an honest, open, sincere young man whose approach to our profession is one of a vocation.

'It is the GRB's opinion that the Garda Síochána is the one service in which only the best can ever be good enough. Not only must our state seek the best people, but it must give them the best pay, and provide them with the best service conditions. These qualities are even more necessary when we consider the restrictions which membership of the service imposes. What other service demands that its membership be on duty 24 hours a day in peacetime conditions, without as yet, compensation for overtime?'

The announcement that the Garda Band was being wound up at the end of November 1965 caused outrage. Immediately Jack Marrinan and executive member Brian Sheehan met the Minister for Justice Brian Lenihan to protest. The official line was that the members of the band were needed for garda duty.

'Our force has been allowed to decline in numbers in recent years, while their needs have multiplied' Marrinan complained. 'The reduction in numbers had affected especially those involved in the prevention and reduction in crime and the regulation of traffic.

'In 1948 our total strength was 7,478 of which 5,917 were gardaí. That year 14,879 indictable crimes were reported, a total of 107,511 vehicles were licenced and 153,879 persons held driving licences. This year the strength of the force is 6,540 and in August last 518,692 people held driving licences and 447,129 motorised vehicles were licensed.' In other words, fewer gardaí were being asked to police almost three times as many vehicles.

'Now 35 musicians have been called on to bridge the gap.'[17]

The claim for a reduced working week was getting nowhere, but pay claims were subject to arbitration and could progress. On 19 March 1966 Marrinan reported that an arbitration board meeting on their claim for eight per cent was due at the end of the month. It would be chaired by chartered accountant William Sandys. The Department of Justice would be represented by an official called O Buachalla, with whom he and Pat Nolan had earlier clashed, and an official called Mac Guill for the Department of Finance. The GRB was represented by Jack Marrinan and Tom O'Leary, an executive member representing Dublin. The official side had strongly opposed the claim primarily on the grounds of the current national economic situation where inflation was becoming a major problem.

In April, Marrinan got good news. The chairman had ruled in favour of the gardaí. He recommended that their wages be increased by six per cent on all points of the salary scale, and that the new rates be backdated to the 30 June 1965. The pay awards of July 1963 and June 1965 taken together resulted in a £3 per week increase in the pay of a recruit garda. At end July 1966 male gardaí aged over 21 years were awarded £1 per week increase.

17    This was a reference to a government White Paper on cutbacks called *Closing The Gap*.

Those under 21 and ban gardaí got 15 shillings. Both awards were backdated to 1 June 1966.

Another straw in the wind was a letter Jack received from Deputy Commissioner E A Reynolds in October 1966 notifying him of changes in the examinations for promotional positions. Henceforth the pass mark would be 40%. Did Marrinan think that was high enough? The Commissioner would like to know. This was Patrick Carroll's management style, consultation followed by decision, not just simple diktat. He had taken over as Commissioner from William P Quinn in March 1967. Neither would be in the job long enough to get much done, but Carroll's collegial tone came as a welcome change.

Patrick Carroll, who took control of the force in March 1967, was a quiet man. As a barrister his appointment as Commissioner raised the bar. He had joined through a cadet recruitment scheme, avoiding the Garda Depot training experience, and was sometimes known as the untrained Commissioner. It was a joke, kindly meant as he was a popular officer. He had progressed through the ranks as a sergeant, inspector and superintendent, and from 1962 as assistant and deputy Commissioner. He knew his gardaí and few in the force were better qualified to meet the many-faceted challenges then presenting themselves. The pity was that his time was so short. He retired shortly before the North began its downward spiral in 1968. He would have been an excellent choice to lead the force through the changes the Conroy report would require. His daughter Mella Carroll became the first female high court judge in 1980.

In March 1967 Sir Albert Kennedy announced a shorter working week for the RUC. Marrinan again pounced.

'They are going to get a 40-hour week, where up to 1964 they had worked a weekly 44 hours. We do not enjoy a fixed working week, and we have no enforceable right to time-off or compensation in lieu. We must average 48 hours per week before we are entitled to two free days. In fact, there is no guarantee that having worked the required number of hours a member shall get his free days at the end of the month. Frequently, they do not.'In holiday resorts members work for months on end without any free day. In these circumstances a member must be excused if, occasionally he is not as cheerful and efficient as he might be when going about his duties. Perhaps a special committee should be set up to advise the Minister for Justice on how best a reduced working week for gardaí can be implemented.'[18]

And that's exactly what happened. However, as mentioned previously, the claim for a shorter working week opened up a split on the management side. Commissioner Carroll set up an all-ranks working party. Chief Supt John Coakley, selected to chair this group, set about devising practical arrangements to implement a shorter working week – on the assumption that it would be conceded at some future date. Berry was infuriated by the implied concession, maintaining that what Coakley should have been doing was to find ways in which costs could be contained without additional expenditure. What Berry really wanted was an operational plan to cut smaller garda stations and employ more civilian staff. And the proposal to close stations was about to reappear on the agenda in spectacular fashion.

On 27 June 1968, newly-appointed Minister for Justice Michael O Morain issued a press release in which he outlined his current vision on the role of gardaí in Irish society. This included a commitment to training, promotion, modernisation and discipline. He wanted to reorganise the force, increasing productivity and closing stations, he said. He spoke of improving public relations, new technology and more transport. He concluded. 'I should like to assure the gardaí that they will be pushing an open door regarding additional funds in these regards.'

18    Editorial *Garda Review* March 1967.

All very innocuous and praiseworthy sentiments from a progressive Minister who sought to modernise the force and was willing to spend money on making it happen, the average reader might well conclude. Marrinan read it very differently. Peter Berry was attempting to stage a coup, side-lining the GRB by junking existing claims – some already well advanced in conciliation – and also hoping to win public acceptance of the need to close some stations under the guise of modernisation.

Immediately, Jack Marrinan wrote to the Commissioner questioning the Minister's statement and saying it had 'caused alarm and distress' in the ranks. The fact that the press release did not mention the existing claim for a shorter working week, or a pay claim lodged the previous month, added to the growing discontent, he said. He sought Commissioner Carroll's permission to hold a special GRB meeting on 3 July 1968 to discuss the Minister's remarks. The delay in processing the claim for a shorter working week would be discussed, the letter said.

Jack Marrinan also wrote to Peter Berry, as secretary of the Department of Justice, reiterating members' alarm and distress, and requesting an urgent discussion with the Minister. Marrinan was telling Berry that he had 'rumbled' his tactic of appealing directly to gardaí and the public, and by-passing the GRB he would fight tooth and nail to stop him.

On 28 June 1968 Jack Marrinan presided over an angry GRB general meeting. A resolution was agreed, saying, 'that the present machinery available to gardaí to deal with, and rectify grievances is entirely inadequate.' It called for an immediate interim pay rise and also called on the government to set up a commission to inquire into and establish appropriate conditions of employment for the force.

On 25 July 1968, the GRB represented by Jack Marrinan, Jim Fitzgerald, Brian Sheehan, Tom O' Leary, Andy Hallissey and Michael Conway met Department of Justice officials. Pay and a reduced working week were the main issues on the agenda. No agreement was reached, and discussions were adjourned.

A week later on 31 July 1968 the GRB executive team met at conciliation to consider an offer made on its claim for parity with clerical officers in the public service. The offer on the table would meet all garda claims up to June 1970. Kerry man Andy Hallissey, along with his staunch ally Pat Tierney, was there. His account conveys the tensions of the time:

'We were at a conciliation meeting on pay and had a good cut at the official side but came away empty-handed. We had the usual de-briefing. I remember Jack saying that there was something in the wind. The following day they were back with "an offer that would have tied us up for two years", Hallissey said. Jack called a side meeting to discuss. Everyone had their say, but we all waited for Jack's response. His decree was to hold tough. When we declined the offer, I sensed that the opposition were taken aback.'

It looks like Jack must have heard a whisper on the grapevine from the Labour Court where Dublin firemen seemed likely to win pay parity with gardaí. Settling in advance of this bombshell becoming public would put the GRB in a dreadful mess. As it happened, the executive trusted Marrinan's instincts.

A week later, on August 8, Dublin firemen were in the Labour Court seeking a pay rise. The chairman P.S. Mac Carthaigh awarded an increase of 25 shillings a week. He refused a claim for pay parity with clerks but said he saw substantial similarities between the recruitment and employment of firemen and that of An Garda Síochána, and found that firemen should benefit from any increase the gardaí received.

Like Marrinan, Berry had got wind of the impending decision in the fireman's claim. Berry had set a trap for the GRB, hoping to tie them into a two-year pay freeze before the fire brigade decision became public. Jack hit the red button.

'Marrinan went on the rampage like a forest fire', Hallissey said. Jack spoke out vehemently on radio condemning the Labour Court ruling out of hand. In his anger he forgot to seek official permission as he was required before doing so. Assistant Commissioner Wymes summoned Jack to appear before him at the Garda Depot the following morning for a dressing-down.

Later that evening at a function in the Garda Club, Commissioner Carroll strode in. He went straight up to Jack and said he was glad that he had made the statement regarding the pay relationship between gardaí and firemen. Carroll finished the job by telling the press:

'My gardaí have duties and responsibilities which are peculiar to their calling and which distinguish them from all other public servants and municipal employees. I cannot agree or accept how the court arrived at their decision, without having before them details of my members' training qualifications and responsibilities, which distinguish them from all other public servants.'

In referring to the force as 'my gardaí' Carroll had gone a long way to acknowledge the essential unity of the force and heal recent wounds, as well as telling the government what he thought of its industrial relations machinery, and incidentally telling Wymes to leave Jack alone. 'To my knowledge it was the first occasion gardaí united from top to bottom to become guardians of their profession and personal well-being', Jack said afterwards. No more was heard from Wymes on that subject. This was Carroll's swansong.

Soon afterwards Michael Wymes succeeded Patrick Carroll as Commissioner. The expectation was that Wymes would be more pliable in the eyes of the Department of Justice. Marrinan was sorry to see Carroll go – he had been able to do business with the soft-spoken man from Stradbally, Co. Laois. It was a pity that he left office too early.

Within 28 days all garda representative associations united to call for a commission to inquire into garda pay and conditions of service. The recently appointed Minister for Justice Micheal O Morain had conceded an inquiry– provided the force accepted a pay increase of nine per cent in line with that offered to other public servants. The GRB said they would accept the nine per cent as a payment on account.

The stage was set for a most significant event in the development of a modern Irish police force – the inquiry and report of a committee chaired by Judge John (Charlie) Conroy.

# 5

# Jack scores a famous victory with Conroy

Understanding what happened at the time of the Conroy inquiry into the Garda Síochána is difficult, made more so by the fact that the winners, the rank-and-file gardaí represented by Jack Marrinan, took a long time to realise how much they had gained. And the losers, Peter Berry and the Department of Justice, never wanted to admit that they had come off second-best. In fact there's a strong possibility that the official publication of the report was mishandled in the hope that the gardaí might reject the entire document. And the report, which ran to 250 pages, covered so much ground that it defied punchy headline categorisation. Was it a pay claim as most newspapers reported? Yes, it was, but it was much more besides, and the pay element was its weakest and least significant point.

Ivor Kenny's racy memoir (*Last Word*, Oak Tree Press, Cork 2006) is as good a place as any to begin to understand what happened. He lifted the lid on the work of the Conroy inquiry. Kenny was a coming man, seen then as a guru of the hip new science of management and in his spare time he coached the Garda Boat Club. He had family connections with the force. He came to know the guard he called Jackie Marrinan and they discussed management matters. One day Marrinan told him that a commission was going to look into garda organisation to see if some deep-seated problems could be resolved and asked if he would like to be part of it. The chairman was to be Charlie Conroy, a senior circuit court judge, and a free spirit as judges go.

The full commission consisted of: Judge John C. Conroy, chairman, Ivor Kenny, director of the Irish Management Institute, Patrick Noonan, vice president of the Incorporated Law Society and a practicing solicitor, Gerard Quinn, lecturer in political economy at University College Dublin, and retired Commissioner William P. Quinn. Joe Chadwick of the Department of Labour would act as secretary, Conroy having shrewdly declined the services of a Department of Justice official who might find himself serving two masters- the more persistent being Peter Berry.

The first meetings were held in what is now the Merrion Hotel. 'Five of us sat on an elevated platform and were addressed as Mr. Commissioner.' Kenny said it was an amazing experience. Some submissions were tedious, and Kenny took to having a nap during them, until a friendly guard warned him that he had been rumbled.

Most of the questioning was being done by economist Gerry Quinn. When they visited rural police stations, they travelled in a hired black Austin Princess limousine. Berry, who was responsible for Department of Justice spending, tried to tell Conroy off for this extravagance; Conroy ignored him, observing that if Berry continued in this vein, the inquiry would be minded to visit the Hawaiian police. This got back to Berry, as Conroy intended, because no more was said about limos.

Something else happened - Kenny was no longer dozing through tedious presentations; he had become engaged by the subject. Here was a police force with many strengths, particularly widespread public support – a priceless asset in itself – capable of doing great good; but badly led, getting itself in a muddle over simple and not so simple organisational matters. This was grist to a management guru's mill and Kenny got stuck in. His prints are all over the final document.

'When it came to writing the report, Charlie brought us to a private room in the Royal Marine Hotel in Dun Laoghaire and he was merciless. He would not let us out for a pint until we had agreed on a chapter', Kenny wrote.

On the final night in the Dun Laoghaire hotel, Kenny said to Conroy, 'Look, we've solved nothing here. Most of the problems stem from the relationship between the Garda Síochána and the Department of Justice.' Conroy told him to write that down and he would make it the final chapter of the report. This was how the infamous paragraphs 1262-7 came to be added to the Conroy Report, lighting a fuse that would sizzle and fizzle to the present day. The greatest offence was caused by the conclusion that there was something seriously wrong with the relationship between the force and the Department of Justice.

This was dynamite. If accepted, it would blow a hole in Department of Justice control of the Garda Síochána. Even the fact that it was included gave great offence. The report was finalised at the end of 1969 and sent to the Minister's office in St Stephen's Green.

The headline on an *The Irish Times* speculative piece on Wednesday 21 January 1970 must have made Jack Marrinan's heart sink: 'More pay for senior gardaí?' The newspaper went on to say that the Conroy report would shortly be published and suggested that the top brass were in for a big payday. Jack's members certainly wouldn't be rushing out to thank him for that. The following Saturday, the news was more promising. 'More pay for all ranks' was the headline over a report which told the world that the report had been published the previous afternoon. But again the point was missed- this was about very much more than pay.

Conroy had accepted the case for a shorter working week, opened the door for the very first time to overtime payments, agreed that garda accommodation needed improvements, endorsed the case for better treatment for garda widows and orphans, called for restoration of the Garda Band and recommended shortening the list of disciplinary offences.

The problem was the small pay increase even though it was backdated to June 1969. Members of the force had been expecting more. *The Irish Times* report deserves credit for noting that the recommendations on organisation and structure of the force would prove to be most significant in the long-term. It also noted that garda representatives had welcomed the report but offered no evidence of any enthusiasm.

Sunday's newspapers told a different story, one of rank-and-file anger over small pay increases. Monday's *Irish Press* reported that Ivor Kenny criticised the Department of Justice for the way in which the report had been released. 'The Commission accepted that there had been widespread and long-standing discontent in the police force. In a highly charged situation like that, I would have thought the report would have been issued with more care. I think the way it has been communicated has been extraordinarily flat-footed. There has been no indication of the government's attitude', Ivor Kenny was quoted as saying.

In publishing the report but not welcoming, explaining or endorsing it, the government had left the general secretary and the executive of the largest garda representative organisation swinging in the wind.

By the time Monday's newspapers appeared, Marrinan was on the back foot, defending the increases and calling for their immediate implementation, while admitting that his members had expected more. *The Irish Times* on Tuesday reported that Dublin gardaí had met and accepted the recommendations, as had those in Bray, but criticised the pay increase. Gardaí meeting in Boyle,

Co. Roscommon had rejected the pay, overtime, rent allowances and stand-by elements of the package. This, let it be said, was quite mad- gardaí gained a great deal out of these concessions. Cavan-Monaghan gardaí had voted full confidence in the general secretary Jack Marrinan but called for a countrywide secret ballot on the recommendations. Kilkenny gardaí also voted confidence in the general secretary but expressed disappointment in the low increase in pay. On Wednesday the Minister for Justice, Micheal O Morain, announced that a Garda Consultative Council was to be set up, indicating acceptance of Judge Conroy's report, but it was too late. Conroy was going to be a hard sell. The report had failed the first test by not delivering the pay rise most gardaí had been expecting.

The GRB was now in freefall. After hurried consultation with senior officers and taking advice from supportive colleagues, Jack summoned area representatives from all round the country to Dublin for an emergency meeting. He laid the problem out before them. Conroy had done most of what the GRB asked, but fallen short on pay. Members only saw the pay increase and it was not enough. Few gardaí had read the full report or had access to a fair summary.

John Hurley, a native of Caherciveen, Co. Kerry, who represented West Cork, was one of those present. One thing that would help was to get the increase paid now, before the rumblings turned to open revolt. 'The dilemma was how to put pressure on the government. Some members wanted strike; others wanted a page in the daily paper that we were going to withdraw our labour. Jack advised that we adjourn and sleep on a solution.'

So John Hurley and delegates went back to their hotels, Groome's in his case, where he was expected to mix with other guests, including out of town Fianna Fáil TDs. The meeting resumed the following morning, he told me. 'It was mostly the same oul guff, until Jack arrived. "Let's go and see the Minister for Finance", he said. So he led a delegation to meet Charles Haughey in his Kinsealy home.

Haughey's response was succinct and to the point. "Whatever you were promised you will get."' Incidentally Hurley believed that this was not the only time that Marrinan visited Haughey at home.[19] 'Marrinan traversed countrywide promoting the Conroy findings', John Hurley recalled. 'He spread Conroy's gospel. He was humble but insistent, and most of all he had the pedigree. Without Marrinan and the GRB, the Conroy report might not have been accepted', John Hurley said afterwards, noting that the Department of Justice officials dearly wanted it to be rejected.

Marrinan's ability to get to Haughey when he needed to proved invaluable and bought time for the GRB leadership to go out and sell the less immediately obvious gains from the Conroy report to a still dubious membership. However, larger wheels were turning on the political scene, and Haughey's tenure as Minister for Finance would shortly come to an abrupt halt.

Throughout the 1960s Jack Marrinan had learned important lessons on the wing. The Macushla stand-off had occurred because the rank-and-file garda had no effective means of pursuing his objectives, justified or not, and the civil servants responsible for the force had little interest in providing one and were distracted by wider economic problems. Typically, when a pay claim came before the representative body it was almost inevitably rejected, whether the claim was merited, partly merited or just a try-on. Claims about poor living conditions, unsuitable uniforms, overzealous enforcement of discipline- almost all were brought to a full stop by the official side within the JGRB framework, turned down with a one-word response: denied.

To circumvent this, Jack Marrinan had decided to make his case to those whose endorsement could be used to twist the arm of the Department of Justice and the Department of Finance, which

19  Jack's friend John Collins thought that Haughey invited Marrinan to his home many times, but he only went once.

controlled the national purse. He had always wanted a judge-led inquiry into the sorry state in which Ireland's police force found itself. Frederick Mangan's service as an arbitrator had been useful, but a district court judge is merely a local magistrate. In contrast Charlie Conroy, a senior judge of the Circuit Court, was a heavy hitter. Marrinan was now replaying the tactics which had won the day in November 1961– applying the American writer Dale Carnegie's precept of winning friends and influencing people- and his forum was the Conroy inquiry.

Working closely with Tom O'Reilly representing sergeants and inspectors, Marrinan had presented well-argued papers which differed qualitatively from pay-focused submissions of the past. The *Submission to Commission on Garda Pay and Conditions of Service* presented by Marrinan in January 1969 lucidly set out the case for the reforms needed for his people to do their job properly. It runs to about 60 pages of closely typed material, amounting to more than 60,00 words and is supported by lengthy and detailed appendices supporting the arguments put forward.

A subsequent document, *Submissions by Garda Síochána Joint Representative Body*, into which Marrinan had considerable input, pulled together the joint position of the three representative bodies on matters of shared concern: guards. It followed the format of the earlier garda rank-only document. The two were bound together, presented and read as one. They provide a detailed snapshot in time of where the force stood in 1969, from the viewpoint of its entire workforce, the force's strengths and weaknesses and how they informed their needs and hopes for the future.

From September 1968 to January 1969 Jack Marrinan and his GRB colleagues were totally engrossed in the preparation of the Conroy submission. A preamble stated that the strength of the force was 6,535, with 4,969 gardaí and 1,566 of higher rank, and put those figures in the context of demands on the force.

'Since the end of the second world war garda numbers had been decreasing and between 1940 and 1950, they had fluctuated between 6,900 and 7,900. During the 1950s the strength had declined and since 1957 it had varied between 6,350 and 6,650. Some 4,946 gardaí were male, with 23 ban gardaí and 417 detective gardaí. During the preceding four and a half decades there had been a continuous upward curve in the workload with indictable crimes rising by 80%. There had also been an ever-increasing volume of general legislation requiring enforcement. Between 1940 and 1960 almost 150 new pieces of legislation were enacted, putting an increasing strain on the diminishing garda force.'

Made accessible by a well-laid out index, the initial January 1969 document consisted of a general introduction followed by an 18-page section on hours of duty. The third section of nine pages covered allowances, a topic close to executive member Michael Conway's heart, and his input to the fourth section on welfare must have been considerable. Five further sections covered reforming discipline (three pages), the need to improve garda status (three pages), uniform, including the need for a summer uniform and the chromium plating of buttons (three pages), the use of vehicles (two pages) and accommodation (four pages). The conclusion followed along with the detailed appendices, with supporting statistics and international comparisons already mentioned.

The *Submission from the Joint Representative Body* lodged in May 1969 followed a similar pattern, dealing with matters affecting the entire workforce. It included procedures about consultation, proposed changes to the conciliation and arbitration scheme, arrangements for the representative bodies, rent allowance, retirement and pension arrangements, the Garda Compensation Act, Gardaí and the Social Welfare Acts, the reward fund and payment of expenses.

To compile today such a lucid and detailed exposition of a case for reform would require a team of full-time industrial relations officials with access to a well-staffed research unit. Marrinan for the guards and O'Reilly for the sergeants and inspectors did it with the help of a handful of volunteers. In doing so they provided a map of some very murky terrain and invited Conroy to examine what lay below the surface at some very challenging landmarks which they identified. But all this discussion was dry and statistical. What leaps out is the account individual gardaí gave of their lives in evidence at the hearings. What follows are some examples of how garda service affects home life, the worries about being transferred, the demands of official duties and the dangers associated with a career as a garda.

At a hearing on Friday 6 June 1969, D. Montgomery, a barrister on behalf of the joint Garda Representative Bodies, examined Detective Garda B. Lynch, Dublin Castle regarding injuries he received during his duties. Garda Lynch said he joined the force on 16 May 1947 and on 17 March 1955, he was attached to the detective unit at Pearse Street station, Dublin. He recounted an incident in Dublin's South King Street which occurred while on duty and which had seriously affected his home and work life.

He and two colleagues had been on patrol car duty when they got a call that there were housebreakers on Taylor Keith's premises at the back of Sinnott's pub, on South King Street (now part of the St. Stephen's Green shopping centre). Lynch and his colleagues climbed over a gate and spotted four youths coming out of a building. Three of them were captured but a fourth climbed on a roof and made to get away.

'I was fast at the time and climbed onto the roof and grabbed the young lad (he was about 14 years of age) by the coat. Suddenly, the roof gave way and I fell about 30 feet on to a cobble-stoned stable. I broke my left hand in three places and injured my shoulder. I injured my knee, which is bad since and busted my shoe.'

*'Were you removed to hospital immediately?'*

'Mercer's [hospital] was the nearest. My colleagues carried me. It was Sunday and there was no radiologist available so after about two hours without an x-ray I was sent home. I was told that as it was Saint Patrick's weekend I should come back on the Tuesday.'

*'Were any efforts made by the force to get you x-rayed immediately?'*

'None whatever. At 11.30 am the Tuesday after the holiday I was x-rayed. At that time my arm was as big as my thigh. I was put in plaster and ordered off work for ten months.'

*'What pay did you receive?'*

'My garda pay and plain clothes allowance. My detective allowance was stopped immediately when I was hurt. My garda pay was queried after six months. The staff sergeant called me and said there was a question of me being put on half pay.

'My response was: if I'm put on half pay, I'll have to consult legal people.'

*'Did you seek compensation?'*

'I was told sorry, but you have no case. It was not malicious. I agreed that the little chap used no violence against me.'

*'You returned to work after ten months?'*

'I was put in the criminal records office, but I was in pain. My head started to turn to the left. Something was happening to my neck. I went to a consultant in the Adelaide Hospital, Mr. Sugars. He said I should not be employed sitting, that I should be walking. It was suggested that I should not drive or even sit in a car.'

*'What were your chances of promotion?'*

'I had a discussion with my Chief Super. He said due to my sick record and injuries my prospects were slim.'

*'How was your sick record prior to the injury?'*

'Prior to same it was perfectly healthy. I've had several bouts of illness since the incident.'

*'What is your present condition?'*

'I was before the garda surgeon about a fortnight ago. He said he was sorry, but he could not do anything for me, and as there was no point in changing horses mid-stream, he was going to send me back to Mr Sugars.'

*'If you were back in the same condition that you were prior to the accident what do you think your promotion prospects would be?'*

'I had the very same chance of promotion as the two members who were with me that day. One of them who was a garda at the time is now a detective inspector and the other who was the same as myself, a garda crime detective, is now a superintendent.'

*'I understand that you have received your wages during your sick periods.'*

'I have, but it will be coming up again next week as to whether I receive full pay. I will have to write about it again, myself.'

*'Are you suggesting that you are living in constant fear that your wages will be cut?'*

'I am living in fear that I will be discharged from the force.'

*'Have you a family?'*

'Two children.'

*'You have received no compensation?'*

'None.'

Det Garda P J O' Farrell, Castlebar station, Co. Mayo, said he was married with nine children aged from 14 years to two months and was given four days' notice that he was being temporarily transferred to Dublin for a period of 82 days. He was to avail of messing and sleeping accommodation in Pearse Street station at a cost of 11 shillings per day for three meals. Along with one light snack per day the total outlay came to £57.8 shillings. During his absence from home he was entitled to 7 shillings and 9 pence for 30 nights and 5 shillings and 3 pence for 52 nights, a total of £25.5 shillings and 6 pence. Thus, he was £23 out of pocket.

Special weekend return train fare was £2.17 shillings and 6 pence and availing of a once-monthly visit ensured savings on accommodation and messing facilities meant that his transfer would cost him in the region of £30. The only way to cut back on expenditure was not to go home.

'My Pearse Street bedroom housed 11 members, who worked different shifts. Some were called for early duty at 5am, others went to bed at 6am, following 10pm to 6am night duty. A few getting up at 9am to attend courts, as well as members having a lie-on prior to their 2pm shift. Gardaí were going and coming intermittently over the 24-hour period which meant I never got more than four hours' continuous sleep. The room was cold and undecorated and poorly furnished, which meant reading was done in bed.'

On the unpredictability of hours of duty, Garda Sean Fulton, Raheny, was a Dublin-based member, married with four children aged eight, six, four and two. He worked in uniform on tours of duty known as the Regular, but which should have been called the Irregular, with tours of 6am to 2pm and 2pm to 10pm on alternative days for two months, followed by a month of nights from 10pm to 6am. The exigencies of the service meant he was on call outside those hours.

'From day one I made it my business to get to know most of the residents in my area. One widow was having trouble with her teenage son. He was away from home a lot and she didn't know what he was at. In plain clothes and off duty, I made a lot of enquiries. I discovered what he was up to and got a reconciliation.

'On night duty I was sitting down to my tea at 1.45am when I got a call that there was a man threatening colleagues with a gun in the extremities of my area. Colleagues had been trying to arrest his brother. I dropped the cup and headed out. After three and a half hours of patient dialogue and contacts the problem was solved in safety.

'I'm often called away from my station at short notice. This means having to "uniform-up" and head off on public transport to wherever required. There is no allowance for travelling time, as the clock only starts on arrival at the designated post. It could be duty at meetings, protests, parades or celebrations. Recently, I left home at 9am to attend court. Having arrived back at 12.30pm I was just in the door when I got a direction from my station to parade at a city centre station. I had no time for dinner and remained on duty until 7pm. I was back home only a short time, when I was called out on an emergency. Off duty at midnight.

'As regards refreshments while away from my permanent station there are no arrangements in place. Some time back I was on duty at a motor racing fixture in the Phoenix Park. A mobile canteen was serving food at three shillings to the public and two bob (shillings) for a garda. This arrangement did not suit the caterer, and he figured it was more beneficial money-wise to serve the public.

'I also had occasion to deliver a baby.'

Garda Thomas J Walsh said he signed on in 1954. He lived in official quarters attached to the one-man sub-station of Glenville, in a very rural area between Fermoy and Mallow, Co. Cork. His rent was £1 per week. He gave evidence that both buildings were in bad condition, with a damp ground floor and woodworm upstairs. There was no bathroom or hot water. The toilet was outdoors. He always worked alone, and his duties commanded him to be available 24 hours for personal callers and telephone. He had no private life.

'A sudden death occurred, and the local doctor declined to issue a death certificate. I was duty bound to investigate, so I notified the coroner who ordered the body to be moved to his jurisdiction. The relatives were annoyed and blamed me. The deceased's doctor could not be located and an ambulance was not available. I moved the remains on a stretcher, with my own two hands. The coroner directed me to transfer the body to a funeral home in a big town. The local curate objected and was uncooperative, and now he will not talk to me.

'An ageless dispute between two neighbours flared up over a right of way; they were fighting over a yard of ditch and a sup of water. Word came that it was getting serious. I got out my shovel and sorted the mess, and the problem.'

Garda Kevin T. Power said he was stationed in Muinebheag, Co. Carlow, and was married with two children. He joined in 1958 and previously served in Castleblayney and Clontibret, Co. Monaghan and Dublin's Coolock station.

'I rent a 100-year-old detached two-storey house. It is structurally sound and in reasonable repair, but very damp. My furniture valued at £300 which I brought with me on transfer is ruined. I now must keep it in an upstairs room. I am obliged to pay £2 rent per week.

'Each day the sergeant performs station duty 10am to 2pm. I take up from 2pm to 6pm and perform standby as required until 9am the following morning. When off duty I cannot be more than three miles from my station and my whereabouts must be posted on the station door. If I'm not immediately available, I am subject to disciplinary charges.

'I use my private car travelling to crime scenes, accidents and serious matters, but I get no allowance. Recently, I was required to perform night duty for three consecutive weeks, including weekends at a dance marquee six miles from my station. My hours were 9pm to 3am. I was directed not to use my car, but cycle to and from the venue.

'I also inspect bulls and make a declaration that they have been castrated. I've investigated housebreakings, larcenies, assaults, common and indecent, malicious damage, traffic accidents and the causes of fires. I've viewed and had to handle dead bodies, arranged for their identification and sympathised with families. I've had an involvement in virtually every happening in my area.

'A while back I was off duty and coming home from Mass with my two young children. A traffic accident had occurred, which I pulled in to deal with. A car pulled away from the scene in a zig-zag manner. I followed. The driver refused to stop, and I had to pull back in fear for my children. The car eventually pulled in at a dwelling and I approached. The driver was drunk, and I told him I was arresting him for drunken driving. He turned on me and struck me with both fists. It was two and a half hours later when I got home. I still had to perform four hours' duty that evening.'

There were many other such tales. In total 107 witnesses gave evidence, many serving gardaí and officers including Ban Sársaint Sarah McGuinness, Garda Dog and Sub Aqua units, garda clerks in headquarters and the DMA, Weights & Measures personnel, pay sergeants, driving instructors and radio technicians. The Garda Commissioner and the Departments of Justice and Finance sent representatives.

On 16 June 1969 Jack Marrinan told his members that during the previous week the final submission from the joint garda bodies had been lodged. He envisaged that the hearing would be completed by the end of August or early September. On 17 July 1969 he forwarded a copy of his final submissions to each garda station and district representative. He said that his objective had been to secure a fair rate of pay, reasonable working conditions, equitable treatment and an acknowledgement of the importance and standing of every garda in the community. To this end he had placed great emphasis on the high order of duties, functions, responsibilities and powers of members of the uniformed section of the force, the main body of its membership.

Early in October 1969 the GRB was notified that the pay of the force had been increased by 25 shillings per week retrospective from 1 June 1969. It was a 'no strings attached' award and consequently male garda pay was increased to £15.7.6 during training, and to £23.7.3 after 10 years' service. Ban garda pay started at £13.7 shillings and 9 pence rising to £20.8.9 pence at maximum.

In a December 1969 Dáil debate, as the Conroy report was being finalised, almost a dozen deputies spoke up for the force. Fine Gael's John Bruton said, 'The Conroy Commission must consider the unanswerable case for a very substantial increase in the remuneration of An Garda Síochána. They are entitled to an increase of the magnitude that the deputies in this house gave themselves not so long ago'.

Labour's Dr. John O'Connell said there was serious unrest among young gardaí, due to insufficient numbers. 'They are expected to work unreasonably long hours, and they will not tolerate the present working conditions.' Another Labour deputy Barry Desmond paid tribute to the members of the force who, particularly during the past four or five months, had to work under a considerable strain in conditions which were far from satisfactory and called for prompt publication of the Conroy Report. 'There is also a special need for specific provisions for overtime payment', he said.

A Cavan Fine Gael TD Tom Fitzpatrick called for help for garda widows. Tom Enright, a midlands Fine Gael deputy, said: 'I have had occasion to visit garda stations and was appalled at the conditions of most of them. If convicted criminals were asked to spend a weekend in some of these stations there would be a public outcry, but these are the stations in which gardaí are expected to work.'

The report issued at the end of January 1970 ran to 250 pages and made 52 recommendations on virtually every aspect of everyday garda service: accommodation, allowances, discipline, education, hours of duty; including new rosters and night duty, pay, pensions, recruitment, training, uniforms, welfare and many others. Conroy introduced two new and exciting terms to the garda vocabulary – rest days and overtime- and he outlined relevant payment conditions. Many of the recommendations issued by Conroy were based on the GRB submissions.

The problem was that none of this had been communicated in any meaningful way to gardaí around the country. Releasing a complex document on a Friday afternoon when most people are switching off for the weekend is an invitation to misunderstanding. The

Minister for Justice Micheal O Morain was not in good health at the time. A detailed and complex report making recommendations that affected almost all aspects of a garda's life became reduced to a headline dealing with pounds shillings and pence. A press conference could have elicited the fact that gardaí had made significant progress on more than 80% of the issues raised. Somebody independent was needed to tell gardaí they had won a considerable victory, the benefits of which would continue to flow for generations to come. Instead, in those inflationary days, no pay award could look like a win, because the next pay claim would yield more, until inflation brought everyone back to square one. The penny hadn't dropped that winning overtime payments was an enormous gain taken with a reduction in the hours worked. Those who shouted loudest about the Conroy outcome probably had not read the report. Those who rejected the finding on hours of work and overtime certainly hadn't.

In his opening remarks Conroy referred to the relationship between garda duty and morale, a recurring theme in Jack Marrinan's submissions.

'The continual emergence of new legislation raises the bar of garda duties and places an ever-growing responsibility on them to know more than was necessary 20 years, or even 10 years ago. Nowadays, the public are better educated, more discerning and more demanding of higher standards from their gardaí. They also expect them to discharge their duties in circumstances which are more difficult than at any time in their history. The net result is that today's gardaí must go on duty armed with high morale, full commitment and exceptional standards.'

Morale, morale, morale, the one big key to understanding and releasing the potential of the Garda Síochána, the point that Marrinan kept making to Berry, that was there in the very beginning of the Conroy report, if only people were reading it. 'The functions of gardaí demand that they not alone enforce the laws of our State, but they must provide a public service by befriending those in need of aid, as well as assisting in any emergency that arises.'

In Chapter 2, Conroy acknowledged the uniqueness of garda service and the importance and value of their calling.

'The occupation of a policeman is unique. When someone joins the garda, they not only take up a job, but a way of life, for which they must have a vocation. Duties have first claim on their lives, with family and social relationships taking second place. More than any other sector in the State the exigencies of their service make them subject to authority. Without any, or any adequate, or prior notice they can be called to serve long hours of duty or may be liable to have leave of absence refused or cancelled.

'Due to disciplinary regulations a garda must obey the orders of their superiors, while at the same time their main functions as a police officer are vested on them by virtue of their office and not by the directives of a higher authority. Also, their powers and duties are with them, whether they are on or off duty.

'Police must also take responsibility for any error of judgement in exercising their powers and are answerable for such errors. They are also exposed to risks of assault or personal injury, and they may have to tackle an armed man or be set upon by a gang. During the months of June, July and August 1969, a total of 55 gardaí were injured while carrying out their duties; 42 of these were the result of assaults.

'Liability to transfer is another unpleasant feature of a policeman's life, and on transfer his children have to change schools, his wife and family lose their circle of friends, and have to start afresh in a new environment. They also risk serious financial loss when setting down roots in a new community.'

On pay Conroy adopted the GRB term 'a rate for the job' widely used in Marrinan's submission.

'There has never been any attempt at a comprehensive assessment of the pay and conditions of members of An Garda Síochána. Their original pay was based on principles laid down by the Desborough Commission, which were borrowed from the RIC. In 1924 garda pay was reduced, for reasons entirely unconnected with the content of police duties, or the value of a garda to his community. Since then, apart from a few arbitration awards, all increases in pay have been limited to giving compensation for rises in the cost of living. At no time since the foundation of the force, does there appear to be any weight given to the changes in garda duties, or to the environmental changes in which these duties have been performed.

'A compelling case has been made by the GRB that the duties and conditions of service of gardaí are unique. We accept their argument that police work has become more onerous, complex and demanding, and requiring of a higher educational standard. These factors should be recognised by appropriate pay and improvements in conditions of service.'

Conroy recommended salary increases with pay rising to £15.7.6 per week during training, increasing to £25.7.3 per week for male gardaí on full increments, with ban gardaí to get £2 less at both extremities of their scales. He also reduced the incremental scale by one year and recommended a pensionable long-service bonus of £1 per week for members who had served for 15 years and had not been promoted.

On hours of work, the GRB had submitted a lengthy claim for a five-day 40 hour working week. They stated that subject to the exigencies of the service a member is entitled to two days leave each month, which more often than not are refused. As recently as July and August 1969, 234 and 269 members were refused such entitlements. The official side said that the claim for working long hours was exaggerated.

Conroy came down on the garda side.

'We are satisfied that many gardaí normally work more than 48 hours per week. This should be reduced to 42 hours, including a meal break. Parading time should be reckoned as time worked. A new duty roster of a 28-day cycle per calendar month is recommended, with each member allowed seven rest days per roster. Where a member works extra duty on any day, he should be allowed time off in lieu on succeeding days on the following basis; if on the three-relief system 1½ hours for each extra hour of extra duty; if performing duty other than above, the member should benefit with time off equal to the extra duty; if time off is not granted they should get overtime pay.'

Regarding night duty Conroy also agreed with the GRB.

'They believe that it involves a real hardship, puts a strain on members' health, and for married men upsets the rhythm of their homes. We agree, and we recommend that each member of the force up to the rank of inspector, who has worked a qualifying period of 40 hours night duty in a 28-day calendar month, should get a night allowance. The allowance should be in respect of the total night hours worked in a roster period and paid at the rate of one seventh of the member's hourly scale of basic pay.'

Regarding garda stations, the official side had admitted that there were many sub-standard stations. During their visits Conroy's team had seen many stations with no running water or drying rooms, and many poorly furnished rest rooms. Conroy identified the Technical Bureau as an example of poor working conditions with valuable and irreplaceable fingerprint records lying around in passages and hallways, as well as old toilets being converted to dark rooms.

Conroy recommended that a minimum standard for all stations should be agreed. New stations should have adequate office space, including storage, interview rooms, proper office equipment and rest rooms, toilets, as well as facilities to cook a light meal.

The GRB submission highlighted the dire quality of living-in station facilities, allied with the likelihood of transfer. Conroy commented:

'In our countrywide visits we noted that some of the official accommodation is sub-standard and not fit to live in. While the National Building Agency and the Board of Works have done some good work providing good quality married quarters, a similar provision should be available for unmarried men. At present most official garda houses are substandard, with standards varying according to rent payable. In this regard the GRB pinpointed individual cases applicable to various locations within the State. They reported that in 1968 a total of 1,388 unmarried members lived in official accommodation. Of these there was 643 men in 208 garda stations that have no messing facilities, and in many stations the only facility for cooking or making tea was an open hearth.

'In the same year there was 1,012 married members who lived in houses or quarters officially provided, while 3,194 married members and 924 unmarried men were not living in official quarters. Out of the 578 married quarters that are provided, 160 have been in existence since 1922; there is no water in 99, and no hot water in 112. 107 have no flush toilets, and a further 22 have outdoor flush toilets only. A substantial array of facts and figures accompanied the GRB summary. They have conceded that different rent allowances should be payable to married and unmarried gardaí. We concur'.

According to the GRB submission, the Garda Code requires a member to use his bicycle while travelling on duty for up to eight miles from his station. Under chapter 34.1 a divisional officer may authorise a member who has a motor car to use it on special tours of duty or on duties of a regularly recurring nature. If he gets such permission, he would be entitled to claim mileage allowance. Conroy commented:

'We are told that this permission is given sparingly and that circumstances often arise where prior sanction cannot be obtained.

We recommend that the relevant code chapters be amended, to enable a district officer to ratify a member to use his private car by a member on duty.'

The GRB claim on pensions raised a difficulty which had arisen over new pension legislation in 1951 and sought to have 76 members who had failed to apply in time for transition arrangements allowed to do so. Conroy ruled that they should be given a second chance to do so.

Conroy had harsh words to say about the Garda Disciplinary Regulations of 1926 and 1942.

'The GRB has claimed that the Disciplinary Regulations are harsh, oppressive, anachronistic, and even occasionally of questionable legality. Some are also vague, unnecessarily restrictive, open to abuse and vexatious in their interpretation. Section 12a states that a member is liable to commit an offence of insubordination or oppressive conduct by his or her demeanour.

'The disciplinary offence of neglect of duty can be committed by a member gossiping on duty, even though the primary role of gardaí is to familiarise themselves with members of the public.

'An offence of intoxication is committed by a member who, while on or off duty shows because of consuming intoxicating liquor the slightest departure from strict sobriety.

'Section 23 prohibits wearing of badges or emblems without the Commissioner's consent, and section 24 forbids members marrying without permission.

'The procedure for investigating allegations sometimes deprives members of rights to which they are entitled to under the current laws of our State, for example Regulation 7 states that an offence against discipline will be aggravated by denial of the charge.

'The GRB have claimed that many disciplinary investigation techniques were out of date. When answering an allegation on a misconduct form, a member must admit or deny the charge without any qualification. Also, the member accused of a disciplinary breach gets no legal warning before making a statement and cannot be represented by a legal advisor at an unsworn enquiry. Furthermore, except in exceptional circumstances, a member charged does not normally get an opportunity of reading the evidence that may be given against him. The member concerned is not privy to the contents of his superior's report, which will accompany his charges and pleadings to Garda Headquarters where his guilt or innocence is decided.'

Conroy recommended that a revised code of conduct be drawn up based on the understanding that gardaí are responsible persons doing responsible work, capable of making up their minds on who to marry without seeking permission from a superior officer. He recommended that the present disciplinary regulations, and those presently being drafted, should be like the regulations used by the English authorities. 'To assist in this comparison, we have included a copy of the British Police Disciplinary Regulation 1967, in an appendix to this report. It is noted they total 31 breaches, while the garda regulations have 69.' For its part the GRB agreed that some progress on these matters had been made recently.

In Conroy's chapters on recruiting, education, training and the standardisation of uniforms for all ranks, he stressed that a new lightweight summer uniform, an improved greatcoat, and a gabardine overcoat with chrome-plated buttons, as well as a new type of uniform shirt with shoulder epaulettes, should be introduced. The material and colour should be the same for all ranks. He also recommended that a comprehensive scheme for the training and development of personnel should be developed. Conroy also recommended the appointment of a welfare officer, a public relations officer, and the employment of civilian workers to do clerical work, as well as setting up a research and planning unit.

In conclusion Conroy recommended that the existing system of conciliation and arbitration be streamlined so that it was not used to put inconvenient matters on the long finger. Recruitment, promotion discipline and suggestions from the Garda Representative Body for promoting the efficiency of the force should be added to the matters for discussion at conciliation, and there should be a 28-day time limit following submission of claims for the hearing to commence. Also, the arbitration board should include claims in respect of weekly hours of work and overtime.

But what caused real problems for Peter Berry and the Department of Justice, who felt they had been unfairly forced into establishing the commission, was the very clear message contained in the concluding sentences penned by Ivor Kenny, here given in full.

'Because of our terms of reference our recommendations are almost all about pay and conditions. We have not had an opportunity, nor were we asked, to look at other factors influencing the morale of force. We are satisfied from the evidence [put before us] that pay and the conditions are only part of the problem. The objective is an effective police force with high morale fully accepted by and integrated with the community it serves. This objective will certainly not be fully attained by merely paying the force fairly and by looking after their physical conditions of employment.

'We would be failing in our duty to the Minister for Justice if we did not strongly urge that an examination be carried out by appropriately qualified people into the role, organisation and personnel policy of the force and its relationship with the Department of Justice.'

This was saying that the Department of Justice was not up to the job of overseeing the running of a police force. Jack Marrinan, for the gardaí, and Tom O'Reilly for the sergeants and inspectors, had made significant gains on two fronts. Firstly, they had won substantial concessions on pay, pensions and conditions, even though their members wanted more. Secondly and more importantly they now had on public record the need for an examination of the role and behaviours of the civil servants who currently pulled the Garda Commissioner's strings.

In vain Peter Berry would protest that Conroy had gone outside his terms of reference. The bell had rung, and as everyone knows, once rung, you cannot un-ring a bell. Jack's wish for the outcome of the Conroy inquiry, expressed soon afterwards to reporter Joe McAnthony, 'I hope that in future a garda would be able to spend more time in real policing, and have a larger say in pay, policymaking and work conditions'- now had the backing of a finding of an official inquiry.

Desmond O'Malley, who succeeded O Móráin as Justice Minister when O Móráin's health worsened, failed to capitalise on a remarkable reform package. He ran into flak over delays in paying back-money for overtime. He argued that overtime *per se* had not been conceded, but time off in lieu of overtime had been granted, with the proviso that if time was not taken within three months, payment would follow instead. As the time off did not materialise, overtime thus fell due to be paid but in arrears.

It was a shoddy manoeuvre designed to hide a total U-turn on the official side. The slow pace of implementation of Conroy was eroding the goodwill which should have followed publication of the report. In late 1970 an editorial in the *Garda Review* set out Jack's views.

'Ten months since the Conroy report laid bare a great bulk of grievances that had bedevilled the force and agreed a formula for removing them, it has become apparent that there has been no goodwill on the part of the government to implement the recommendations.

'While [improvements in] pay scales have been welcomed, they have lost some of their lustre with the recent pay offer to Dublin traffic wardens. The fixed working week and night duty allowance is appreciated, but not one penny of overtime has been paid even in respect of extra duty carried out as far back as last April. There has not even been compensation with time off in lieu. Neither has the recommended rent allowance accepted by the government been paid, even though these provisions played a significant part in getting the force to accept the commission's findings. Similarly, recommended disciplinary regulations have not become operational, with members rapidly souring [because of] the clear injustices accumulated during the old system.

'In addition, 1,700 garda widows whose hopes were raised when they read the commission's recommendations are sadly concluding that they will have to continue to struggle on £5 per week or die before they are paid the agreed ex-gratia pension.

'By promptly conceding and implementing the benefits recommended by the commission, which have been accepted by gardaí, the government could have achieved a degree of gratitude and goodwill which is now being gradually flittered away.'

On Wednesday 31 March 1971 a lengthy Dáil finance committee debate took place, more than 14 months after the Conroy report had appeared. O'Malley opened the proceedings, by moving a supplementary estimate of £2,550,000 for garda costs.

'As deputies are aware, two new widows and children's pensions schemes are also being introduced for the force, along with a contributory scheme, like that in operation in the civil service. This will apply to members serving on or after 23 July 1968, the date of commencement of the civil service scheme. Under the second scheme of ex-gratia pensions, equal in most cases to half the benefits under the contributory scheme, this will be payable to the widows and children of members of the force who died or retired on pension before 23 July 1968. These ex-gratia pensions will be paid with effect from 1 October 1969, or the date of commencement of the widow's existing pension, whichever is the later.'

Too little, too late, Minister.

The Conroy report was accepted by the GRB, although without enthusiasm. In time Jack Marrinan and his allies would win over members, as the gains became more obvious. Today's policemen and women see in the work of Judge Conroy's committee the foundation stone of a new era in policing in Ireland. This view was not shared by the rank-and-file garda looking at his or her payslip in 1970. It is now generally agreed that the report of the Conroy inquiry was Jack Marrinan's finest achievement.

After he retired, Jack Marrinan was fond of saying that the most important lesson he learned from the Conroy process was something which Ivor Kenny had quoted to him: 'People are generally better persuaded by the reasons they have themselves discovered than by those which have come into the mind of others.' [20]

20    Ivor Kenny was quoting the French philosopher Blaise Pascal (1623-1662).

# 6

## Sheer bloody murder

Policing was about to get much more difficult. The Northern Troubles arrived on the streets of Dublin. Garda Richard Fallon was the first to lose his life. A republican splinter group calling itself Saor Éire (Ireland Free) was robbing at gunpoint a Royal Bank of Ireland branch on Dublin's Arran Quay, close to the Four Courts. The Mountjoy patrol car driven by Garda Pat Hunter responded to an alarm triggered by a cut telephone line. It arrived at the scene on Arran Quay while the robbery was in progress. Two uniformed gardaí, Dick Fallon and Paul Firth, both unarmed, confronted three armed gunmen. The robbers fired at least six shots, and when Fallon reached out to grab one of the gunmen, he was shot in the head at close range. The bullet severed his spinal cord. He was dead on arrival at Jervis Street hospital. Another bullet had entered his left side shattering a bone in his arm.

'Gardaí are exposed to risks of assault or personal injury, and they may have to tackle an armed man or be set upon by a gang', Conroy had said a few months earlier. The three robbers fled the scene having stolen £2,000. Saor Éire was an alias for IRA supporters trying to extend their activities south of the border. In 1970 Dick Fallon was in his 45th year, with a young wife and five children under the age of 12. He was the first member of the Garda Síochána to be murdered in the line of duty for almost three decades. I was 23 years old and in my third year of service in Whitehall station when the news came through. The station sergeant, a bulky man, was typing out some reports. All was quiet in the rest room and I was dozing quietly in the spring sunshine. The telephone began to ring. The sergeant answered it giving his name, rank and 'Can I help you?'

After a brief pause, the sergeant began to bellow. I was off duty, heard the commotion and ran to the public office to find out what was happening. 'Stop. No. Shut up. Don't dare pull that one on me. What are you saying?' The sergeant, the mildest of men, had gone out of his mind, or was having a fit, I thought. He was stalking back and forward across the public office, his arms flung wide, his head shaking, whimpering like a child. The phone receiver lay on the public counter. The sergeant leaned over his desk shouting at the mute receiver. 'No, no, no.' I picked up the phone but there was nobody there. I replaced it on its cradle. The sergeant was shouting. 'Mother of God Almighty. Cold-blooded murder. Unarmed. Shot dead. What's to come of us all?' His next outburst nearly floored me, or maybe it was the puck of his fist that accompanied it. 'What are ye looking at? Get out. Out. Put on the blue and get the lads out. Everyone. We must parade the uniform and have a show of strength.'

Hearing the racket, another guard appeared. A normally placid man, his face was twisted in anguish. Dick Fallon was dead, he said. Dick from the Joy was dead. Garda Richard Fallon, from nearby Mountjoy garda station, was dead. 'Shot in a bank raid on the quays.'

The sergeant roared at them both. 'Get up them steps, on the double.'

A thousand blue uniforms paraded at the Church of St Paul of the Cross in Harold's Cross, South Dublin for Dick Fallon's funeral. Afterwards they formed up and marched in formation into the city as far as Parnell Square, watched from the pavements by quiet respectful people, many with joined hands, bare heads, lips moving in silent prayer. An old woman rushed forward out of the crowd and tugged at my arm. 'May God forgive those who did such a terrible thing.' Saying 'amen', I gently dislodged her hand and marched on. At Parnell Square, the gardaí got on buses to take them to Balgriffin cemetery, where they said a final good-bye to their fallen comrade.

There had been earlier straws in the wind. Less than two months earlier there had been a bank raid in Rathdrum, Co. Wicklow, during which the raiders took control of the village, cut it off from outside contact, and held Garda Joe Arrigan at gunpoint while they stole £2,000 from a bank, and a gunsmith's shop was raided. Similar raids took place in other villages and towns. There had been 12 armed raids since 1967[21]and the Garda Central Detective Unit (CDU) knew that Saor Éire was involved in many of them. In response, the banks cut back on the amount of cash held on vulnerable premises, so the takings usually did not exceed £2,000. Still the fact remained that at Rathdrum, a quiet village barely an hour from Dublin, the rule of law had been suspended by armed men.

The Central Detective Unit (CDU) under Detective Chief Superintendent John Joy was on to Saor Éire. Detectives knew that indirect contacts existed between Saor Éire and two Ministers – Charles Haughey and Neil Blaney – and that Garda C3 intelligence division was aware of this. They also knew that Haughey's brother Jock was in contact with Martin Casey, a leading Saor Éire member, while Blaney's brother Harry had been meeting other Saor Éire members. Saor Éire first denied any involvement in the robbery but later changed its tune. 'We deny that Garda Fallon was killed in the course of protecting the public. He died protecting the property of the ruling class, who are too cowardly and clever to do their own dirty work.'[22]

---

21  *The Guarding of Ireland*, p.30

22  Irish Republican Marxist History Project. "Statement by Saor Éire Denying Responsibility for the Raid on the Royal Bank Arran Quay, Dublin." Irishrepublicanmarxisthistoryproject, National Archives Ireland, 7 Apr. 2017, irishrepublicanmarxisthistoryproject.wordpress.com/2014/12/27/statement-by-saor-eire-denying-responsibility-for-the-raid-on-the-royal-bank-arran-quay-dublin/.

Bad and all as the murder of an unarmed guard undoubtedly was – Dick Fallon was a young man and his wife Deirdre now had five children to bring up on her own – the political and social implications were also appalling. Fallon's posthumous Scott medal recognised his courage but did not close a troubling chapter. Three men were subsequently charged with murder and acquitted by a jury which had, many observers feared, been 'got at', either suborned or intimidated. One accused was known to have visited the home of a prominent Dublin journalist on the day of the bank raid. Another suspect was helped to escape across the border into Northern Ireland by a Donegal-based Minister in the Fianna Fáil government, according to Gerard L'Estrange, a Fine Gael TD. Lestrange did not name anyone, but it was widely believed among gardaí that Neil Blaney was responsible.

More generally the IRA, claiming kinship with 'liberation struggles' elsewhere in the world, was seeking to be made 'respectable'. A sense that despite the IRA's excesses, in some sense Northern Ireland 'had it coming' began to spread into schools and universities, trade unions, sport, social and professional associations. Press and broadcasting were not immune. Old ways were being discarded piecemeal. In Europe what began as the 'peace, man' flower-child revolution of the 1960s was giving way to hard-edged radical activism in the 1970s. This was the era of the Baader-Meinhof terrorist group, responsible for more than 30 deaths in Germany, and the Italian Red Brigades who took the life of former Prime Minister Aldo Moro in 1978. Britain's so-called 'Angry Brigade' recruited among Irish students at UK universities. Also in the Irish community in Britain, the Connolly Association raised funds for 'freedom fighters' in Northern Ireland, and Clan na Gael rallied support among the Irish diaspora in the United States and Britain.

Above all this was the heyday of the 'snakin' regarder' phenomenon identified by *The Irish Times* columnist John Healy. To be found in pulpits, official and otherwise, at parish and council meetings and on barstools, the 'snakin' regarder' was a peculiarly nasty phenomenon of the time, speaking out of both sides of his mouth. In the wake of the latest IRA atrocity, voices could be heard spouting 'Say what yiz like about the lads, but it takes courage to stand up and be counted at a time like this', delivered with a knowledgeable smirk.

Jack Marrinan recognised this tolerance for what 'the lads' were doing for the mortal danger it was and went on the attack, insisting that the price of such public misconceptions and political ambiguity was liable to be paid by a garda going about his or her daily duties left bleeding to death on a city street or in a disused farmhouse.

In the immediate aftermath of the Fallon murder, Marrinan also tried to broaden the discussion in an editorial in the *Garda Review* in April 1970.

'While sincere sympathy was evoked by Dick Fallon's death the realities of the way he carried out his duties were missed. The public, and indeed the media seemed to have no realisation that his death was the result of his being confronted with a situation which made a call on his sense of duty that is not required from any other member of our community.

'There are members of the force who are beginning to genuinely wonder where the public stands in relation to the running skirmish between law and crime, which has become the salient feature of a policeman's job in a modern society.'

Marrinan was telling his members, and other readers of the *Garda Review*, including politicians and civil servants and society at large, that the context in which policing in Ireland was operating had changed for the worse. In 1969, a civil rights march from Derry to Belfast was ambushed at Burntollet bridge by about 300 loyalists; about a third were said to be off-duty part-time policemen, known as 'B Specials'. The unionist-dominated parliament at Stormont had banned the march and the

RUC members on duty did little to protect the marchers who were pelted from a nearby hillside with rocks from a local quarry. According to historian Paul Bew, this was the spark that lit the fire of the Northern Ireland conflict. But the tinder had been accumulating for much longer.

A piece of reforming British legislation from 1944 providing secondary education for all had unforeseen consequences. In Northern Ireland, the first generation of Catholics thus educated came of age in the mid-1960s. This generation, inspired by the black civil rights marches of 1965 in the USA, was now ready to challenge the unionist dominance. The initial demand was for civil rights, the right to public housing on equal terms, the right to vote on equal terms in local government elections, and an end to discrimination against Catholics and nationalists in recruitment. In the background was the IRA, its campaign of violence aiming to reunite the island by force having been seen off as recently as 1956. The brutal way in which the Stormont regime responded to peaceful protest, firstly banning marches then letting loose the RUC, which had a few Catholics in its ranks, and/or loyalist gangs on those taking part, allowed the dormant IRA to emerge again and the stakes were raised in a conflict which would claim 3,000 lives. That all this would somehow be contained within Northern Ireland nobody really believed.

When the 'Battle of the Bogside' erupted in the flashpoint city of Derry in August 1969, three days and nights of fighting between the RUC and nationalists ensued, and the minority called for intervention by the Irish government to protect them from their own police force. TV networks worldwide showed the RUC baton-charging peaceful demonstrators. According to journalists Patrick Bishop and Eamonn Mallie, 'Both communities were in the grip of a mounting paranoia about the other's intentions. Catholics were convinced that they were about to become victims of a protestant pogrom; Protestants that they were on the eve of an IRA insurrection.'[23]

On 13 August 1969, the Taoiseach Jack Lynch broke off his holidays to call for the intervention of United Nations troops on the streets of Northern Ireland. In a televised speech he said it was clear the present situation could not continue:'It is evident that the Stormont government is no longer in control of the situation. It is clear also that the Irish government can no longer stand by and see innocent people injured and perhaps worse. It is obvious that the RUC is no longer accepted as an impartial police force.' Lynch ruled out British army intervention and called for UN forces to be sent in. 'We have also asked the British government to see to it that police attacks on the people of Derry should cease immediately.'

In the aftermath of the Derry street riots, the British government dismissed Lynch's comments but commissioned two inquiries. The more significant one by Lord Scarman, a judge, found that the Catholic minority no longer believed the RUC was impartial. Another by Lord Hunt, a respected mountaineer and explorer, recommended that the part-time B Specials constabulary, which had been involved in sectarian attacks, be reconstituted as the Ulster Defence Regiment within the disciplines of the British army.

There was a significant lesson for the Garda Síochána. Gardaí could count on public support for now, but that could change. If shooting at members of the RUC was acceptable, it would not be long before a garda was in the firing line. And that is what happened, sadly. Dick Fallon was the first of many. After April 1970, Marrinan and his colleagues on the GRB executive knew that nothing would be the same. As did every garda spouse, noting that when a loved one went to work, there was now a worry about him or her ever coming home.

---

23    Bishop, Mallie, *The Provisional IRA*, p103

For Commissioner Michael Wymes, and the men and women of the force, these were very dangerous times. As had happened in the 1920s during the Civil War, support from significant politicians and their followers could not be counted upon. A close link existed between the murder of Garda Dick Fallon and what was to become known as the Arms Trial. Both involved efforts by the nationalist minority in Northern Ireland to obtain arms. Both had a common purpose. The bank raid was to get money to buy arms illegally; the Arms Trial was about Northern nationalist efforts to get the Dublin government to supply them with arms legally.

There were in fact two arms trials. The first was a mistrial. The verdict in the second – in which a senior government Minister, an army intelligence officer, a Belfast republican and a Flemish nationalist were acquitted of conspiracy to import arms – was rejected by Taoiseach Jack Lynch in very questionable circumstances. Questionable because, as we now know, Lynch's government had secretly given the go-ahead to import arms.

The head of the Garda Special Branch reported directly to the secretary of the Department of Justice on matters of state security. On 17 April 1970, barely a fortnight after Dick Fallon was murdered, Chief Supt John Fleming informed Department of Justice secretary Peter Berry of the imminent arrival at Dublin Airport of arms from Vienna. Berry phoned Charles Haughey, then Minister for Finance, and told him that he knew a shipment was of arms was coming into Dublin Airport and that he had given orders for gardaí to seize it. Haughey called the shipment off.

The cat was out of the bag. Lynch dismissed Haughey and Blaney as Ministers: they, Kelly and Albert Lukyx, a Flemish nationalist and Blaney associate who had taken Irish citizenship, were then charged with conspiracy to import arms. Blaney's prosecution was dismissed at district court level. At the Central Criminal Court, the jury found the four remaining defendants not guilty, though Lynch would challenge this verdict. The jury found that an operation in-stigated by a Cabinet sub-committee and overseen by the Minister for Defence Jim Gibbons was not a conspiracy against the state. The morality of a democratic government covertly providing arms to members of an armed conspiracy in an adjoining territory was neither here nor there so far as the court was concerned. Politically Lynch had lost control of a situation where senior members of his government were prepared to supply arms to the IRA.

The Arms Trial and its aftermath need not detain us here except insofar as it affected the Garda Síochána. In the whole sorry tale few emerge with credit. Peter Berry, a civil servant who stood up to powerful Ministers, was a shining exception. Here was a lesson which Jack Marrinan and his GRB executives clearly understood. In a fight on the fundamentals on which policing in a democratic state rested, when politicians trimmed to the wind, you could count on Berry, despite being difficult, obstructive and bloody-minded on other matters.

Accounts of this turbulent period have tended to consider the resurgence of the IRA, the murder of gardaí , tensions within gov-ernment on security policy, the fracturing of the political consensus on Northern Ireland, the appearance of hard drugs on the streets of our towns and cities, and a general increase in serious crime as sep-arate phenomena. They weren't. Michael Wymes and his force had to face all these challenges at the same time, and an increasingly worried public had to be reassured that the force could and would cope. Like Berry, Wymes deserves credit for standing firm in the face of an onslaught which was about to get worse.

In his annual crime report covering the period ending 30 September 1970, Wymes reported a steadily deteriorating situa-tion. Indictable crimes had risen from 23,104 in 1969 to 30,756 in 1970, with burglaries and robberies increasing from 7,563 to 9,577. Almost two-thirds of these crimes were in Dublin. There were 10 murders: four in Tipperary and one each in Clare, Roscommon, Laois and Cork, and two in Dublin. Crime in 16 of the 17 countrywide divisions showed large increases. There were increases of over 40% in the divisions of Longford-Westmeath, as well as Galway and Tipperary. Laois-Offaly and Sligo-Leitrim had increases of almost 30%. Some 12 armed robberies were committed, mostly in post offices and banks, with eight in Dublin city and one each in Kerry, Monaghan, Galway and Wicklow.

The following year, Wymes reported that the total number of indictable crimes was 37,781, which was 33% greater than the previous year; 26% of these crimes were committed in Dublin. The detection rate was 44%, down 6% from 1970. Larceny from the person, housebreakings, robberies, and offences against property with violence had increased by 30%. There had been 30 armed robberies, almost double the previous year's total of 17. Likewise, theft of motor vehicles had doubled in a year. Some 70 people had been charged with possession of cannabis, with 32 having other illegal drugs.

Wymes attributed the increases to:

Criminals on bail committing further crimes. A total of 383 repeat offenders had committed 1,570 crimes while on bail.

Lack of security along with growth of urbanisation and industrialisation.

Increased mobility of criminals.

More professional criminals with greater legal knowledge.

Wymes said the Garda Crime Prevention Unit had been expanded, and a special task force for Dublin had been set up. Also the Juvenile Liaison Scheme was extended to all other cities and eight major towns.

Yet another new challenge appeared on the streets of Dublin in early 1970, much less serious than terrorism and the professionalisation of crime, but it still required another policing skill to be mastered and required deployment of considerable manpower by an over-stretched force. As 1969 ended and 1970 began, a South African rugby team was touring Britain and Ireland. There were large and sometimes angry demonstrations outside the stadiums where the 'whites only' Springboks were playing. The Irish Anti-Apartheid movement had support from idealistic young people, and trade unions and other civil society organisations joined them in opposing the rugby tour. The stage was set for an angry confrontation at Lansdowne Road stadium on 10 January 1970. The visiting team was due to stay in the Royal Hotel in Bray, and a day before they arrived there was an explosion in the grounds. A man was subsequently charged with possession of explosives.

The day before the international rugby match, the Springboks team visited Leinster House at the invitation of a Fine Gael TD, Dr Hugh Byrne. Gardaí clashed with demonstrators in Molesworth Street. On the day of the match, about 6,000 people joined an anti-apartheid march from the city centre to the grounds. The demonstration was peaceful until a group of 100 protestors broke away and tried to open a gate into the ground. There were some scuffles and the gardaí held them at bay. *The Irish Times* reported that the gardaí did not draw batons, and the police operation was conducted with good humour.[24] The match result was a draw, and so also it appears, was the stand-off between gardaí and the protestors.

Afterwards Jack Marrinan told *Sunday Independent* reporter Joe McAnthony, 'If you take the recent demonstration against the Springboks, some members on duty would have liked to have seen the match and others would have liked to demonstrate. Instead, they all had to work. Their job happened to be the preservation of individual's freedom under the law. And that is what they did.'

He also spoke of the pressures on himself in representing gardaí. As the only full-time official in the GRB, he had 740 stations to look after, and even with local representatives to deal with matters

24    *Garda line holds rugby pitch gates, The Irish Times. 12 January 1970.*

in their area, most of the decisions were made on his desk. On average he worked 14 to 15 hours per day.

During the second half of 1971 Jack Marrinan used the columns of the *Garda Review* to warn senior officers and the Department of Justice that planned cutbacks were affecting the morale of members, and that existing cuts had bitten deep enough.

'In many garda districts our members are severely critical of senior officers who tend to insist that manning of patrol cars and beats has become a low priority function, while others insist that it is due to lack of resources. Last month we had the Minister for Justice on the floor of the Dáil proclaiming, "There has been no diminution of essential garda services." By his reckoning [the word] essential does not include larcenies, unauthorised taking of vehicles, and vandalism, much of which receives little garda attention. This can be observed first-hand with a visit to the control room in Dublin Castle where a diminished staff struggle hopelessly to give some sort of service to a city clamouring for attention. The cutbacks are equal in their effect to the withdrawal of full-time services, including overtime, of 900 members of the force.'

He then raised a problem which was symptomatic of the pressures the force was experiencing.

'A recent meeting of our association discussed the concern that there is a hardening of attitudes by certain district and some divisional officers towards local representatives when they make representations regarding genuine problems. Unless this idea is dispelled very quickly it will lead to a total eclipse of the representative bodies, and they will be obliged to undergo a complete review of their position and adequacy. Perhaps, this is long overdue anyway?'

A New Year's Day 1972 editorial in the *Irish Press* said that Catholics in the north had suffered enough. In the background there had been talks aimed at defusing the standoff between the IRA and loyalists. 'Attempting a settlement without involving the

IRA would be like America ending the Vietnam war without reference to the Viet Cong.' In other words, the IRA could murder gardaí, members of the RUC and the British army, it could kill, maim and injure the public at large and be rewarded with a place at the conference table. This was not a sentiment that anybody trying to enforce the law and protect life and property could contemplate with equanimity.

Two days later the IRA, true to form and doubtless taking comfort from the support of the armchair warriors of the *Irish Press*, set off a bomb in Callender Street in Belfast, injuring more than 60 people, many of them women and children. Worse was to come, much worse. On the afternoon of 30 January 1972, British troops fired live ammunition into a civil rights demonstration in Derry, killing 13 and injuring 13 more. The TV newsreel image of Derry priest Edward Daly holding a white handkerchief trying to recover the injured and the slain from the streets of a British city shocked the world. The cry of murder most foul went up.

The morning after the slaughter in Derry, crowds of protestors gathered outside the British embassy in Merrion Square, Dublin. Chief Supt Eamonn Doherty (The Doc) deployed a cordon of uniformed gardaí around the front of the embassy building. The demonstration was initially peaceful, but this did not last. The next morning an incendiary bomb was thrown over the heads of the gardaí setting the embassy front door alight. Bricks and stones were hurled at the blue uniforms, but the line held. It became obvious that the men on duty were outnumbered and ill equipped for their ordeal. They had no riot gear. Doherty ordered his men to draw their batons to drive the angry crowds back. Two baton charges followed, but the situation remained unresolved. On Wednesday evening Doherty ordered his exhausted men to withdraw. The crowds raced up the steps into the building and within an hour it was burning merrily. Short of deploying the army to drive back the crowds, which were being stewarded by known IRA members, there was nothing else to be done.

Premises belonging to British businesses in Dundalk, Dun Laoghaire and Limerick were also attacked. The Northern Troubles had well and truly crossed the Border.

On 22 February the Official IRA planted a car bomb in Aldershot military barracks, home of the Parachute Brigade, killing five women preparing meals in a canteen, and a Catholic chaplain, Fr Gerry Weston. This, they said, was a response to the deaths in Derry. The cycle of violence continued. The Provisional IRA bombed the Abercorn restaurant in Belfast. Two people were killed and 130 injured, including two young women shopping for a wedding dress, both of whom lost legs. On 20 March six people were killed and more than 100 injured by a 100lb car bomb detonated by the Provisional IRA in the centre of Belfast. Two off-duty policemen were killed as they tried to lead people to safety.

For the garda force there was some good news on the pay front. On 16 April 1972 Minister for Finance George Colley signed the Garda Síochána Pay Order 1971. This set out three pay increases from June 1, 1969 , April 1, 1970 and 1 January 1971. The pay increases were:

- For men in training: £15.7.6 to £18.3.0.
- On completion of training £17.10.0 to £20.15.0. In the ninth year: £26.7.3 to £29.13.0.
- Gardaí with 15 years' service – long service increment of £130 per annum.
- Ban gardaí started at a lower rate of £13.7.9 to £16.13.0, on completion of training £15.8.9 to £18.14.0, and in the ninth year: £22.8.9 to £26.5.0.

A campaign was building for equal pay for women in the force, as it was in wider society. An equal pay claim had gone to conciliation in 1971 without being settled. Almost four years later, in 1975, it was said to be close to being conceded. In fact equal pay would happen reasonably soon after that, triggered by the obligations of EEC membership – rather than any official sense of fair play for female employees.

# 7

---

# A booby trap bomb on the Border

eanwhile in Whitehall station, a landmark on the main road from Dublin city to the airport, I was trying to advance my career. By 1972 Sergeant Dick Keating had served as my mentor for almost 12 months. After the Macushla revolt in which Keating had played a major part, officers had realised that there was more to him than they had previously realised. When an energetic superintendent named Edmund Garvey was appointed to lead the Pearse Street detective unit, he gathered around him a talented bunch of detectives including the colourful Blackie O'Brien, Bill Ronayne, Joe Campbell, Dick Keating, and others. Their profile was enhanced with the solving of the Ballast Office robbery, and the 1969 theft of the Brian Boru harp from Trinity College.

In the early 1970s, Keating had applied for promotion and was made a sergeant in Whitehall, where I had my own ambitions to become a detective. I had much to learn. Whenever I ran into a problem I went to Keating, who usually heard me out in silence, sitting leaning forward, with one leg thrown over his other knee, his hands folded mid-thigh, his head back and eyes skywards, pondering his response.

Here I can take up the story.

One night, in early June 1972 I was on beat duty and Dick, as my section sergeant, was bound to certify 'my all correct' in his beat card. That night his normal 'Richard Widmark' grin was absent, and there was no chat. I respected his silence. This time the silence was prolonged. Eventually he spoke, his words twisting as his lips struggled with what he was trying to say. 'An inspector had died in an explosion.'

Inspector Sam Donegan was killed by a booby trap bomb at the Border between Cavan and Fermanagh on 8 June 1972. He was serving in Cavan station, and had the reputation of being a conscientious officer. A native of Ballymacormack, Co. Longford, Donegan was 60 when he died and beginning to look forward to retirement after 37 years in the force. Lt John Gallagher of the Defence Forces was injured but not killed in the explosion. Two gardaí had minor injuries. Sam Donegan's death tends to be forgotten now; he was one among many to come. He left his wife Mary and six children.

A retired member of the Garda Technical Bureau later gave me this account:

'Visiting a scene where a colleague lost his life is unforgettable and I will never forget the June day when I was dispatched to the Border crossing where Sam Donegan lost his life. At the time there was about 120 crossings in the Cavan-Monaghan division, 80 which were open and 40 closed. The place was known locally as Drumbo, an abbreviated version of an almost unpronounceable Irish name.

'On arrival I discovered that Sam's death had occurred just north of the Border. I know I shouldn't even consider crossing without permission, but an overwhelming desire and reverence for a fallen comrade had me walking in his footsteps. The RUC had completed their examination as the road had been re-opened.

'Back on the southern side I was informed that a short time before Sam's murder a similar box scrawled with the word BOMB had been cleared as a hoax by experts on another crossing a short distance away. Following its elimination, the locals appealed to Sam Donegan to open the road which was blocked by a similar device. When he lifted the box, it exploded killing him instantly. Having dealt with similar devices I knew it to be what subversives called a 'come-on-bomb'. These were deadly devices with no command wire, but capable of being detonated by a spring-loaded circuit switch when lifted. It was like a light going on when you open a fridge.'

Samuel Donegan was buried with full garda honours. Six fellow inspectors escorted the hearse through the streets on Saturday June 10, 1972, escorting his remains from Cavan Cathedral, where the Bishop of Kilmore Dr Quinn presided over Requiem Mass, to Killygarry cemetery three miles outside the town. The Garda Band played the Dead March from Saul and Chopin's Funeral March, and the Army provided a guard of honour.

A couple of days later Deirdre Fallon, widow of Dick, received her husband's gold Scott medal for bravery and Garda Paul Firth, who was with him when he died, received a silver one from the Minister for Justice Desmond O'Malley at a service in Dublin. That ceremony also marked the 50th anniversary of the founding of the force and was attended by President de Valera and Taoiseach Jack Lynch.

The following day, Rev Barry Wymes, son of the Garda Commissioner, celebrated an anniversary Mass at the Church of the Holy Family in Aughrim Street, Dublin, with 1,800 serving and past members of the Garda Síochána present. They included Garda John Laffin, the longest surviving member, born in 1898, near Stradbally in Laois. He had served in Limerick and west Cork and had retired in 1959. Those present heard that 20 members had died in the course of their duties, the latest being Sam Donegan. A commemorative ceremony was also held in St Patrick's Cathedral in Dublin. Among those attending was Andrew Ward who had succeeded Peter Berry as secretary of the Department of Justice.

The year 1972 proved to be the worst year of the Troubles in Northern Ireland. There were 467 deaths, more than 10,000

*Jack as a Garda Recruit, 1953.*

*Garda Recruits, November 1953.*
*240 recruits in total. Jack Marrinan is number 9 from the left in front row. See list of names on page III.*

Maurice Landers
Patrick Scott
John Mcniffe
Michael Gaughan
Edward Kelliher
John Maxwell
Michael Gilhooly
Timothy Malone
Christopher Mcnamee
Christopher Mccaffrey
John Mcfadden
James Hanrahan
Hugh Mcguire
Patrick Rynne
John Mccormack
John King
Charles Mclaughlin
Joseph Carey
Edward Gordon
Denis Hurley
Roderick Treacy
John Driscoll
Walter Whelan
John Magee
Denis Sullivan
Robert Daughton
Patrick Murphy
James Connolly
Ignatius Higgins
Gerard Cronin
Connor Beirne
Martin Costello
Sean Quinn
John Sullivan
Edmund Smyth
John Ogara
Patrick Fegan
Patrick Hughes
Michael Mcnulty
Cornelius Cahalane
Thomas Mulcahy
Denis Griffen
John Kennedy
Patrick Mcnamara
Timothy Shea
Patrick Turley
Michael Kelly
Nicholas Moore
William Creighton
Thomas Maher
Thomas Nestor
Martin Corbett
Patrick Mcdonagh
Augustine Hynes
Thomas Burke
Patrick Walsh
Denis Odonnell
James Deasy
Patrick Glavin
William Oneill
Michael Golden
Patrick Morrisroe
Francis Odonnell
Michael Dooley
John Omahony
Michael Healy
John Boyle

Patrick Keane
Ciaran Ualionain
Patrick Mccool
Denis Teahan
John Cronin
John Galvin
John Geary
Edward Sheehan
John Cotter
Thomas Madden
Patrick Campbell
Timothy Fallon
Philip Okeeffe
Brendan Sullivan
Jeremiah Oconnell
Maurice Short
John Guerin
John Osullivan
Thomas Duffy
John Reynolds
Terence Kelly
Anthony Oconnor
Vincent Fanning
William Oshea
Brendan Moroney
John Barrett
Joseph Mcgovern
Martin Burke
Michael Keevans
James Kerins
Cornelius Smyth
Thomas Flatley
Daniel Oconnor
Christopher Deely
John Mcgonigle
Patrick Mccarthy
Patrick Derrane
Timothy Foran
Patrick Murray
Cornelius Murphy
Michael Colton
Thomas Casey
Thomas Brennan
James Carpenter
John Danaher
Jarlath Monahan
Dermot Winston
John Sugrue
James Mcevoy
Bernard King
Daniel Osullivan
Cornelius French
Thomas Heneghan
James Duffy
William Ferguson
Michael Guthrie
Thomas Walsh
John Quirke
Thomas Dowling
Martin Ohora
Patrick Sloyan
Patrick Anglin
Patrick Courtney
William Oleary
John Guinane
Kevin Ohara
William Williams

John Flynn
John Crowley
Thomas Omara
James Kirwan
John Marrinan
Cornelius Mccarthy
John Dunne
Murty Grealish
Patrick Lyons
Michael Smyth
Michael Connolly
Michael Hanrahan
Michael Curran
William Ryan
Patrick Daly
James Connolly
Niall Heron
Terence Macmahon
John Mitchell
Michael Moran
Timothy Okeeffe
Thomas Hegarty
James Walsh
John Odea
Donald Duff
Daniel Rahilly
John Buckley
Anthony Oconnell
Patrick Corkery
Peter Mcloughlin
Patrick Duffy
Michael Daly
John Trevaskis
Matthew Kelleher
Eugene Doddy
William Dwyer
Thomas Hanratty
James Mahoney
Bernard Boyle
Thomas Casey
Donald Mcguire
John Gahan
Bartholomew Faherty
Patrick Reilly
Francis Lyons
Desmond Mcsherry
John Oconnor
Edward Rossi
Patrick Early
John Lawlor
John Oconnor
Michael Oreilly
Patrick Murray
Cornelius Ocallaghan
Maurice Hinchion
John Conheady
Michael Hussey
John Kelly
Peter Carolan
Charles Tynan
Thomas Moran
Richard Heffernan
Cornelius Duggan
Francis Odoherty
Francis Donnelly
Maurice Boyle
James Walsh

Thomas Hanahoe
Michael Smith
Thomas Osullivan
Patrick Blanchfield
Albert Burke
John Nolan
Patrick Organ
Andrew Gallen
Timothy Sheehan
John Osullivan
Charles Ocarroll
James Mullin
Martin Hennessy
John Murphy
Joseph Orourke
Bernard Sheridan
James Mcgarry
Daniel Sullivan
Bartley Joyce
Laurence Obrien
Patrick Reynolds
John Sullivan
John Lyons
Luke Gartlan
Michael Lonergan
James Nugent
John Morrisey
Patrick Hayes
Thomas Keating
Patrick Moore
Patrick Orris
John Fitzsimons
John Stapleton
Pascal Mcardle
Christopher Manton
John Kilmartin
Stephen Rowe
James Lawlor
John Kavanagh
Patrick Mcguire
Anthony Cahill
James Flynn
John Finnerty
Brendan Gilleece
Patrick Greene
William Walsh
Brendan Conway
Michael Hughes
Thomas Dunne
Michael Brennan
Patrick Obrien
William Kennedy
John Madden
Joseph Higgins
John Walsh
Thomas Tannon
Francis Mulligan
Michael Johnston
Thomas Naughton
Luke Mcnulty
Joseph Coyne
John Casey
William Shannon
Patrick Brennan
Michael Noonan
Jeremiah Kerr
James Carmody

Denis Osullivan
John Dullea
John Fogarty
Patrick Mahon
John Kelly
Joseph Scott
Kevin Lavin
Martin Connor
John Mckenna
John Muldowney
Michael Blake
Patrick Linnane
Patrick Brannigan
Thomas Healy
Francis Mchugh
John Holmes
Peter Lee
Patrick Kitt
Philip Bergin
Charles Mcgovern
John Fitzpatrick
John Odonnell
Peter Casey
Martin Purtill
Sean Mcconologue
Michael Ashe
Patrick Hartigan
Thomas Kilbane
James Nolan
Patrick Walsh
James Ocallaghan
Cornelius Gallagher
Patrick Daly
Benedict Odwyer
Michael Mcginley
John Flannery
Michael Riordan
Thomas Maguire
Joseph Mcardle
Hugh Odonnell
Patrick Fox
Patrick Morahan
Patrick Guest
Patrick Fallon
Michael Rochford
Patrick Conroy
Patrick Daly
John Golden
James Kelly
Simon Connell
Edward Fitzpatrick
Patrick Tuohy
Joseph Callanan
Patrick Donohoe
Edward Mcguinn
Jeremiah Odonovan
Timothy Smiddy
Peter Devany
Augustine Conry
John Chatten
Thomas Egan
Michael Mchugh
Thomas Martin
Matthew Killilea

*Presentation to Vincent Boyle on the ocassion of his transfer to Donegal in 1958.*
*Photograph taken at John Whelan's Bar in summerhill.*

*Front L-R: Joe Dunleavy, Ginger Carroll. Second Row L-R: Dan McCale, Seamus McKiernan, Vincent Boyle, Tom Moriarty, Michael Guthrie, Barney Mc Shane, Michael Smith, Dick Fitzgerald, Jim Daly, Tom Hogan, Billy Roynane, John O'Connell. Back L-R: John Carty, Tom Langan, Tom Donohue, Paddy Moriarty, Edward ryan, Michael Hanrahan, Tom Reilly, Gerry Courtney, Eamon Moriarty, Paddy Reynolds.*

*Jack Marrinan's notebook.*

*Record from Jack Marrinan's notebook on the date of his dismissal.*

*Record in Jack Marrinan's notebook following his re-appointment as a garda.*

*Initials of Superintendent Eamon Doherty in Jack's notebook.*

*Jack and Mary's Wedding, 1963. (L to R) Tom (Jack's Father), Elizabeth Dempsey (Mother of the Bride), Jack, Mary, Mary (Jack's Mother) and Anthony Dempsey (Bride's brother).*

*Jack and Mary with their first child, David.*

*Jack, Mary and family (Clare, David and John) at his conferring in Trinity College.*

*Mary Marrinan, Jack's Mother, the night of his retirement.*

*Garda Representative Association (GRA), circa 1965 at Garda Depot in Dublin*
*Front row L to R: Michael Conway Treasurer, Jack Marrinan General Secretary and member of the*
*Arbitration Board, Jim Fitzgerald Chairman, Brian Sheehan Executive Committee, Thomas J. O'Leary*
*Executive Committee and member of the Arbitration Board. Back Row L to R: Andie Hallissey, James Reidy,*
*Ted Roche, Jim Hughes and Patrick Tierney. Note: Patrick Keaney, Executive Committee Member, was*
*unavoidably absent on GRB business.*

Members of the newly elected Representative Body for Guards, photographed with the Body's
Consultant, Senator Garret Fitzgerald, at their meeting in Dublin on the 10th May, 1968. Pictur-
ed are (left to right) front row: Dan McNamara, Thurles; John Marrinan, General Secretary;
Jim Fitzgerald, Chairman; Senator Fitzgerald; John Hurley, Bandon; Tom O'Leary, Dublin Executive Committee. Back row: Brian Sheehan, Dublin, Executive Committee; Leo Kenny, Ball-
ina; Frank White, Milford; Co. Donegal; M. G. Sheridan, Ballymote; Seamus Quaid, Wexford;
Andie Hallissey, Waterford and Michael Conway, Headquarters, Treasurer.

*Members of the newly elected Representative Body for Guards.*
*Iris an Gharda, Meitheamh, 1968*

*Jack Marrinan at his desk in the late 1960s.*

*Garda Representative Association (GRA) Conference 1981.*

*Garda Representative Association (GRA) Conference 1981.*

*Garda Representative Association (GRA) Conference 1981.*

*Garda Representative Association (GRA) Conference 1981.*

*Garda Representative Association (GRA) Conference 1981.*
*L to R: Eamon Doherty, Jack Marrinan, Paddy McLoughlin, Jim Ivers and Gerry Collins.*
*In the background is Michael Conway.*

*Event for the Garda Benevolent Society in the RDS circa 1980s.*

*GRA Central Executive Committee Conference at Wexford 1983*

*Back Row L. to R. – Pat Mahon, Tony Hand, Bill Dunne, John O'Sullivan, Paschal Feeney, Donie McDermott, Aiden Woods, Bernie Keating.*
*Middle Row – Noel Kevane, Philip O'Callaghan, Mick Guerin, Sean Brennan, P.J. Davey, John Hartigan, Peter O'Connor, Donal Ó Gallachoir, Larry Duffy.*
*Front Row – Christy Lonergan, Michael Conway, Brian McCabe, Mick Halpin, Frank Mullen, Jack Marrinan, Tim Hurley, John Ferry, John Mulloney.*

GRA Central Executive Committee elected Septemeber 1984.

Front Row L. to R. – Martin Walsh, Harry Murphy, Tim Hurley, Brian McCabe, Frank Mullen, Mick Halpin, Jack Marrinan, Mick Guerin, Barry Martin, Aidan Woods.

Middle Row – Noel Kevane, Tony Fagan, Christy Lonergan, Frank Gunn, Julian Ryan, Pat Mahon, John Ferry, John Mulloney Pat Curtin, Sean Brennan, Pat Fox.

Back Row L. to R. – Donal Ó Gallachoir, John Faul, Peter O'Connor, Mick McNamara, Tony Hand, Frank Consodine, Matt Givens, Michael Lawless, Bernie Keating.

*GRA Central Executive Committee at Annual Conference, Bundoran, Co. Donegal. April 1985*

*Front Row L. to R. – Tony Hand, Mick Lawless, Harry Murphy, Brian McCabe, Mick Halpin, Frank Mullen, Jack Marrinan, Tim Hurley, John Ferry, Aidan Woods.*

*Middle Row – Pat Mahon, Sean Brennan, Matt Givens, Frank Considine, Martin Walsh, Julian Ryan, Barry Martin, Frank Gunn, Pat Fox.*

*Back Row L. to R. – John Mulloney, Mick McNamara, Pat Curtin, Peter O'Connor, Christy Lonergan, Donal Ó Gallachoir, Bernie Keating, Mick Guerin, Noel Kevane.*

*GRA Central Executive Committee, 1987-1990.*

*Front Row L. to R. – Frank Consodine, Mick Guerin, John Ferry, Christy Lonergan, Jack Marrinan, Mick McNamara, Brian McCabe, Pat Fox.*

*Middle Row – Sean Brennan, Bernie Keating, John Sugrue, John Greene, Tony Hand, Brendan Flynn, Larry Duffy, Aidan Woods, John Sullivan, Pat Lydon.*

*Back Row L. to R. – Gerry Treacy, Donal Ó Gallachoir, Mick Lawless, Jim Doyle, Eddie O'Donovan, Matt Givens, Martin Walsh, Tony Fagan, Pat Higgins, Frank Madden*

*Jack Marrinan and Commissioner Eugene Crowley on his retirement night.*

# AGENDA 38

THE SUNDAY BUSINESS POST *September 29 1996*

## personal finance

# ESB and Garda gain in health schemes

**Several private health care schemes – all Irish – are already giving the VHI a run for its money, reports Gail Seekamp**

Ireland's Voluntary Health Insurance (VHI) is about to feel the full weight of competition from BUPA, the British-based giant.

But two home-based rivals have challenged the VHI on its home turf for several years. These schemes run exclusively for employees of the ESB and Garda Síochána, respectively, cover an estimated 75,000 people, including dependants.

"Neither scheme can — nor wants — to compete on the open market. Nor are they charge that both have captured a loyal client base, providing benefits that would make some VHI customers green with envy.

What do members get for their premiums? And can the VHI, now rethinking its future after extended dependence of chief executive Brian Duncan, learn from these small but successful operators?

## Garda scheme

The St Paul's Garda Medical Aid Society is bucking some and a longer list of benefits. It started life as a Friendly Society in June 1934, but has steadily expanded to — since then, to quote Pat Mahon, the society's secretary.

The scheme gives about 45,000 people its optional plan, ordinary and comprehensive, for

## Good news

Jack Marrinan appreciates his private health scheme — with good reason.

Six years ago, this former general secretary of the Garda Representative Association had heart by-pass surgery at the Blackrock Clinic in Co Dublin. It would have cost in the region of £10,000, but his bill for small

The operation was precipitated by a severe bout of angina and carried out at very short notice. "The result is positive," he says. "I can walk up stairs and play 36 holes of golf in one day. My quality of life has improved tremendously."

His medication bill, now about £300 a quarter, is met by the scheme and Eastern Health Board.

shootings, and almost 2,000 bombs placed. Consider those figures for a moment and what they mean: on average more than one death a day, approximately 35 bombs per week. All this could not be contained on the north-eastern corner of a small island. Many IRA volunteers fled across the Border where fellow travellers gave them a hero's welcome and fed and housed them.

Commissioner Wymes's crime report for the year ending September 1972 stated that serious indictable crime was increasing year on year, with violent offences against the person up by 1,000. Drug abuse was also increasing with 124 people charged, including a small number of people from Britain, USA, South Africa and one from Ghana. Jack's friend John Collins was a driver at the Garda Depot. Occasionally he was assigned to drive Wymes, a duty he very much enjoyed. "Before we set out the Commissioner would fill two glasses of Irish and offer a toast for a safe journey. Once, I think it was during the Conroy sittings, I drove him to the Department of Justice in total silence. When he was getting out of the car, he remarked to me: 'Say a prayer for me. I'm going to meet Peter Berry.'" Wymes retired in January 1973, having held the line for just over four very tough years. He was succeeded by Patrick Malone.

In the 1973 general election, Liam Cosgrave had become Taoiseach of a coalition government, with Fine Gael as the majority partner and Brendan Corish of Labour as Tánaiste. The justice brief went to Patrick Cooney of Fine Gael, a midlands solicitor. Cosgrave chaired a Cabinet sub-committee on security. The other Fine Gael members were Patrick Donegan, Minister for Defence, and Cooney; Labour nominated James Tully, Minister for Local Government and Conor Cruise O'Brien, Minister for Posts and Telegraphs.

But two weeks after taking office, the new government got a salutary reminder of the scale of the security problem when five tons of arms destined for the Provisional IRA were seized from a

Cypriot-registered ship, the *Claudia*, off the Waterford coast. The arms had originated in Libya, where Britain's MI6 had spotted IRA veteran Joe Cahill from Belfast and tipped off Scotland Yard, which contacted the Garda Síochána. The Irish Naval Service intercepted the *Claudia*. Cahill got three years in prison for his trouble. While this looked like a success for the authorities, the background was more chilling. Lethal weaponry in large volumes was being supplied to the Provisional IRA. The Naval Service and the Garda Síochána had been lucky this time, but the coastline was long and impossible to control. The assumption had to be that more weaponry would soon be on its way, as it was.

Patrick Cooney began his ministerial term by visiting garda stations along the Border. There he found a mixed bag of dissatisfactions, including the slowness of the pace of reform post-Conroy, poor working conditions and worse living accommodation. In September the focus shifted to Mountjoy Prison where IRA inmates were demanding to be treated as political prisoners. A hunger strike began and gardaí and soldiers were sent to Mountjoy to assist the prison staff in keeping order. On 31 October, a hijacked helicopter landed in the prison exercise yard; three leading IRA men scrambled aboard and were gone. Prison staff, seeing the helicopter approach, thought it was a Minister making an unannounced visit. The IRA had scored an outstanding coup; the government, the prison staff and gardaí had all been taken totally by surprise and humiliated. The following day the remaining 90 IRA prisoners were taken by bus to Portlaoise prison, which was henceforth designated as a high security unit.

A subsequent report by High Court judge Thomas Finlay pointed to the absence of advance knowledge of the rescue and emphasised the need for better intelligence-sharing between the Garda Síochána and the Defence Forces and increases in staffing. Garda intelligence had been concentrated on the Official IRA which had been on ceasefire since 1972. The breakaway Provisional IRA, which now posed the most serious threat, had been neglected.

On 25 October 1973 Commissioner Patrick Malone published the crime figures for the year ending 30 September 1973. Crime had increased by 160% from 1962 to 1972. The number of murders committed was 21; the highest since 1926. The year 1973 showed an increase of 25% in the serious crime against person category, but thankfully in Dublin there was a decrease of 6%. Border duty was a consistent drain on resources, and greatly reduced the visibility and influence of guards in other areas, he said. The radio service was now operating in all divisions. A traffic corps had been established, in which 300 staff would eventually be employed. Drug possession and use was on the increase with the appearance of heroin. There were 270 arrests.

On 9 December 1973 at Sunningdale, Berkshire, British Prime Minister Edward Heath, along with Taoiseach Liam Cosgrave, and the leaders of the Northern Ireland political parties signed a document which became known as the Sunningdale Agreement. It provided for power-sharing between nationalists and unionists. Section 15 of the agreement stated that in order to improve policing throughout Ireland both governments would cooperate under the auspices of a Council of Ireland through their respective police forces. To this end the Irish government would set up a police authority.

Jack Marrinan considered the police authority proposal very significant, and he responded positively.

'The Garda Representative Body recognises this as one of the most momentous developments in the force since its foundation. Our first reaction must be that it would be totally out of keeping with the traditions of our force if we did not support wholeheartedly any development likely to bring peace and tranquillity to the communities in all parts of our island.'

A garda authority had been high on Marrinan's shopping list of structural reforms from early on. He was to be disappointed. Power-sharing collapsed in May 1974, under the weight of unionist opposition and a loyalist strike.

In 1974 another element in a very volatile mix came into play. On 17 May the loyalist Ulster Volunteer Force set off car bombs on the streets of Dublin and the town of Monaghan. Some 26 people, including a pregnant woman, died in three blasts in Dublin city during the evening rush hour, followed by seven more in Monaghan about an hour later at 7pm.

A subsequent report by retired judge Henry Barron found that within days of the bombings, the Garda C3 division had obtained the names of the bombers from RUC Special Branch. Barron said the big obstacle in bringing the culprits to court was the understanding that there could not be full co-operation between the Garda Síochána and the RUC due to [Irish] government policy. 'The inquiry has been told by a number of gardaí that there was a general policy of not allowing the RUC to question witnesses or suspects in the state', Barron said. The investigations were thus doomed from the start. Gardaí could not ask the RUC for assistance knowing that they could not reciprocate. Barron was unable to say if the Department of Justice was aware of this restriction. Of course it was.

However, the RUC had been able to help in another way. The bombers were picked up and interned in Northern Ireland. Another report into this sad muddle by experienced criminal lawyer Paddy McEntee concluded that the hesitation to have a particular suspect interviewed by the RUC in Northern Ireland may have been justified in the fraught circumstances of the time. Secret negotiations aimed at reducing violence could have been jeopardised by arrests of prominent activists or their supporters. It was a thin justification stretched too far and McEntee, a clever lawyer with a good mind, knew that. The Irish government was running scared of a backlash against extraditing IRA members to face charges in the North. Extradition worked two ways; they couldn't extradite loyalist murderers if they harboured IRA murderers. Muddy waters indeed, and no help to beleaguered police trying to combat terrorism.

In this period, Jack Marrinan continued to use the *Garda Review* to engage with the public as well as members. In his hands it was a tool with which to engage the public, and politicians, to push senior officers and the Department of Justice along the road of reform for the Garda Síochána.

The force was getting a bad press. The operation of the law in the district courts was being put under the microscope in *The Irish Times* by journalist Nell McCafferty. Her daily reports from the coalface – made chilling and compelling reading. She painted a picture of self-important district justices sitting in seedy rundown courthouses, solicitors arguing badly prepared cases, guards who appeared only too willing to provide whatever evidence was needed to obtain a conviction with scant care for the truth, and confused members of the public, accused, witnesses, and victims of crime, milling around the courthouse at sea among impenetrable legal procedures.

Marrinan challenged the authorities to speak up for the force. He said that Nell McCafferty's *The Irish Times* column, called 'In the Eye of the Law', had for many people become the main source of information on what was happening in the courts and how justice is administered.

'Miss McCafferty is an exceptionally able, articulate journalist, and that is why her articles have succeeded in focusing public interest on an area that has been ignored for too long.

'However, one must wonder is it not time for the garda authorities to start answering back, especially where the criticism had been unwarranted? Much of what she writes is true; too many gardaí fail to prepare their cases properly; too many justices are unnecessarily rude to defendants, bailsmen, and even witnesses; too many people are forced into crime out of poverty, ignorance, and inadequacy as distinct from simple criminality. The law as we know it is often iniquitous, harsh and cruel. It is at best a blunt instrument. But it is hardly fair to place the blame on the doorstep of the gardaí. They only enforce the laws which communities, through Dáil Éireann, have authorised for the better ordering of our society.'

Marrinan continued in this vein.

'Miss McCafferty's columns portray garda enforcement as harsh and insensitive, and in doing so distorts the public image of the force. Her column is read, absorbed, and talked about – and 90 per cent of the talk is detrimental to the gardaí. So, what are we going to do about it?

'One cannot deny the right of a journalist to write what he or she sees fit, and it would indeed be a pity to see an end to her penetrating articles. They show the community what crime, poverty, deprivation and prison is all about. But there is no justification for allowing the Garda Síochána to be blackened in the eyes of the community, because for so long the penal reform question has been ignored. The public understandably interprets silence as guilt. And when very serious allegations are laid against the gardaí by journalists we must answer back swiftly and strongly, and in detail.'

This is an example of Jack Marrinan's pen at the service of his members and the public at its very best. The tone is measured, the sting of criticism of gardaí is acknowledged and drawn. Word-by-word, line-by-line, he builds his case for the appointment of a garda press officer to improve relations, not just with the press, but with the public.

In the same issue he reminded members of the progress that had been made.

'Since Conroy, the job has become more humane. Previously members were packed off on transfer from one station to another with little regard as to whether they could get a house for their

families. As a profession, policing has many opportunities for satisfaction which a job should offer to a dedicated person, who wants
involvement in their work; however, a lot of our members feel that
being a garda simply entails carrying out routine duties ordered by
someone in authority.

'Many gardaí feel they are now less team members and not really
part of the organisation. Too often they are simply handed tasks
to do; theirs is not to reason why, with little time taken to involve
individual members in planning or policy making. I believe gaps
between ranks are disappearing on the social level but expanding in
on-the-job situations.'

And he had a word for his critics.

'I've been asked if our GRB representation has become too close
to its authorities and the Department of Justice and is drifting
somewhat from its membership. I believe if you asked the Garda
Commissioner or the Minister for Justice they would not agree and
comment that it was very much the reverse. The GRB has been the
single most pressing influence for modernisation in the force, and
we have taken a lead in demanding many of the beneficial changes
which have taken place since we were set up. Perhaps on occasion
we paced our campaigns and appeared to some members as being not fiery enough, but on many occasions we secured benefits
by negotiation which would probably have taken strike actions to
achieve in other occupations.'

He listed other concerns.

'The relationship between the Department and the Commissioner
deprived the latter of a good deal of personal responsibility and initiative that one would expect from a man of his eminence. What we
are seeing nowadays is recruiting to deal with temporary political situations. I worry about our authorities rushing to employ extra gardaí
and packing them off to the Border armed with 18 weeks' training
without any clear long-term plan. Too many members spending time

on posts and roadblocks have no chance of on-the-job satisfaction or getting inside their profession. Some enlightened innovations have been born, developed and abandoned. The Juvenile Liaison Scheme was an imaginative scheme, but it's still no more than an infant. It has been more than 10 years since it was heralded as having a bright future- now it is being resuscitated in its cradle by a few dedicated juvenile liaison officers.'

Another aspect of Marrinan's *modus operandi* in those years was provided by Christy Lonergan, from Tipperary town, who joined up in 1958 and served in Dublin. He recalled GRA meetings he attended with Jack.

'In 1973 as Conroy's recommendations were unfolding, I became involved with Eugene Lynch and Paul Kearney. I also teamed up with Jack and travelled down the country to deal with local issues.

'On one occasion a member launched into a ferocious tirade. He listed them all; pay, promotion, discipline, directives and duty hours, welfare, accommodation, and transfer. Jack sat back silently and never interrupted the rant. He adopted an expression of supreme concentration. Now and again he would purse his lips, scrunch up his face, and adopt another of his legendary mannerisms. Then, in a most conciliatory tone, he assured the member that his submission was valued, and he would consider it carefully, and reply in due course.

'Not a pen or notepaper in sight.

'In his car Jack turned on a tape recorder and repeated the harangue verbatim. In a few days he would write to the member concerned addressing his every thought and word. It was one of his secrets of his success and longevity.'

In 1974 Jack Marrinan invited Patrick Noonan, a member of Conroy's original inquiry team, to comment on the implementation of their recommendations. Noonan said he was dissatisfied with the progress in improving professional aspects of the force.

'One of our [Conroy] conclusions was that the government had too much control over the garda organisation, when it should only be remotely regulatory. Conroy recommended that a full examination be carried out on the management structures and administration and directed that the Minister should distance himself from the day-to-day running of the force; however, the implications of the Sunningdale Agreement pinpointed that the control still existed.

'I would like to see a new garda authority, having its own budget as well as overseeing recruitment and promotion', Mr Noonan said. He criticised superintendents for spending too much time in court and too little on managing the force.[25]

To Jack Marrinan's consternation, Patrick Cooney announced that he had commissioned management consultants Stokes Kennedy Crowley (SKC) to examine the administration and structures of the Garda Síochána to see what improvements could be made. SKC was a major accountancy practice branching out into management consultancy, and accountants, as Jack Marrinan well knew, always look to save money. That the national economy was in trouble after the first wave of oil price rises, and that government was hard stretched to meet current obligations, was very clear. Cuts in on-street patrols were by now obvious to all but the blindest citizen. But Marrinan had another more fundamental objection, largely based on the final paragraphs of Conroy. He spelt it out in the *Garda Review* in April 1975. Determining the role of An Garda Síochána was not a job for management consultants, no matter how eminent. 'As our society becomes more developed and complex our role must change. It is no longer merely keeping peace; our workload has increased enormously. Drug taking, highly organised mobile and armed criminals and white-collar crime, have all increased while at the same time emphasis has been placed on the rehabilitation rather than the punishment of crime offenders.

25   *Garda Review, February 1974.*

'To us it seems more appropriate that any questions about the garda role over the next decade should have been settled before the consultants come in. If this does not happen, SKC must be required to make recommendations on how best we should be structured to fulfil all the functions of our ever-broadening role. Otherwise, their first task will unfairly require them to make recommendations on the type of garda service this country should have, and make decisions based on legal, economic, political, and sociological considerations, which may well not be within their compass.'

Elsewhere Marrinan described the SKC exercise as choosing wallpaper for a house long before it was built. He was not alone in this. Garda historian Gregory Allen had also spotted the hole in the consultants' approach. He had this to say about SKC inviting civil servants and gardaí in the force's research and planning unit to accompany them on a tour of police establishments abroad.

'In a five-day week they swept through the police forces of the Netherlands, Norway, Sweden and Denmark. Their understanding was that computer programs would now determine the value of a garda in economic terms by reference to crimes, and offences committed, and other incidents dealt with during beats and patrols. There were few governments in the world who had not engaged in this pointless exercise; pointless, because police cost-effectiveness can only be accessed within the context of crime prevention. It is a paradox for garda management that success in its primary role was self-defeating [as it] led to stations closing and other economies.'[26]

Marrinan's position hardened. In June 1975 he reported that the first meeting with the SKC team took place on 16 May.

'Over two hours we related our expectation that their survey would be a follow-up to the Conroy recommendations, and stressed that the long-term discontent which Conroy unearthed has not been resolved. Since then it had become obvious that only

26  *The Garda Síochána*, Gill and Macmillan, Dublin 1999, p202.

the representative bodies have remained constant in their demands for the full implementation of Conroy's recommendations.

'We re-iterated paragraph 1266 which concluded that an examination be carried out by appropriately qualified people on the role, organisation and personnel policy of the force, and its relationship with the Department of Justice.'

Marrinan went to say that the SKC process had been 'captured' by the authorities and it would do their bidding. The GRB and the other associations were excluded despite lip service to the contrary. The full editorial containing these sentiments in the *Garda Review* was reproduced in the Dublin *Evening Press* of 26 June 1975 under the stark headline 'Garda future on the line' much to the annoyance of the Minister and the Department of Justice.

This prompted Marrinan to observe that:

'Disputes between the Garda Síochána and the Department of Justice over pay and conditions often tend to become acrimonious and unpleasant before a compromise is reached. This is unfortunate as it is unnecessary and indicates a malaise more fundamental than simple disputes. In recent years three representative bodies have clashed with the official side, and in almost every case there has been a substantial loss of goodwill through prevarication, delay and bad communication.'

Marrinan had hit on two sensitive points. The inability to have an adult exchange of views over claims was something that could, with goodwill, be overcome, if those charged with leading the force could be brought to understand that at the negotiating table aggression is no substitute for reasoned argument.

There was another point that needed to be understood. The GRB and its successor the GRA were not trade unions with the freedom that went with that status. In a disciplined force there could be no strikes, nor even the threat of them. Those in authority needed to recognise the implications of this restriction – not just

CHANGING OF THE GUARD

exploit the advantage it gave them. Gardaí expected the benefits to which the trade unions had settled access. Senior officers and the Department of Justice had to recognise their responsibility not to let the kettle boil over again, Macushla-style. Firmness in negotiations accompanied by creativity, leadership and good manners, rather than merely relying on confrontation, would be a start.

And bubbling away below the surface, under attack from too many sides, morale was becoming fragile. For some senior officers, discipline was a means of putting manners on pushy youngsters who didn't know their place. Too often lively young guards fell afoul of petty regulations. Promising careers were blighted because of minor transgressions; an overdue haircut, buttons missing from a uniform, or a dirty patrol car. Conroy had made some progress on simplifying the code of discipline, but some officers of the old school still demanded blind obedience. Seán Brennan, whose father and uncle were also members of the force, recalled that abuse from those in authority was a feature of his own early career.

'I remember an evening in 1964. The officer hardly looked at me as he directed me to roll up my raincoat and present myself at the All-Ireland Fleadh Ceoil in Enniscorthy the following day. The sunny south east and thoughts of picnics were not on my mind as I rolled up a crust of bread in a newspaper. Enniscorthy was 130 miles away from Limerick where I was posted. On arrival I was turfed out on a checkpoint and forgotten. I was on top of a hill outside the town with a sour taste in my mouth. Later, I discovered the place was known as Vinegar Hill.

'Due to the irregular hours I developed a stomach problem and had to attend the Garda Depot. Surgeon Quigley diagnosed a minor gall bladder ailment.' Brennan applied for and got a transfer. 'After that I began to advise younger members. I discovered that many recruits lacked enthusiasm, and this was due to not having any understanding of the authority regime that was flourishing.

'Having thought it out, I had the beginnings of a plan; the district and divisional clerks were the key. They knew the disciplinary regulations inside out, did most of the officers' work, reading correspondence, making decisions, and typing up instructions. They could "read" officers. They had knowledge which could help a young member stay out of trouble, or if in trouble, they knew how to deal with it.'

Brennan replaced Anselm Walsh as Limerick GRB representative. 'One day I approached Jack and told him my idea of having experienced members to mentor the younger lads, though we didn't say mentor then.' He said, 'Let me think about it.' Within minutes he was back with a suggestion for calling it the Panel of Friends. Next, he advised me to put it in a motion for the next AGM. It passed with flying colours, and in no time, it was extended countrywide, and it became a great success.

Where the problem was minor and the officers sensible it was often possible to resolve the matter without much fuss. Noel Kevane explained:

'The purpose was to get the young garda back on track with as clean a record as possible. If the officer in charge was out for blood, we usually laid it on Jack's table for a discussion. At heart he was a real policeman, adept at considering all the angles, including the track record of the member concerned, as well as the reputation of the board. He was great at divining what he termed, "extenuating circumstances."'

I was off duty on 11 September 1975, playing a Gaelic football match at a ground in Raheny. I was doing a stint as a trainee detective in Store Street station, and lined out for the 'Storemen' against a selection from stations west of Dublin. These games were played under 'garda rules', a euphemism which permitted 'anything goes' bloodletting.

Referee Senan Finucane, a sergeant, had left his notebook in his tunic pocket. He blessed himself before encouraging us to let the game flow. And flow it did, along with copious amounts of bodily fluids. I was knocking lumps out of Bill Mugan, a Roscommon-born garda, and he out of me when the whistle blew for half time. Both teams huddled and conferred as far away from each other as we could manage. Then came word that one of our lads had been shot in St. Anne's Park.

We raced the 50 or so yards to Raheny village, where a checkpoint was in place. We were directed to spread out and cover the park exits. Half of us went along Watermill Road, and the balance spaced out along Raheny road to the limit of the park near Sybil Hill. We discovered that our colleague had been shot dead on the avenue side of the Nannikin stream, which bisects the park from west to east. That afternoon I discovered the real meaning of garda comradeship, and what above and beyond the call of duty meant.

Later, I discovered that Mick Reynolds had been off duty and driving the family car with his young wife Vera carrying their two-year-old baby daughter Emer on her lap. At the Bank of Ireland at Killester, a car pulled across their path at excessive speed, and Mick gave chase. The occupants had just held up and robbed a bank. Mick's intervention upset their getaway plans, and being a trained garda driver, as well as being on his own terrain, he forced them into a cul-de-sac. A short time later they abandoned their vehicle and fled on foot. Leaving his wife and child in the car, Mick gave chase and having collared one robber, another shot him in the head. There was a huge public outcry, but thanks to a magnificent response from the public, and an outstanding investigation led by Det Chief Supt John Joy, one of the most uncompromising crime detectives that ever took up the chase, the culprits were quickly arrested and brought before the courts.

Michael Reynolds had been a member for five years. He worked as a patrol car driver out of Clontarf station. I knew him well from being at Whitehall; our patches adjoined.

'We often joined forces on the fringes of our jurisdictions. Mick was first into every action, and never took a step back. The term off-duty did not exist in his code, as suspicious behaviour or criminality any time or any place spurred him into immediate action.'

And that was what led to his death on a sunny September afternoon in a peaceful public park on the northern edge of the capital city where the leaves on the trees were turning gold. Michael Reynolds was 30 years of age, a native of Ballinasloe, Co. Galway. Like Dick Fallon, he was awarded a gold Scott medal for valour. Commissioner Edmund Garvey, in his first week in office, told *The Irish Times,* 'He was one of the finest men we had'. The list of the recently fallen was lengthening: Fallon, Donegan, Reynolds. A very bloody period of garda history had got under way.

At the end of September 1975 Commissioner Garvey had published the annual crime report for the previous year. The figures were horrific. Serious crimes of violence had increased by almost 10%. There had been 51 murders, including 33 committed in the Dublin-Monaghan bombings, where fatalities included men, women, and a one-month-old infant. Nobody had been charged. There had been 17 cases of attempted murder. On 22 April shots were fired at a sergeant and two gardaí in Co. Leitrim. On 12 May shots were fired at a detective garda in Co. Mayo. On 4 September shots were fired at a sergeant and two gardaí in Co. Donegal.

The release of Dutch industrialist Tiede Herrema, kidnapped in Limerick by the IRA for ransom, provided some welcome good news in November 1975. Painstaking police work had traced IRA members Eddie Gallagher and Marian Coyle to a house in Monasterevin, Co. Kildare, where Herrema was being held. There was a two-week stake-out, with a ring of steel around a small council house, and the world's media camped outside. When prolonged attempts at mediation to get Herrema released looked like being successful, the phone rang in an *The Irish Times* journalist's Dublin home early one morning. A voice spoke but did not give a name. 'You'd better get your arse down to Monasterevin, there's something happening.' Conor Brady was on the road minutes later.

# 8

---

# A coward's war

In 1975 the challenges were immense– an armed conspiracy, the Provisional IRA and its splinter groups, and the threat of a repeat of the loyalist Dublin and Monaghan bombings. Added to that was the danger that Northern Ireland would erupt in a way that could sweep away or seriously damage the democratic structures of the republic. Unemployment and inflation were rampant and funding for all essential services including policing and security was under threat. But the problem went deeper than that. If garda morale buckled under the onslaught of terrorism, the game was up. This could not be said aloud. However, important developments had been taking place within the GRB in 1974, and they merit back-tracking and consideration.

In mid-1974 a new executive committee of the GRB took office. Jim Fitzgerald remained chairman. Welcoming the new members, who included John Ferry representing Sligo – his eventual successor as general secretary – Jack Marrinan spoke of further delays in the long-promised summer uniforms. Dan Kennedy, a new member representing Store Street, remembered that first meeting.[27]

---

27  Other members included Jim Fitzgerald, Chairman. T.B. McNamara, Limerick, J. Ryan, Tuam, N. Campbell, Castlebar, J. Kirwan, Clara, Michael Conway, Garda HQ, V. Mullen, DMA, Jim O'Shea, Tipperary, A. Kelly, Training Centre.

'There, I met Jack Marrinan and sat around his horshoe-shaped table in Dublin Castle. He spread his arms wide to include us all in the debate and decision-making. I remember a much-discussed issue at the time was that the GRB was not fit for purpose.'

Kennedy was right. There was an internal reconstruction needed. The reformed GRB which arose out of Macushla had been a big improvement on what went before, but it was not equipped to represent members in the expanded force with greater challenges that had emerged. Despite the pressure of daily events, this had to be tackled. Marrinan set up a working party consisting of activists he had come to rely on, people like Jim Fitzgerald, Julian Ryan, Dan Kennedy, Ben McNamara and Michael Conway. Their job was to come up with new representative body regulations. As he said himself:

'Most of the 1950s men were on their pension lap, and with the constant drum roll of new recruits, new blood on the representation side was needed. We needed representation in the Border region, and our desks needed to be dealing today with issues that happened today.'

Marrinan recalled many years later that when he set out to reform the GRB, he wanted to double the numbers taking active part in representation.

'The force had become larger, with almost 9,500 members in 1977 and would shortly exceed 10,000. Society became better educated, and unafraid of questioning authority figures. Internally we found that negotiating of grievances with local high ranks was becoming more and more ineffective. As a result, it was a basic necessity that we increase our representation, thereby improving our bargaining power', Jack Marrinan said, looking back in 2014.

The 1974 half-yearly GRB meeting was held in October over four days with over 150 items on the agenda. Marrinan told the gathering:

'The arbitrator's recommendations on claims for special pay for duty at weekends, public holidays, and nights are now being presented to government. Without any increase in premiums we have succeeded in securing a 10 per cent increase in cover under the garda insurance scheme, provided by the Caledonian insurance company. We have adopted a resolution to introduce the new rate of cover from 1 December next, if possible, to coincide with the 15th round national pay increase. Under the above award our basic pay will increase by £7 at the top of the scale; however, the rising cost of living will negate any real benefit from the increase, even before it is due.' [28]

Approaching Christmas 1974, Jack Marrinan had invited members to attend a special Mass at Mount Argus in Dublin for the comfort and recovery of Garda colleagues and relatives in ill health. The celebrant– Fr Clarence Daly, a Passionist priest and a big man in every sense of the word– was the force chaplain and stood with it in good times and bad. Many marvelled at his unfailing devotion, visiting sick members in hospital, attending garda funerals, ministering to the families of the deceased, and helping out whenever and wherever he could. Successive garda Commissioners acknowledged Fr Daly's contribution, according to Greg Allen. [29]

Eamonn Barnes became Ireland's first Director of Public Prosecutions (DPP) on 1 January 1975. Previously the attorney general, a political appointment, had decided which cases would be prosecuted. Jack Marrinan welcomed this change as removing the suspicion of political interference. Like the DPP, the Garda Síochána administered the law as they found it: those who sought change needed to go to Leinster House, not the local garda station, if they wanted reform, Marrinan reminded readers of the *Garda Review*.[30] As Fr Clarence Daly was fond of saying to members– stay away from politics. Marrinan refined that message to counsel members to respect those who hold public office and to

---

28  *Garda Review*/GRB News. November 1974.
29  The Garda Síochána, p.178.
30  *Garda Review, January-February 1975.*

avoid party politics. That wasn't always easy in a climate of terrorism and financial stringency.

The joint conciliation council met on 6 February 1975 to discuss claims including subsistence allowance, boot, cycle, plain clothes, detective and juvenile liaison allowances, along with a claim to have time-off in lieu of overtime discontinued. Michael Conway's ingenuity of finding reasons for allowances was deployed in obtaining an improved system of travelling expenses for members making return visits to their families while on extended duties away from their permanent stations, for dog-handlers, in eliminating disparities in overtime rates for men and women, and adding New Year's Day to the holiday entitlements. Between pay claims which were hobbled by national agreements, the 'old reliables'– allowances– could be called upon to deliver.

An April 1975 the *Garda Review* editorial raised a more fundamental matter. After a routine swipe at the national pay agreement negotiations from which the force was excluded, and his ritual denunciation of the SKC process, Marrinan went to deliver a serious warning:

'It must be evident by now, even to the most unperceptive observer, that the frequency of personnel disputes within our force derives from something more fundamental than simple dissatisfaction over pay. Over recent months this column has chronicled disputes involving chief superintendents, superintendents, inspectors and sergeants, and more recently we have the dispute by garda clerical staff. All these matters can only be resolved by a radical appraisal of the force's personnel policy.'

There was one common factor in all of this. Relations with senior garda authorities had worsened. What was billed as a special meeting to discuss options for improving garda work practices, including an appropriate roster inclusive of weekends, took place shortly afterwards, but there was no meeting of minds. A meeting with the SKC team followed, but Marrinan's insistence on revisiting the Conroy recommendation on clarifying the role of the Department of Justice got nowhere.

Across the summer of 1975 *Garda Review* editorials spelt out what was afoot.

'Our force has become more diverse with a need for our association to get involved in other matters including recruiting, training, promotion, personnel policies and force management. These initiatives are vital to maintain morale and job satisfaction, as well as ensuring a strong vocational commitment.

'In the meantime, our association must remain strong with frequent meetings, delegate conferences, regular information bulletins, with active and concerned local committees. Only active members democratically elected by their local comrades at grassroots level will guarantee our success. Our strength and success emanate from each and every one of our members.

In mid-1975 Marrinan reported to members on increased benefits payable by the Medical Aid Society and his hope that it would join forces with St Paul's Benefit Society. He also noted that the last phase of the national wage agreement had ensured wage increases of 10% on all points of the scale. However, there was unhappiness with the failure to continue the in-service training school begun at Fitzgibbon Street station in Dublin the previous year, an initiative backed by the garda research group of which Marrinan had high hopes and which had its genesis in Conroy.

In autumn 1975 Marrinan expressed good wishes to the retiring Commissioner Patrick Malone, as well as welcoming his replacement Edmund Garvey; whom he described as 'a man of action who gets things done'. This changing of the Commissioner prompted some editorial musings.

'Leading a national force the size of An Garda Síochána is no job for someone lacking in confidence, strength and determination. The 1970s have been difficult, and we are grateful that we have been directed by a Commissioner with precisely these qualities. Patrick Malone has led the force through the most difficult period since the early days of the state. The task of the Garda Síochána in the 1970s has required much more than simple police efficiency. It has required the exercising of tact, diplomacy, and much common sense– areas which Commissioner Malone has been exemplary.'

It was a nicely judged compliment and a reminder to Garvey that much was expected of him.

By September 1975 the tone had changed.

'August has been the month of cutbacks', Marrinan declared. 'It was the month which we learned that in the opinion of those who administer us we could be turned off like a tap and done without– at least on many occasions, and in many places where previously our services were regarded as so important that leave could be denied and personal conveniences disregarded.

'Duties, the neglect of which could warrant dismissal one day previously, were henceforth to be left undone, and it seemed that duties and responsibilities vested on our members by the law were now contingent on whether or not they incurred overtime. Overtime has become a factor in the charging of prisoners and granting of bail. Small wonder that morale has taken a battering as gardaí begin to question the real validity of other rules that were always considered binding. Priorities have become relative, and the availability of our service is no longer judged in terms of human well-being but in pounds and pence. Members working in reduced numbers are being exposed to dangers, as witnessed in several incidents over the recent weeks. Garda back up, which is their strength, may not be there when they call for it. Anything between a third and a half of our operational strength is tied up on the Border, as well as Portlaoise prison, and other security commitments were already draining Dublin of its patrol strength even before the reduction. One can only hope that sanity will prevail to reverse recent directives.'

This was challenging stuff and raised hackles in official circles. Airing it in the *Garda Review* meant that Jack Marrinan had tried other less public avenues but failed. In his post-retirement interview with me he admitted using the columns of the *Garda Review* provocatively at this time.

At the end of 1975 Jack Marrinan wrote:

'At year's end it is difficult to remember a period in which all-round relations between our authorities and our members were ever as bad. The new Commissioner Edmund Garvey has taken over a vessel whose crew, though loyal and efficient, have little confidence that their best interests and that of their profession are being given sufficient support in the corridors of power.

'While our commissioner may not be at fault, he is the man who must carry the problem of garda unrest on his shoulders, and the fact that he has had no part in creating the problem does not make the task lighter for him. Garda commissioners have always been constrained by governments, and indeed by the civil service, which at present is giving absolute priority to financial economies. It is in these quarters that one must look for enlightenment and for a realisation that piecemeal remedies such as have been applied since 1968 will not solve existing problems.'

Marrinan then turned to the SKC report.

'The Minister [Patrick Cooney] has told us that the present management survey will be the panacea for many of our present ills. He says it will be a comprehensive and a soul-searching evaluation, probing the very foundation of our organisation. We say that it has not been commissioned a moment too soon, and we can only hope that when it does conclude, its findings will be circulated to the force and immediately implemented in such a manner that the present running sores of bad morale and discontent can be cured once and for all.'

In this issue he also cited continuing disputes involving senior officers and garda clerks as evidence that the personnel policy was not working. This point was taken up by the *Sunday Independent's* Wigmore columnist who asked a pertinent question. If rank-and-file gardaí could find within their membership a person of the leadership calibre of Jack Marrinan, why couldn't the senior ranks produce someone similar, able to take the force's personnel problems by the scruff of the neck and do something about them?[31]

Going into 1976, Jack Marrinan in his editorials kept the pressure valve fully open and aimed at garda leadership and the Department of Justice. On the ground, there were some positives. In April, Kyran O'Mahony was appointed garda welfare officer. Because much of what they did was confidential, the value of welfare officers is often overlooked. Without fanfare, they helped members to sort out personal problems and had access to a wide range of expertise. They often quietly put an end to local abuses like bullying.

And two new Dublin representatives had been elected to the GRB executive: Det Garda Brian Sheehan of CDU and Garda John O'Brien of Whitehall station. Sheehan had long service on the conciliation council and was particularly passionate on two subjects- the garda credit union and a clothing allowance for detectives- while O'Brien was the youngest member of the GRB executive. Both men would have considerable impact in the years to come, and Marrinan was conscious that he had already passed the halfway mark in his time as general secretary. In January 1976, Marrinan complained again about the exclusion of his members from the SKC process. 'The authorities must give credence to legitimate grievances and complaints, and if this neglect continues, we are seriously considering the right to strike.'

In garda representation terms, this was the nuclear button. Just mentioning the word strike raised the stakes. In June 1976 the strike threat surfaced again. Reporting the outcome of a meeting

31  Wigmore. Sunday Independent. November 23, 1975.

to consider the new association to replace the GRB, Marrinan said that members presently strongly backed having the legal right to industrial action and ultimately the right to strike.[32]

This prompted a ministerial riposte. The Minister for Justice Patrick Cooney said in the Dáil that the *Garda Review* did not reflect garda policy and that the crime rate in Dublin was lower than in some English cities. At a presentation of Scott medals in Templemore, Cooney warned gardaí against panicking the public and defined loyalty as the willingness of the force to stay silent even when suffering from a legitimate grievance.

In turn that brought a blazing response from Jack Marrinan. In summary, he said:

'If this is the advice the Minister is receiving then one cannot be surprised at our body's desperate throw [calling for strike]. Indeed, one can only be astonished that such a refusal to admit realities has not long ago resulted in far more drastic and spontaneous action among our members.'

He went on to say that the response of the GRB national executive to the Minister's words was to demand the right to strike. Due to garda cutbacks criminals were ruling the streets and the countryside, he said. The criminal was winning.

'In a large city district in March of last year a total of 16,000 hours of patrol overtime was worked. This year the figure for the same month was 4,200. In a midland district with several busy towns the gardaí worked 273 days less in March this year than last year.' (Cooney represented a midlands constituency.)

In a lengthy rebuttal of Cooney's Templemore speech, Marrinan gave copious examples of cutbacks. He concluded by taking the high ground:

'The Minister need not fear for our loyalty and the impartial protection of all our citizens. When we ask for loyalty from the

---

32  GRB Newsletter June 1976.

government it is loyalty in the form of sufficient manpower to allow us to complete what the public expect, it is not the loyalty that has us frogmarched to self-destruction by requiring us to achieve mutually incompatible ends.'

This was fighting talk, no mistake. Whatever they made of it in the Department of Justice, over in the Garda Depot Commissioner Garvey was hopping mad with Jack Marrinan and the GRB airing 'dirty linen' in the *Garda Review*. So mad was he that he sent a deputation of senior officers to tell the new Director of Public Prosecutions to do something about him. Garvey wanted Barnes to charge Marrinan and four others with usurping the functions of government– citing an editorial in the *Garda Review* issue of June 1976.

'The five involved were the editorial board of the *Garda Review* including the general secretary Jack Marrinan, his assistant Michael Conway, chairman Jim Fitzgerald, as well as Inspector Patrick Culligan and Sergeant Derek Nally who represented the Representative Body for Inspectors, Station Sergeants and Sergeants (RBISS)', *The Irish Times* said. The newspaper offered some clues as to what had pushed Garvey's button. 'The [Garda] associations had questioned promotions made by the Commissioner, and there was also disquiet about his directive to each garda to secure 200 convictions for traffic and other minor offences each year.'

The unofficial version of the scene when senior officers met the DPP was more interesting. A senior garda officer formally read out a prepared statement to Barnes and a couple of his officials. Beside the officer who was speaking, another senior garda was making strenuous efforts to avoid eye contact with the DPP or his staff because if anyone present laughed at what was being said, he was afraid he might join in. Barnes listened impassively. Then he replied. While he would give the Garda Commissioner's request due consideration, he didn't think it was likely that his office would press charges. The whole notion was ludicrous, everyone except

Garvey could see that. Of course it got back to Marrinan. There the matter rested until *The Irish Times* unearthed the story in January 1978. On one level this was light relief, but another reading of it showed Edmund Garvey – 'the man who gets things done' – making decisions while under very severe pressure from all sides.

On 21 July 1976, the British Ambassador to Ireland, Christopher Ewart-Biggs, and a Northern Ireland civil servant Judith Cooke were killed by a booby trap bomb which detonated under the car they were travelling in close to the embassy residence at Sandyford, Co. Dublin. This was a dreadful lapse and there was no getting away from that. Questions were asked about the garda protection for the British ambassador, and it emerged that he had expressed concerns to his superiors in London about it. As a direct response to this outrage, Taoiseach Liam Cosgrave and the Minister for Justice Patrick Cooney moved to introduce a bill allowing for terrorist suspects to be detained for questioning for seven days. Because the Dáil was in recess, this legislation was not introduced until the autumn, when the measure was strongly opposed by the Fianna Fáil opposition led by Jack Lynch.

On the evening on which it was to be voted on in the Dáil, 16 October 1976, gardaí received an anonymous tip off. It said that IRA members were gathering at a vacant farm at Garryhinch, near Portarlington Co. Laois. They were planning to target a prominent local Fine Gael TD and Minister Oliver J Flanagan. Five members were sent to investigate: Det Garda Tom Peters, Sgt Jim Cannon, Det Garda Ben Thornton, Garda Gerry Bohan and Garda Michael Clerkin. When they got to the disused farmhouse, they saw nobody there. Clerkin, aged just 24, went around the back, climbed in through a half-open window and went to open the front door to admit his colleagues.

The door was booby-trapped. Mick Clerkin died on the spot and the others were injured, some badly. Tom Peters was permanently blinded and lost much of his hearing. The bomb was the work of the IRA in South Armagh and was a direct response to the Emergency Powers Act 1976, as it was known. Sgt Jim Cannon told a reporter that searches like that were routine: 'You know, we check out places like this every day.'

This was war, a dirty war, a coward's war.

In November 1976 Commissioner Garvey published the 1975 crime report. Indictable crimes rose from 40,096 to 48,387, showing an increase of 30% over five years. Violent crimes had increased by 20%. The overall detection rate was 43.4% down from last year's 48.1%. Garvey commented that the crime situation could only be described as disturbing, with criminals becoming more vicious, with attacks on the elderly and disabled in rural communities becoming more widespread and menacing. There had been three bomb fatalities; one in Dublin Airport, and two in Dundalk. The number of serious robberies was 703, up 130 from the previous year. 153 were armed robberies, with 119 committed in Dublin. Drug prosecutions rose from 293 to 333, involving 10 nationalities. During the year 566 motor vehicles were stolen, an increase of 25%, and larcenies from cars rose by 34%. This last was the result of removing foot patrols, gardaí believed.

Early in 1977 Jack Marrinan maintained relentless pressure on the government. A measure of how bad the situation had become was a meeting with the Minister for Justice on 28 January. Over two hours, Patrick Cooney heard the GRB's views on efficiency, morale and welfare. Marrinan focused on over-zealous enforcement of disciplinary regulations, excessive use of transfers, and a questionable promotion regime. He also raised the dangers associated with the introduction of one-man patrol cars, describing it as an arrangement which was opposed by every garda in the country, and put individual members at serious risk. Difficulties with Commissioner Garvey were mentioned. Finally, Marrinan outlined the effects of financial cutbacks.

Cooney's response was conciliatory. He was prepared to extend the conciliation and arbitration scheme to cover discipline, promotion and transfers. Jack Marrinan welcomed this 'significant development, which in the future could lead to the removal of many sources of irritation and grievance that our members experience'. The unanswered question was – what about Garvey? That problem would fall into the lap of a new Minister for Justice. In June Jack Lynch led Fianna Fáil to a landslide victory, and Gerry Collins, a former teacher from Co. Limerick, was appointed to the justice brief. Cooney lost his seat and did not return to the Dáil for four years.

Another problem was bubbling away in the background. On 31 March 1976, the Dublin-Cork mail train had been held up at Sallins, Co. Kildare, by members of the Irish Republican Socialist Party, another republican splinter group. Some £200,000 was stolen and five IRSP members, Osgur Breathnach, Nicky Kelly, Brian McNally, Mick Plunkett and John Fitzpatrick, were arrested. All except Plunkett signed confessions but maintained that they had extensive bruising and injuries they claimed were inflicted by gardaí. In February 1977, over the course of five days, *The Irish Times* published a series of reports stating that brutal interrogation methods were being used by a group of gardaí nicknamed the 'Heavy Gang' questioning suspects of serious crime, and this tactic was a response by Garvey to pressure from Fine Gael Ministers to secure convictions. In other words, the men accused of being the Sallins train robbers had been beaten into confessing – whether they committed the crime or not. The newspaper stressed it was not accusing the whole force of brutality, just a small group within its ranks.

The existence of this memoir stems from when I was working as a detective in Store Street. The city centre was tense. Cars with out-of-town registration plates and people with unfamiliar accents were regarded with suspicion. Bomb scares were everywhere. Armed robberies were everyday events. The threat of further atrocities hung in the air. An unexplained parcel could set nerves jangling. The usual pattern of city policing was replaced by an altogether more jumpy relationship on the streets. Allegations of garda rough handling of suspects became prevalent, and an important plank in the defence of some suspects. Graffiti saying 'Help the guards – beat yourself up' began to appear on the streets of Dublin. The city detective unit to which I belonged was fully stretched. During the course of an investigation serious allegations of assault were made against me, and I was charged with a number of criminal offences. This was serious, I was a young guard, married with two children, and my wife Agnes was expecting another. I could be discharged from the force. I could even have found myself in prison.

John Robinson was my superintendent. He had been friendly and encouraging to young gardaí like myself. Since administering the caution, conversation with the superintendent had ceased. However, one day Robinson shoved an envelope into my hand. I took it away and opened it suspiciously, fearing more trouble. Instead it contained a copy of the *Garda Review*, and a section describing how the GRB defended members in trouble had been clearly marked so that I wouldn't miss it.

Soon afterwards I was knocking on a door marked General Secretary in the Phibsboro office of the GRB. Jack Marrinan sat me down and put me at his ease as the words came out of my mouth in a torrent. When I finally finished, Marrinan spoke calmly:

'You swore the Garda Síochána oath to do your duty without fear, favour, malice or ill will. If you were doing the job with those precepts in mind you weren't doing much wrong.' He named two eminent lawyers, Hugh O'Flaherty, Senior Counsel, and John Gallagher, a former garda turned barrister. They would represent me.

Before the court hearing, Jack Marrinan kept in touch with me, focusing on the specifics of the charge, avoiding blame or criticism of others involved. His final advice to me on the eve of trial was encouraging: 'March into the court, head held high, mentally armed with answers to each and every allegation'. On my way into court, I was waylaid by a senior officer. He almost dragged the top-coat from my shoulders as he sought to take possession of my garda identification card. He warned me that I was no longer a member of the force. District justice Seán Delap heard the case over two days and reserved judgment. Back in Store Street, Det Inspector Billy Kelly set me to work as if nothing had happened. The days were endless, but Kelly made sure I had plenty of work to do. Eventually Delap announced his verdict: not guilty. I was promoted to detective sergeant two years later, with the support of Supt Robinson and Det Chief Supt Joy. My gratitude to Marrinan gave way to a fascination with the man whose measured response saved my career and led to the research and writing of this memoir.

At this stage Jack had not quite given up hope that the SKC report would deliver structural reform as Conroy had done earlier. He called on Patrick Cooney to publish the reports– the process focused on many aspects of the force, and individual reports were issued separately – before the goodwill and spirit of trust (arising out of the January 1977 two-hour meeting) had evaporated. [33] Cooney kept his word on preparing the GRA legislation, but it did not get through parliament before a general election was called.

The 1977 election was held in a spell of very warm weather and as parties published manifestos and hopeful candidates pounded pavements, the *Garda Review* told members that they were about to be balloted on the new representation structure. 'Our executive has accepted the proposals in a spirit of willingness and good intent, in the belief that partnership between management and gardaí on the ground can ultimately bring the force out of these difficult times into a fuller and more productive alliance', Jack Marrinan wrote in the June 1977 issue of the *Garda Review*. The proposals were

---

33   Editorial *Garda Review*, March 1977

accepted by a margin of almost two to one, but implementation had to wait for the new government to be formed.

In July Marrinan noted the departure of Patrick Cooney.

'We did not always see eye to eye with him on some details, but we fundamentally agreed on the important issues. He believed in a strong force, well officered, well turned out, and equipped. He will be remembered for his unflagging defence of our force when it was under attack from the outside.'

This respectful farewell masked the fact that Marrinan had never warmed to Cooney. Now he would have to deal with a very different kind of politician in Collins. The initial omens were good. Shortly after his appointment Collins met Marrinan and the GRB executive for nearly three hours. The talks covered welfare, personnel relations, transfers, restoration of beat toler-ance, two-men patrol cars, and an increase in garda services to the public. Collins was asked to review the practice of using ban gardaí in prisons.

'It was a friendly, cordial meeting and Mr Collins promised ear-ly consideration of all the matters. He assured the members that it was his aim to remain in close contact with the forces' representa-tives', Marrinan said afterwards.

*Garda Review* editorials were pushing hard for increased allow-ances and strengthened criminal legislation. The July 1977 issue told members that the GRB was fighting at conciliation for in-creased rent allowance, pensions and equal pay for ban gardaí. Some progress had been made by removing the requirement for women to retire on marriage, but Marrinan complained that the negotiations on equal pay had been tiresome and fruitless. The case for equal pay for equal work had been proved beyond doubt, yet nothing had happened. Other claims such as those based on garda clerks, meal breaks, night duty allowance, and substitution allow-ance were also before the council.

'The recent upsurge in the use of firearms by criminals in Dublin and Donegal has raised the question of arming gardaí. Members have been held up at gunpoint, taken prisoner, pistol-whipped, and tied up. With the exception of Great Britain, the Garda Síochána is virtually alone in Europe as an unarmed force. To clamp down on lawlessness the government must give us sufficient numerical strength to maintain a vigil on society. They must also remove the financial shackles on gardaí, improve the justice system to meet the needs of the new crime spree, and ensure speedier trials', Marrinan told his members. Arming the force to deal with armed terrorists had become a hot topic. In August, the *Irish Independent* reported that Jack Marrinan was in Donegal 'for an on-the-spot assessment following the ruthless and brutal attacks on unarmed garda patrols along the Border.' He said he had received many calls from parents, wives and families of gardaí seeking greater protection for their loved ones on Border duty.

'At the weekend three gardaí from Ballybofey were savagely attacked by a 10-man gang who smashed through a checkpoint on the Ballybofey to Glenties road. The gardaí gave chase, forcing the gang to stop, but the gang produced sub-machine guns and pistols and made their getaway. On Thursday, in a separate incident, a gang opened fire on gardaí on a lonely Dunlewy road, and yesterday a stolen patrol car was recovered in a Castlefinn bog. Also, an attack was carried out on the garda station in the village of Carrigans', the newspaper said. [34] Donegal was being used as a safe haven for terrorists operating in Northern Ireland.

Answering increasing calls for gardaí to be armed to defend themselves, Marrinan side-stepped, thanking the army for coming to the aid of garda members under attack. 'We are an unarmed force', he said, 'and it has always been our policy to remain so, and only if there is a substantial swing in favour of us bearing arms

---

34   *Irish Independent*. Monday 29 August 1977.

would the GRB put forward such a proposal.' He was always a staunch believer in an unarmed force, with members only having weapons for very specific purposes. At times like this with deadly bombs being placed under culverts and squad cars coming under fire from sub-machine guns that stance was bound to be questioned.

In 1977 when Gerry Collins became Minister for Justice, he found on his desk the completed GRB submission on reforming the body and reconstituting it as the Garda Representative Association. The GRA it envisaged would represent all members of garda rank and be organised countrywide with 110 districts and 26 divisions. It consisted of an elected chairman, secretary, and a minimum of three members per division with a delegate to the yearly annual general conference. Members would serve a three-year period.

The legislation was passed, and Munster delegate Jim O'Shea was elected to chair the first annual conference of the GRA in 1979.[35] Jim O'Shea recalled being impressed by Jack's demeanour at meetings.

'He carried a file, but never needed to open it, never took out a pen or notepad. He made it his business to know the oppositions' strengths and weaknesses. I recall a meeting with a government advisor when we had a claim. Just as we were called in the AGSI delegation (sergeants and inspectors) exited the room. We asked how they had got on? They brushed past and said we'd be reading about it. Jack led us in, and we got a better deal. All the higher ranks– many of whom were not in his corner– benefited from his negotiation.'

More than the name would change when the GRA replaced the GRB.

---

35   The other members were Michael Gallagher, Donegal, Noel Campbell, Castlebar, Michael Halpin, Galway, A.J. Walsh, Limerick, Noel Kevane, Bandon, T.J. Hurley, Union Quay Cork, Mick Guerin, Wexford, Jim Marshall, Portlaoise, Frank Coll, Cavan, Brian McCabe, Drogheda, M K Connolly, Garda Headquarters, Martin Hogan, Dublin Castle, Frank Mullen, Dalkey, Patrick Fox, Irishtown Dublin, J. Campbell, Dublin Castle, Christy Lonergan, Bridewell Dublin, with Jack Marrinan as general secretary and Michael Conway as assistant general secretary. This cohort included four future GRA presidents – Halpin, Lonergan, Mullen and McCabe– who would lead garda representation throughout the 1980s.

The new organisation's executive committee had tripled in size, increasing the association's engagement with members throughout the country. Recent recruits had a harsher introduction to policing than their older colleagues. In response to the terrorist threat more than 5,000 were recruited in the 1970s. Many had been posted immediately after training to carry out exposed patrols in Border areas. Unlike earlier generations they did not have the structured 'apprenticeship' of being allocated in small numbers to stations up and down the land, arriving at intervals of two or three years that gave the previous cohort time to settle in. Too often the latest recruits were pitched straight into the front line, learning the job from a relatively inexperienced previous intake.

In short, the culture of An Garda Síochána had been changed by the pressure of events, and the accelerated arrival of many new faces brought other changes. The fact that the first GRA executive in 1978 was roughly three times the size of the GRB executive it replaced meant that the general secretary could no longer rely on a majority in favour of his tried and tested approach as he had done in the past. The common experience of the post-Macushla wave of activists no longer held sway. Some younger members had less patience with Jack's gradualist approach. Most older hands who had witnessed steady progress under Marrinan knew him and trusted his methods, while some of the new intake tended to want things to happen faster.

Many new executive members had yet to find their feet in representing individual members, to learn what worked and what didn't. Taking them through that learning process was time-consuming. It wasn't necessarily the case that the younger activists were hostile to the Marrinan approach– some were, and some weren't– but there was a new militancy in the air. At a stroke the workload on the general secretary of the GRA had doubled.

# 9

---

# Ban Gardai enhance the Force

Another change had taken place, slowly at first. The story of women in An Garda Síochána is a complex one and merits a book in itself. On the industrial relations side Jack Marrinan led the moves for equality between the sexes, as we have seen. During the commissionership of Patrick McLaughlin, the uniform was updated to include trousers for women and ban gardaí, as they were still known, were no longer hindered in the physical exercise of their duty by wearing skirts. This reform was both symbolic and significant. At this point a brief account of how this came about illustrates their progress to full participation in the development of the force.

Women first joined the Garda Síochána in 1959. Commissioner Daniel Costigan had been very keen to have women in the force. He wanted them to be visible, not hidden away in offices doing clerical work, nor like the handful of DMP 'matrons' looking after children who came into contact with the law. Costigan wanted to see women doing frontline police work alongside men. Thus 12 women began their six-month training at the Garda Depot in the Phoenix Park on 9 July 1959.

The previous year, Oscar Traynor, the Minister for Justice, told the Dáil that women would soon be recruited for garda training.

During the discussion which followed, P.J. Burke observed that if the women were attractive, 'they will not be in the force long enough to draw a pension'. Another Dublin deputy Frank Sherwin offered a suggestion to counter this. 'While female recruits should not actually be horse-faced, they should be plain women and not targets for marriage.' Sherwin, a dapper man who wore a bow tie and in an earlier life taught ballroom dancing. Another TD, Joe Brennan from Donegal, warned about the dangers of emphasising glamour at the expense of efficiency. 'There should not be too much concentration on the smart cut of the uniform and the angle of the hat', he warned. No frivolity then. The official class photograph, taken with instructor Sergeant Doreen Prissick on loan from the Liverpool city police force, shows a group of 12 handsome, well turned out and confident young women.

When they presented themselves for training in July 1959, the first uniform provided was a dark blue boiler suit. After about two months they were sent to Arnott's department store in Dublin to be fitted for proper uniforms. Each one was provided with three full sets of tunic, skirt, gloves and stockings, plus two hats. The skirts were designed with an extra pleat in the back – to allow them to run faster when in pursuit of an offender.

Bríd Wymbs, originally from Kinlough, Co. Leitrim, recalled how surprised the public had been to see the new women in uniform. 'Another girl and I were walking along in uniform on O'Connell Street in Dublin the first or second day we were out. The traffic slowed down, and everything came to a standstill. At all the windows along by the Savoy Cinema and the Gresham Hotel there were people looking out', she told *The Irish Times*.[36]

'We approached a male guard, how innocent we were, and we said to him, "What's going on, is there something happening?" He said, "Would you go away from me, for heaven's sake, it's

---

36   *First women Gardai honoured, The Irish Times, 10 July 2019.*

yourselves they're looking at.'" Wymbs was a sergeant when she retired in 1993.

The other 11 women in that first class were: Mary Gilmartin nee Browne, Galway; Angela Leavy nee Burke, Dublin; Noeleen McGrath nee Cooke, Cavan; Elizabeth Dwyer, Sligo; Kathleen Kelly nee McFadden, Donegal; Sarah O'Sullivan nee McGuinness, Longford; Helena Sparrow nee Hayden, Kildare; Bridgeen Deale nee Sharkey, Donegal; Margaret (Peig) Brown nee Tierney, Galway; Mary O'Donnell, Limerick, and Deirdre Killeen, Dublin.

Peig Tierney was promoted to sergeant instructor for the 1962 intake. Though she was enjoying her stint in the force, she decided to get married. She was very annoyed with a sergeant because she thought he'd been unfair to her. She decided to go and have it out with him; six months later they decided to get married. This meant she would be leaving but with less than six years' service she was ineligible for a gratuity. 'I was damned if I was leaving without it. The marriage gratuity was a month's salary for every year of service. As a sergeant I was getting nearly nine pounds a week. I was not letting that go. Realising that if I went a day before my service was up, I stuck it to the last minute and got my due.'

Peig was replaced as sergeant by another first joiner, Mary O'Donnell.

'In 1996 when I arrived in Limerick, ban gardaí patrolled the streets the same as the men. During my time in Henry Street station I was attached to a unit and did shift work. As time passed all the ban gardaí under me were integrated into shifts. Each unit had four sergeants and about 30 gardaí. I did exactly the same work as a male sergeant.'

In slotting in beside their male colleagues and getting stuck into the work without fuss, Peig Tierney, Mary O'Donnell and the other first and early joiners showed their male colleagues that having women on the team was a good thing for everyone. 'The station mess was less of a mess after the women came', more than one male guard noticed. But it was much more than that. The banners – as they were known – had a humanising effect on the day-to-day life of a garda station.[37]

There was a price to be paid for being an early joiner.

'Photographers treated us like film stars. Every time you opened a newspaper you were looking at yourself', said Kathleen Dixon. 'For a social life we had to travel outside the city.'

Her colleague Teresa Mitchell remembered walking with her along O'Connell Street in Limerick. Both women were in uniform. There was a patch of wet concrete ahead where the pavement was being repaired.

'A young fella was walking along staring over at us, not looking where he was going. The next thing we knew he was up to his knees in wet concrete.'

Teresa Mitchell, who was in the 1962 intake along with Kathleen Dixon and Mary O'Donnell, remembered the training as different to anything she had previously experienced. Previously a teacher, she found herself enjoying the drilling and marching. 'In drill formation I was known as the "right hand man", the term applied to the member who was number one on the parade.' Sergeant Jim Dwyer was a fantastic drill instructor, she recalled. Many others agreed.

There were other new experiences for the women. O'Donnell's colleague Dympna Moore was dismayed to be detailed to search a pregnant woman suspected of stealing money. She felt badly about touching a woman in that condition, she said, 'Instead I just quickly frisked her'.

There were no reports of women at the Macushla meeting in Dublin, nor is there any trace of them attending the support

---

37  Brid O'Sullivan, a history student at Limerick Institute of Technology, did valuable research on the first five ban gardaí allocated to Limerick city in her thesis *The Introduction of Women into An Garda Síochána* from which the accounts of Peig Tierney and Mary O'Donnell are quoted, with thanks. Her parents Tim and Kathleen were members of the Garda Síochána, and also her siblings Maura and Jim.

meetings which followed in November 1961. Women in the Garda Síochána were frozen out of the 1961 award in the same way as their young male colleagues.

The first major sighting of ban gardaí in the workings of the GRB under Jack Marrinan came in 1963 when he submitted a claim for a pay increase of 25% for men and 14% for women. It was a start, but the inbuilt discrimination in framing the claim suggests that the male GRB executive had some way to travel before accepting the case for equal pay.

In 1969 the GRB submission to the Conroy commission did not break any new ground on that front, although one of the witnesses called was a sergeant called Sarah McGuinness. There appears to have been about 25 female members at that time. Not only would management decree that men would get better paid than women, but the pay rises sought by the GRB would increase the gap. In this, the Department of Justice and Garda Representative Body were in line with popular sentiment which held that married men needed to be paid more than single women, especially when jobs were in short supply. Married women had no business taking jobs from unemployed men with families, it was thought. As Peig Tierney had discovered, ban gardaí had to resign on getting married, as was the practice in other state jobs. Marrinan succeeded in getting the 'marriage ban' lifted in January 1974. In 1972, the recently formed Drugs Squad consisted of nine detective gardaí and two ban gardaí. A problem arose then which was that the men got paid extra as detectives; the women who they worked alongside did not. This problem persisted into 1976, and by then there were complaints about the excessive reliance on ban gardaí for prison duties at Limerick.

In 1975 Jack Marrinan had reported to GRB members that negotiations for equal pay for ban gardaí were continuing and 'we are confident of a successful outcome.' Around the same time an editorial in the *Garda Review* complained that the campaign for equal pay for women and increased allowances for the general member-ship had been long and tiresome. On equal pay for ban gardaí, Marrinan argued, 'in every single respect they meet the criteria of equality'. During the discussions the official side have given no rea-sonable explanation why they are not granting the concession.' The Department of Finance had been trying to stave off the inevitable. Equal pay for work of equal value was enshrined in the Treaty of Rome, which applied to Ireland since it decided to join the EEC, as the EU was then called, in 1973.

By 1981 the strength of the force was 10,000 and the number of female members was increasing substantially. One of the 1981 re-cruits was a Dublin woman, Noirín O'Sullivan. She would become Garda Commissioner in 2014, the first woman to hold that office.

The 1982 annual general meeting of the GRA in Ennis provid-ed another milestone. It was the first and thus far only such confer-ence addressed by a Minister for Justice who had been a member of the Garda Síochána – Sean Doherty. He had served in uniform and also in Special Branch but left to devote himself to politics. This conference also saw the culmination of a 12-year campaign to update the uniform. It was displayed for the first time at the West County Hotel, in front of Commissioner Patrick McLaughlin and hundreds of delegates from all over the country. Ann Marie McMahon, the first ban garda to wear trousers as part of the uni-form, took to the stage with local Garda Kevin Birmingham and Garda Christy Lonergan from Mountjoy station in Dublin in the first public appearance of the new uniform for all members. The platform party and delegates rose to their feet and welcomed the new uniforms with a thunderous round of applause.

The background is best explained in the words of GRA Limerick city representative Sean Brennan.

'One evening I was on patrol car duty in Limerick with Ban Garda Deirdre Darcy, one of my best colleagues. We responded to a call to a disorder outside the railway station. The place was jammed with an unruly crowd. We began to separate the ringleaders, and they started to break up, moving backwards and sideways. A few stragglers moved towards Deirdre, and she held out an arm to show the direction they should take. She moved back a pace, one of her heels caught on the kerb, and she fell backwards, with her skirt momentarily in disarray. I was angry that Deirdre's uniform was no way suitable for dealing with such incidents, nor appropriate for the ever-increasing need for public order interventions.

'Later I said to Deirdre that a pair of slacks [trousers] would be much better for such duty. She agreed and the idea took life. We canvassed the rest of the women in Limerick, and they all agreed.'

The timing was right. The question of updating the uniform generally was coming to a head at the time. The GRA had long wanted all ranks to wear the same uniform and was also seeking other updates, as lighter fabric was becoming available, more suitable for modern policing. Brennan asked Jack Marrinan to include him on the GRA uniform delegation. He duly prepared a submission and made a proposal, which Marrinan and his colleagues approved.

'One day I went to the Garda Depot and got a roll of uniform material out of the stores. Then myself and Ban Garda Ann Marie McMahon took it to a Limerick tailor who measured her and made up a tunic and slacks to fit her. The first time the uniform appeared outside the tailors was in my home when Ann Marie modelled it for my wife Maeve, our young daughter Valerie, and myself. We were so taken by the event I took a few photos.

'On seeing the photographs, Jack Marrinan said that he would support it 100%. Next, I put my case to Commissioner Paddy Mc Loughlin. His answer – Is tomorrow soon enough?'

Thus Sean Brennan can fairly claim to be the man who put the first ban gardaí into trousers.

The following year, Ban Garda Brenda Hyland was crowned Rose of Tralee 1983. Stationed in Dublin, she was a familiar face around the city centre, much admired for her looks and her friendly manner to one and all.

In 1983 Jack Marrinan also announced that garda pension scheme arrangements for women would be on the same basis as for men. The implicit assumption that women didn't need pensions as they were bound to quit and get married had finally been dropped. The numbers were rising; ban gardaí would number 300 in 1983, including three inspectors and eight sergeants.

And the barriers to women were falling fast. In 1984 the *Garda Review* had this milestone to report. 'Mrs Mary Vaughan (nee Gibney) is the first married recruit ban garda to join. In 1979, the Garda Regulations removed the marriage bar on men and women. Since then many married men had joined but no women.' She had two uncles working as detectives in England, the report said, and her great-grandfather had been a sergeant in the DMP in Fitzgibbon Street and Kingstown, Dun Laoghaire.

In November 1987, Jack Marrinan told readers of the *Garda Review* about another happy first at a recent passing-out parade. 'Among those who passed out was Mrs Rita Walsh from Military Hill, Cork. She is the first mother to pass out as a ban garda. She was pregnant when she was called for her medical and her two children, Andrew, two years, and Stephanie, eight months, were looked after by her husband Tom during the training period.'

A stark picture of what faced the recruits – male and female – as the drugs epidemic took hold of Ireland's cities and towns was given by a 1990s recruit,[38] when she was told to report to Fitzgibbon Street.

A pretty and heavily pregnant young woman was being questioned about injuries to her infant son. As a male inspector and a younger guard interrogated the woman, who was a drug addict,

---

38   O'Connor, Mary T. *On The Beat. , Gill and Macmillan, Dublin 2005.*

Ban Garda Mary T O'Connor sat in as observer and later was directed to take over the interrogation. She described the desolate woman. 'Her father, her brothers and all her lovers had beaten her throughout her lifetime. That was all she knew.'

O'Connor said she understood.

She didn't, how could she?

'With that, she threw herself down at my knees and cried. "Will my son die? When I came back, I found him stuck between the bed and the radiator. It was on full blast," she said. "I was out getting a score [drugs]. I was gone a long time."' The young garda and her male colleagues were having to confront desperate problems that policing alone could not resolve.

Supt Catherine Clancy, writing in 1997 after the distinction between gardaí and ban gardaí had been dropped, noted that following the initial 12 women in 1959, subsequent increases were less dramatic. They trickled into the force in small numbers until 1975 when 10 women joined. In 1978, 46 were appointed. Now women had the power and training which rendered them capable of conducting their own investigations, instead of merely assisting male colleagues, she said. In 1979, following an increase in numbers, ban gardaí were fully integrated into the work of the force.

Writing in *Communique*, the garda management journal, Supt Clancy noted that the first women did a fine job in difficult circumstances . 'The present status and acceptability of women within and without the Garda Síochána is due in no small measure to the pioneers of 1959.' Catherine Clancy reminded readers that this group of smart and determined women changed a male-dominated culture for the better of all. 'Society at large and the police force in particular benefited from the contribution of female gardaí evidenced by work practices which demonstrate a more caring, humane and balanced organisation', she wrote.

At a ceremony in 2019 to mark 50 years of women in the force, Commissioner Fachtna Murphy noted that the make-up of the force had changed considerably since then. There were now more than 3,000 female members, with women accounting for 22 per cent of the force. By the time the 60th anniversary came around in 2019, there were 3,780 women making up 27% of the force.

# 10

---

# Mountbatten murdered – GRA takes on the GAA and wins

Garda Seamus Lohan reported for duty at Granard Garda Station Co. Longford at 8am on Monday 27 August 1979. Granard was a newly built district headquarters situated on the Cavan side of the town.

'It was just after the weekend of the all-Ireland *Fleadh Ceoil* in Buncrana, and Vincent Fanning who was the sergeant in charge of our station was on duty up there', he told me in 2012. 'I was rostered to work that morning along with Gerry Geraghty who was station orderly. I was down for car driver on my own. After a brief chat and few pulls of a cigarette I started up the patrol car and began with a check of the town. All was quiet and so I decided to stop a few cars on the Edgeworthstown-Longford Road about 50 yards from John V Donoghue's pub. The first vehicle that passed was my superintendent Pat O'Donnell on his way to work. We exchanged friendly waves.

'Shortly after that I noticed a car coming from the same direction. It was travelling slowly and as it approached, I noticed the occupants were two men, the driver and a front seat passenger. The time was exactly 8.55am. It was a red Ford Escort registered number LZO 915 with a black vinyl roof, and I stepped out, raised my right hand, and signalled it to stop. I approached the driver as the car drew to a halt. I adopted a casual and friendly approach. As I got within a foot or two of the driver, I noticed that his face was flushed, and he seemed to be anxious and very nervous. I asked for his name and address and he immediately gave it as Patrick Rehill from Kilnaleck, Co. Cavan. He added that he had left home at 8.30am that morning and had gone to O'Hara's car scrap yard in Longford to buy a petrol tank for a Hillman Hunter car. Timewise his account did not make sense to me.

'Still casual, I asked him to open the boot. His hand shook so much that he was unable to open it. Without a comment I took the key and opened the boot which was empty. I told him to sit back into his seat and when he did, I asked his passenger for his name and address. He was calm and cool and gave this name – Thomas McMahon from Carrickmacross– and said that he had been thumbing from Mullingar and got a lift. I made no response, but my thoughts were that anything I had heard so far did not make any sense.

'By then I began to feel something was wrong. I felt nervous and isolated on my own and decided to call for assistance. I told them I was going to check their car and I sat into the patrol car and radioed for assistance. Gerry answered. I asked if the super was there. "Right beside me", he answered. I told them that I had a car stopped with two male occupants and the driver was extremely nervous. I said that I needed back-up.

'Supt O'Donnell said they were on their way out. Both he and Gerry arrived within minutes. I explained my story and the super-intendent decided that we should bring them to the station. He hadn't spoken to the men at this stage. I brought McMahon with me in the patrol car while Gerry drove the Ford Escort with Rehill, and the Super followed us in his car. On the way to the station

McMahon asked why he was being taken in, as he had only been hitching a lift. I replied: "It's as well that you come in so that we can confirm your name and address."

'Back at the station I discovered that Margaret Doran, a young civilian clerk, was holding the fort. Gerry and I stayed with the two boys while the Super went upstairs to check out the names and addresses. After a few minutes, the Super beckoned me to one side and said the pair were well known to the gardaí in Cavan and if we dispatched a car, they would provide a file on both their backgrounds. Detective Johnny Murren went to get it.

'The Super also asked me what sergeants were working and I told him that Vincent Fanning had been on duty at the All-Ireland *Fleadh Ceoil* in Buncrana the previous night and he wouldn't be too long in bed.

'He directed me to get him straight in. Vincent's home was only a few hundred yards away, and when I called his wife May said that he was in bed having been on duty all night. I quickly explained the urgency of my presence, and she immediately went upstairs to call him.

'I can still remember Vincent arriving in the kitchen wearing a string vest, his pants and carrying his shoes and socks in his hands. I quickly explained the reason for my visit, and I will never forget what he said. "If either of them wants to go to the toilet under no circumstances should they be allowed to wash their hands." Even though he was half asleep and half-dressed he was a highly intelligent and an able dealer, thinking ahead. He arrived in the station soon afterwards.'

At 11.50am Rehill was charged with having possession of a stolen car and McMahon of being carried in a stolen car. Five minutes earlier some 80 miles away, Lord Louis Mountbatten, the 79-year-old second cousin of Queen Elizabeth, along with three of his family and a local boy, Paul Maxwell (15), were murdered by a bomb on their boat while fishing just off the harbour at Mullaghmore,

Co. Sligo. Their garda escort watched horrified from the shore. The Mountbatten family were regular visitors to Co. Sligo and their security and well-being had never appeared in doubt. It was a lovely summer morning. One of the survivors, Tim Knatchbull, then age 14, remembered the scene on board the *Shadow V* in Sligo Bay:

'My grandfather [Mountbatten] was using full power and we were cutting through the water at about 15 or 20 miles per hour. He obviously intended on staying at the helm, so I decided to get up on the cabin roof as an extra pair of eyes. It seemed anyone who had a boat was on the water that morning. Dick and Elizabeth Wood-Martin, in whose borrowed pram Nick[39] and I had passed a good deal of time as infants, were out in their boat, as was the Church of Ireland clergyman Canon Thomas Wood with his son.'

At about 1pm Seamus Lohan went home for a bite of food.

'My wife was busy with general housekeeping and I put a few rashers and sausages on the pan. At about ten minutes past one the doorbell rang, and I answered. It was Supt O'Donnell and he spoke, all in one sentence.

'"Did you hear the news? Lord Mountbatten and a few others have been blown up in Sligo, the two we have in must be involved, be back as soon as you can..."'

He didn't wait for an answer.

Lohan admitted afterwards that at the time he didn't know who Mountbatten was, let alone know he was a member of the British royal family.

'Back in the station I was told that Supt O'Donnell had contacted Garda Headquarters, advising them of the men we had in custody; their possible links with the Mullaghmore bombing in Sligo, and requesting assistance in furthering the investigation. He had also arranged with the Army to provide security around Granard garda station. I learned that both of the men had been identified.

---

39  Nicholas Knatchbull died in the explosion, he was Tim's twin brother.

While McMahon had given his correct name and address, Rehill had been positively identified as Francis McGirl from Ballinamore, Co. Leitrim by Jack Reynolds, a detective in Mullingar.'

Reynolds was from Ballinamore and the McGirls were prominent republicans in that area.

Sometime later John Courtney, head of serious crime investigation, arrived in Granard.

'Earlier that morning along with his family he had left Dublin for a fortnight's leave in Kerry, but when the call came, he was not found wanting', Seamus Lohan said. 'He was accompanied by Detective Inspector Mick 'The Rock' Canavan and Det Sergeant Paddy Cleary – both top class investigators. Their presence and professionalism made me proud to be a part of their team.'

The IRA was not finished with its deadly work that day. In the afternoon, 18 British soldiers were lured to their deaths by two roadside bombs near Warrenpoint, Co. Down, detonated by the IRA's South Armagh brigade. The patrol was blown up by a remote control bomb from the safety of the southern side of a narrow inlet straddling the Border. When their comrades arrived to help the injured and recover the dead, a second bomb was detonated, causing further deaths and injuries. Graffiti appeared in republican areas of Northern Ireland claiming the attack was revenge for Bloody Sunday in Derry:

'*13 gone and not forgotten, we got 18 and Mountbatten*'.

IRA member Thomas McMahon was later convicted of the Mullaghmore murders. He had planted a booby-trap bomb on *Shadow V* the previous night at its mooring in Mullaghmore harbour, close to Classiebawn Castle which belonged to Mountbatten's wife.

The fact that thanks to Seamus Lohan's diligence two suspects were in custody when the explosion took place did not stop the British press having a field day at the expense of the gardaí and indeed the whole Irish security apparatus, already seen as 'soft' on terrorism because of the refusal to extradite IRA suspects wanted in the UK. That the IRA could brazenly murder a prominent member of the British royal family under the noses of his garda escort was an embarrassment to cap all others. Margaret Thatcher, the British Prime Minister, was incandescent when she phoned Taoiseach Jack Lynch to complain about the latest lapse in security. The murder of the British Ambassador had been bad enough, but now this!

The events of that day prompted Castlebar Co. Mayo native Seamus Lohan to reflect on his early life. His father had been a first-time joiner having taken the oath in 1923. His registered number was 5250. Jim Lohan dearly wanted his youngest son to follow in his footsteps and join the gardaí. Seamus was much more interested in heading for England to work 'on the buildings' and the money and craic that went with it. His cousins were already there. To please his father, Seamus sat the garda exam in 1970, failed it and left for England. But when he came home for a family wedding, his three older sisters and brother ganged up on him to sit the exam again for his father's sake. He passed and his first posting was to Mullingar in Co. Westmeath in early May 1972. That was a soft posting, others in Templemore with him were sent to hardship stations on the Border, and it looked like the elder Lohan had called in a favour. Now Seamus was stationed in Granard, and the work suited him, provided he didn't have to spend too much time behind a desk. Getting out and about, talking to people and getting the measure of what was going on, that's what he liked about his job. That was what sent a lone guard, acting on his own initiative, out to set up a roadblock on a summer morning and in doing so detain two people involved in one of the worst atrocities in a very troubled period in Irish history before their bomb was timed to go off. A year to the day later Garda Seamus Lohan, registration number 18066A, was awarded special promotion to the rank of sergeant. His father Jim Lohan nearly burst with pride, he said afterwards.

The GRA and its general secretary had other problems on its plate. According to garda historian Greg Allen, when Gerry Collins, Minister for Justice, asked academic Louden Ryan, professor of political economy at Trinity College Dublin, to conduct a review of the Garda Síochána, it was a response to several simmering disputes which were affecting morale in the force- including one on its way to the High Court involving superintendents.

Ryan's committee was to look into five points: garda pay across all ranks up to and including chief superintendents, problems with payment of overtime, the possibility of recruiting civilians to release garda members for police work, a cadet scheme, and whether the force should recruit some specialists on a one-off basis. The political background was unfavourable, inflation was rampant and conceding leapfrogging pay claims made no sense. Jack Marrinan had lobbied for Ivor Kenny to head this inquiry, but the Department of Justice wouldn't hear of him. Once bitten, twice shy.

Yet with the Provisional IRA campaign of violence in full spate, no government could countenance a serious showdown with the force. The immediacy was underlined within days of Louden Ryan's appointment by a bomb on the Dublin-Belfast train north of the Border, killing one woman and injuring two others. Politically speaking Ryan's purpose was to provide a justification for concessions to be made to gardaí. It wasn't that the gardaí didn't deserve more, they did, but most of the rest of the working population felt they did too. Price inflation was rampant. Trade unions were queuing up looking for raises. ESB power station workers were serial strikers. There was also an 18-week postal strike in 1979, bank staff had been on strike twice in the 1970s and could do so again. In addition, stresses in society led to demonstrations and marches which put demands on the police, and this aspect would get much more difficult in the heightened tensions of the lead-up to the republican hunger strikes of 1980 and 1981.

In December 1978, Marrinan produced a spectacular rabbit out of the hat. This rabbit was called 'greater productivity'. He told members that the GRA had commissioned Howard Greer of the Irish Management Institute (IMI) to measure the productivity of the force since 1969 and also to suggest areas where productivity might be further increased. Greer's findings would provide factual support for the GRA case to the Ryan commission for substantial pay increases. 'Here's proof that we've done more work, now pay us more' was the play.

'Gardaí expect money, quite substantial money, from the Ryan committee', he said. 'They are at the sharp end of lawlessness and violence. As a result, they have had to become tougher, and our working lives have become far less congenial than it was. The fact is that virtually everyone charged with crime of any consequence is legally represented in the courts.'

The crime figures for 1978 had contained much to support the GRA case. Commissioner Patrick McLaughlin reported that the total value of property stolen was £10,372,354.000, with just over 10% recovered. The possession and use of illicit drugs continued to rise with 501 persons charged, against 381 for 1977. Also, the death rates on roads were still increasing, with 620 fatalities, up 51 from the previous year.

The Ryan report was published on 19 April 1979, just five and a half months after the committee was appointed. Almost immediately Gerry Collins announced that, 'he was hugely impressed by the speed in which they had completed their task, and he was happy to inform everyone that their commitment to speed was matched by the promptness with which the government agreed to implement the recommendations on pay– just two weeks after they submitted their report.'

In private both Gerry Collins and Jack Marrinan probably would have agreed that Ryan's report came out too soon. Marrinan was hoping for something more considered he could build on, as had happened with Conroy. Collins had probably hoped that he could buy more time.

Louden Ryan's pay award gave guards with two years' service a pay increase of 6%, from £3,599 to £3,675. Those with five years got 11%, £3,998 to £4,275. Members with nine years' service, including the long service increment, were awarded 18%, from £4,375 to £5,200. For married and single gardaí rent allowance increased to £631 and £423 respectively. The estimated cost of the increases was £14 million, *The Irish Times* reported. Seeing the trap posed by the pay rises being heavily skewed in favour of older members, Marrinan gave the Ryan report a cautious welcome in the *Garda Review,* choosing to concentrate on the non-pay elements.

'Recommendations on training, recruitment, promotion and civilianisation which are presently [being negotiated] before conciliation will be of crucial importance, and we are expecting progress. Another of our bugbears is believed to have been agreed: the opening of a garda college, as well our recommendations on the reconstitution of Conroy's joint consultative council, which should be independently chaired.' He said GRA was happy with proposals to provide health insurance to garda members.

'The tragic events at Mullaghmore and Warrenpoint have once again thrown the security question into the sharpest focus. The hysteria and accusations of security lapses by the British press hurt the Garda Síochána perhaps more than anyone else. When an incident assumes major political significance, gardaí must rely on politicians to defend their performance and shield them from unjust accusations.'

He praised Collins for backing gardaí after the Mountbatten murders. 'It is not the Minister's fault that the Fleet Street press ignored his comments and persist with a portrayal of the gardaí as being soft on terrorism. For several years we have been pleading for action on bail; any working garda will confirm the facts of the present farce. It is called bail; where persons accused of robbery, shootings, rapes, and murder are released often within hours to their normal life, with their trial a distant prospect stretching for several months. It is well known than many of those on bail for criminal offences are committing further crimes. Would it not be possible to create a new offence for such activity?'

Publication of the Ryan report in May 1979 came shortly after the first annual general meeting of the new Garda Representative Association at the Dublin Sport Hotel at Kilternan. In his opening address as president, Jim O'Shea won a standing ovation for this ringing call– addressed to Minister for Justice Gerry Collins and Commissioner Patrick McLaughlin.

'As a garda if I find a suspected person in a most compromising circumstance, say in a serious rape case, I cannot compel him to even give his name. Without his consent I cannot take his finger-prints, samples of his hair, or have him swabbed. Neither does he have to give me an account of his movements. On the other hand, if I suspect that he is in breach of section 30 of the Offences against the State Act 1939, I can compel him to provide his fingerprints, or if I suspect a person of driving while drunk, I can compel him to give blood or a urine sample. There is no consistency here. I believe that a person suspected of committing a serious crime should not have an absolute right to anything. He certainly should not have an unqualified right to silence.

'Frequently, with the assistance of free legal aid, the person before the court is well versed in avoiding the consequences of his actions. The price the public pays as the victim of criminal activity is grossly more than any questionable advantage an individual's rights might have for society. There is also a dire need to change the right to bail.'

At the end of 1979, an editorial in the *Garda Review* deplored the fact that much of Ryan's increase had been clawed back by high rates of income tax.

In his 1979 crime report Patrick McLaughlin stated that he was disturbed at the numbers of assaults on gardaí, which had increased by 352 from the previous year to 2063 in the current year. In 1976 the tally stood at 1274, while in the overall period from 1976 to 1979 the total increase was 61.9%. 'This trend is evidence of an increased antagonism towards gardaí by some segments of our society, and it is imperative that the public are aware of these deplorable attacks, and that their concerns are reflected in court decisions.'

This, though few noticed it at the time, was a major departure. Garda commissioners recited the crime statistics year after year as they were duty bound to do. McLaughlin used this platform for the first time to signal that the consensus which allowed unarmed policing to take place was under attack in a new and sinister way. He had Jack Marrinan's backing for this. Neither knew that the force was about to be hit by a deadly spate of murders, but both knew that public support for the force had weakened enough to worry them.

Marrinan may have been feeling a bit defensive at this time. Some members suspected he was close to the Commissioner, too close perhaps. Many expected that McLaughlin was going appoint him as an Assistant Commissioner to deal with personnel matters. On the face of it, it was no bad idea- Marrinan would have been an ideal choice. In practice it was impossible. Jack Marrinan's die was cast in the days immediately after the Macushla. He chose the representation route, knowing then that with his talents he would have made senior officer, with a tilt at the top job. In many ways he chose a more difficult path of a reformer, working from the ground up. That Jack Marrinan would have made a fine Commissioner or Deputy few doubted, but that door was long since closed.

In January 1980 Jack Marrinan issued a shocking statement to his members. He told them that some recent recruits were sorry base characters, rejects from organisations with higher standards. It was a remarkably frank statement from one whose job included defending members who got into trouble.

'The Garda Síochána has always been fortunate in its recruits. Police work has long been regarded as a high calling – a vocational means of serving, relatively secure and well paid. With the growth in affluence, and the increasing complexity of society, the force must adapt with a carefully thought out and balanced recruitment campaign. That time has come, but unfortunately the parallel development of a proper personnel policy has not. Conroy stated it baldly a decade ago.

'Recently, the Ryan commission touched on it and called for extensive changes in recruiting and training. It is true that we are still getting many fine recruits, but that is no thanks to our selection system. We are also getting some sorry, base characters, rejects from organisations whose standards have been lifted higher in keeping with rising educational standards. We are getting young men whose personal lives are such a mess that a well-paid and secure place in the gardaí is seen as a refuge.

'This is not easy to say in public, but we have been saying it in private too long. Louden Ryan's report sets out certain basic standards. Now, we need to act speedily on his recommendations before the Garda Síochána goes deeper into the morass which is now our recruitment system. We agree with the Minister for Justice when he says that many persons joining are Leaving Certificate holders. However, we would be more at one with his statement if he would only agree that such a standard is essential if a recruit garda is to assimilate his training, fully understand his role, and later exercise powers, duties and responsibilities of his increasingly complex career path.'[40]

---

40  *Garda Review,* January 1980.

Paddy Harte, a respected Fine Gael TD for Donegal, support-ed Jack Marrinan. 'This statement was only made after long and serious consideration', he noted. 'The members of a police force must be impeccable in character', he told *The Irish Times* on Friday January 18, 1980. The following day, a *The Irish Times* editorial congratulated Marrinan for taking 'a thoroughly professional ap-proach' and praised his courage and patriotism. GRA members in the north Dublin stations of J district, Clontarf , Raheny and Howth, were less impressed. An angry meeting in Raheny station issued a statement rejecting Marrinan's views and declared him 'un-fit to hold the office of general secretary'.

Subsequent criticism of the 'sorry, base characters' editorial, voiced by Gerry Collins among others, accused Marrinan of con-fusing two issues, character defects and educational achievement. A Leaving Certificate was no guarantee of good character, they ar-gued. Marrinan never said that passing examinations would trump moral deficiencies. As the text quoted above shows, he was clearly making two separate points. Taking the long view, he had identi-fied an uncomfortable truth and being misunderstood and misrep-resented was the price he would pay.

The stresses of his job had begun to take their toll. One morning in February 1980 Jack was clearly very unwell. Mary Marrinan de-scribed the scene at home in Templeogue. Jack needed help.

'My car wouldn't start, and I recall agonising over who I could call. Tom and Eileen O'Leary were close friends. Eileen came over and we drove Jack to St Vincent's. Everybody in the hospital seemed to know him, but wanted to talk about everything and anything except his illness. It seemed that they couldn't believe he was ill. For a long time, there was no sign of any treatment. We were about to go home when a porter passed and greeted Jack by name. As always Jack had a smile. Another man passed by and the porter shouted: "Professor Quigley. Would you ever look after Jack Marrinan, please?"'

Surgeon Peter Quigley immediately put him under his care. Jack had a heart triple by-pass and was kept in hospital to convalesce. When colleague Noel Kevane heard of Jack's illness, he and Tim Hurley travelled from Cork to visit him. When they arrived, the ward sister said he was too ill to see anyone. The conversation in the hospital corridor got a bit heated. Then they heard Jack's unmistakeable voice calling, 'I need to see those two men urgently. They are my brothers from Clare, and they are here to settle my affairs.'

Noel Kevane and his wife Patricia had become friends with the Marrinan couple. 'On one occasion they attended a wedding in Kinsale, after which Mary and Jack stayed overnight in our house in Bandon. Before settling down for the night, Jack said he would be gone at dawn the next day. The next morning, when I got up Jack was unusually agitated, while Mary was outside happily swinging on the children's swing. The previous night Jack had locked his keys into his car. In later years when negotiations got tough, I would produce my car keys and shake them in his direction', Noel Kevane recalled in 2016.

The second GRA annual delegate conference was held in the Great Southern Hotel, Galway, on 9 and 10 April 1980. Jack Marrinan set the tone:

'During the past years our association has had its successes and failures, our good days and disappointments. Last year was the year of Ryan, and it opened with huge expectation, but was dampened somewhat when the final report was published.

'The new pay scales were barely enough to make them acceptable (by a majority of 290 votes out of total of 7,000) but their acceptance restored morale and made the force more contented. The big question now is to maintain the pay structure niche proposed by Ryan. This we must do. Little progress has been made in other outstanding matters, with no change in recruitment standards, with aptitude and psychological tests for applicants appearing to be as far away as ever.

'The entrance examination remains at its old and unexacting level, and young gardaí are put out on the beat after only five months training, expected to exercise on their own – and at their peril – much of the complicated duties and responsibilities of a garda. While a working party has been set up, there seems to be no serious intention to introduce a more satisfactory system of selecting and training members for promotion.'

An indirect result of the engagement with Louden Ryan was the long overdue conferring of Jack's degrees. A photograph of Jack in academic robes appeared in *The Irish Times* on 1 November 1980. The caption told readers that he had Bachelor of Arts and Bachelor of Commerce degrees conferred on him by Trinity College Dublin. The conferring came almost a quarter of a century after his studies.

On the industrial relations front, matters were getting heated and the flashpoint was pay. Brian McCabe was coming to the fore as a GRA activist. His insider's account[41] takes us into the meeting rooms to give a vivid picture of the cut-and-thrust of the times:

'I became seriously involved in GRA business when I was elected to the CEC (Central Executive Committee). 1980 was a turbulent year in pay negotiations. I recall we got an offer at conciliation and it was my job to sign on behalf of the GRA. My opponent on the official side said: "Last week when the ESB signed off they did so with gold Cross pens, but all I can offer you is a Bic biro".

'On 16 December 1980 a special delegate conference was held in the Montague Hotel, Portlaoise to consider the pay award. It was stormy, with a sizeable element out for blood. There was talk about the younger members not being looked after. While we never talked down to any members, our private view was that while all increments were important, the higher up the service scale our members were, the higher the salary needed. For example, a member on 12 or 15 years' service with a growing family being educated, as well

---

41    Speaking in retirement to me in 2015.

as a mortgage, always needed an extra few bob. Also, pensions and gratuities were based on the top scale.'

Brian McCabe was from Northern Ireland. Born in the parish of Clogher, Newtownbutler, Co. Fermanagh, he had no police connections apart from his friendship with Garda Peter C Conlon from Drumully, Co. Monaghan, he told me. 'He encouraged me to join up saying there was little enough to do, and plenty of time to play football. I went to Clones garda station and spoke to Sergeant Tom Sloyan, who afterwards ended up as an eminent chief, to apply to join the force. I heard no more for a while until I got a letter informing me that as I lived outside the jurisdiction I should apply in writing to Garda HQ.' McCabe was called to interview in the Phoenix Park, and– perhaps inevitably– asked if he had applied to the RUC. He hadn't and joined the Garda Síochána on 21 September 1963, and there he began to hear stories about the legendary Jack Marrinan.

In the *Garda Review* of May 1980, Jack Marrinan returned to a favourite topic.

'Last year the Ryan committee stated, "More money will not in itself resolve the problems of the force. Conroy had uttered the same words a decade previously. Our recommendations relating to recruitment, selection, training, promotion, and management are of much greater importance. If these are accepted and developed within a Garda Consultative Council, we believe that the force will be able to achieve more fully the primary objective of its members – to be good police officers."

'What has happened in the meantime? Virtually nothing. The consultative council on which the Ryan committee placed so much hope has not got off the ground. Meanwhile, the pay benefits which were achieved have lost much of their lustre and Ryan's recommendations which were so keenly felt are rapidly slipping away.'

In July 1980, the *Evening Herald* took a close look at crime figures for the Dublin area: 'In the 10 months up to October last year [1979] a total of £1,747,766 was taken in 203 post office robberies; a raid almost every single day. This showed a slight drop in the 2,303,686 that armed robbers stole on 217 occasions during the previous year.'

Reporter Helen Rogers quoted Jack Marrinan:

'There is still almost one armed robbery per day somewhere in the country for every day the banks and post offices are open. The only difference now is that only the big ones make the news. It is a far cry from previous years, for example 1969 when just 12 took place, and 1963, when there was none. The sharp rise started in 1972 when 132 raids netted £162,719.'

'Despite alarming increases in the number of raids the proportion of the government's total budget spent on our force is just under four per cent. Apart from vehicles, other crime detection equipment had a budget of £1.5 million; slightly more than the cost of garda uniforms.'

Things were about to take a turn for the worse, as Marrinan and McLaughlin had predicted. On 7 July 1980, Gardaí John Morley and Henry Byrne were shot dead by INLA bank robbers at Loughglynn, near Ballaghderreen, Co. Roscommon. Sergeant Mick O'Malley and Garda Derek O'Kelly were lucky to escape with their lives. The four had answered a call to an armed robbery. The lives of two gardaí were extinguished by gunmen on a quiet road in their community. Morley was a giant of a man, much feared on the Gaelic football pitch. Age 37, he was married with three children. Henry Byrne was 29 and married with two children.

Archbishop Joseph Cunnane of Tuam told the 10,000 funeral mourners at Knock Basilica in Co. Mayo:

'The bullets that killed these two gardaí also found their way into the lives and homes of many others. They wrecked whole lives, dreams, a marriage, a home, a family built up with love, and the labour of years. It left a void that can never be filled, a wound that can never be fully healed in the hearts of the widows and children, as well as parents, brothers and sisters.'

I also attended. I marched with thousands of colleagues behind John and Henry's remains. Approaching Knock graveyard my eyes beheld the green fields only a few miles from where he had run, jumped, and kicked, until he became a legend of Gaelic football. Beside his grave the expertly cut swards of sods were piled in a cairn arching skywards. My mind's eye took me back to earlier that summer when I togged out in Mullingar for a DMA selection against a Roscommon-Galway selection in the Garda All-Ireland football championship. Early on we were on top, but the atmosphere changed when tumult on the side-line signalled the arrival of John Morley. He was endowed with leadership qualities sufficient to lead his teammates to victory.

The two men's garda colleagues were totally devastated. One of them, John Greene, described the aftermath.

'The outrage and shock drew us together and on the night of the funerals we packed out Roscommon's Royal Hotel to vent our feelings. The gathering was almost ready to explode with emotion when Jack Marrinan arrived. That was the first occasion I witnessed the general secretary chair a meeting, and it was breath-taking to see him in action. Having addressed us for a short while, he sought commentary and questions. Anger came from the floor in veritable waves. He sat, impassive and unmoving, until gradually the floor settled. Methodically he dealt with every query and demand. He didn't talk down, but seemed on the same level of understanding, almost reading our minds, and putting reassuring words in our thoughts.'

Speaking to me in retirement Jack Marrinan also recalled that meeting clearly. 'The men there were driven mad with grief and anger', he said, 'they could have gone anywhere and done anything.' He had been worried that nobody could calm them down. For his part John Greene was so impressed by Jack's handling of that situation that he went forward as a delegate for the 1987 annual general meeting. Welfare was a big interest for him, and he later took part in the Panel of Friends and became chairman of the Garda Benevolent Society.

In October 1980 Det Garda Seamus Quaid was shot dead by the IRA at Ballyconnick, Co. Wexford. Det Garda Donie Lyttleton, who was on duty with Seamus Quaid, was also shot but escaped with his life. Quaid and Lyttleton were on alert in the Wexford area to prevent armed bank robberies. Around midday they received information that a town in a nearby county had been 'bottled up' and two banks robbed under arms. Being suspicious of a local individual they discovered that he was not at home. They stayed out on duty until almost midnight when he returned home, and they discovered he was the culprit. Following an altercation Seamus was fatally wounded. 'Seamus Quaid was a pleasant, soft-spoken member, who for many years represented Leinster in the GRB and GRA', Jack Marrinan said.

In retirement Tony Fagan, a Kildare man stationed in Enniscorthy recalls that following his training his instructor remarked, 'that's a great station, you'll never want to leave it',[42] and he never did. Tony also remembered Quaid well. In conversation with me, he recounted how Seamus was revered by everyone in the south east, especially in Wexford where his service was exemplary.

'As a garda he was renowned as a conscientious and fair applicant of law and order. Limerick-born he hurled for his native county, until after his transfer. He teamed up with Garda John Mitchell and formed two-thirds of a powerful full back line in a great Wexford hurling team that swept all before them and became the 1970 All-Ireland winners.'

---

42  Nor did he leave it. Tony Fagan spent his entire service from passing out to retirement in the beautiful village overlooking the Slaney in Co. Wexford.

Tony Fagan was inspired to become active in the GRA by Jack Marrinan. He was also motivated by the charismatic Derek Nally of Bunclody, whom he described as a model sergeant for a Model County. 'He advised me to go forward when the previous incumbent Michael Guerin became assistant to Jack, and that's how I became an area representative for the GRA.' The two general secretaries, Marrinan for the GRA and Nally for the AGSI, were visionaries in Tony Fagan's book. He served on the GRA executive committee from 1983 to 1990. Tony Fagan later visited Germany along with Jack as guests of the Berlin police force, and he witnessed there his gift for getting along with everyone, friend and stranger alike, remembering names and charming everyone they met. But the serious occasions are those that count. 'I also recall his attendance at the funeral of Seamus Quaid and remember vividly his respectful stance in the guard of honour. Unlike some high rankers Jack always stood with garda families in good times and bad.'

It would be madness to say that something good came out of these dreadful murders. But something did happen. It began in Kerry with Mick O'Connell, the greatest Gaelic footballer of all time, according to many. In the annals of Kerry football nobody stood taller than Micko from Valentia Island, as any Kerryman will tell you. He strode into a county council meeting in Tralee where he was an independent councillor, in the days following the murder of Seamus Quaid. Fortunately, reporter Donal Hickey was present.

Micko was hopping mad. As Hickey's report in the *Cork Examiner* told it, O'Connell got stuck into the leadership of GAA for not showing proper respect to the recently slain Seamus Quaid and John Morley, both guards, both prominent GAA players. 'Not one match was called off in Wexford, and the Roscommon county final was played a week after John Morley's murder.' O'Connell urged members of Kerry Co. Council to voice their disapproval to the government in the strongest possible terms, as well as demanding that loopholes in the law be closed and gardaí protected.

After the meeting, when a motion condemning the murders had been passed, Mick O'Connell was still in full spate. He said that while he did not believe that the GAA supported the perpetrators of violence, 'when President John F Kennedy died every match in Ireland was called off, and if the deceased gardaí had gone abroad and entered political life they would have better chance of being treated with respect.'

Was anyone listening? Two significant people were. Jack Marrinan spoke out first, claiming the GAA were misguided in who and what they supported. He also said that playing rebel songs like 'The Men Behind the Wire' on GAA public address systems on match days was deeply hurtful to those who daily risked their lives confronting terrorism.

Marrinan demanded a meeting with the president of the GAA, Paddy McFlynn. He cited GAA ambivalence toward the use of violence, instancing a problematic resolution passed at the 1979 GAA congress. He reminded the GAA that they had previously noted, 'There has always been a close relationship between the Garda Síochána and the GAA; indeed, two of our most heroic members were top exponents of Gaelic games.' And he was joined in this by former Taoiseach Jack Lynch who knew that an 'umbilical cord' joined the two organisations, GAA and An Garda Síochána, reaching into every townland and parish in the country. The *Sunday Independent* was happy to join the fray. Under the headline 'Lynch tells the GAA to settle garda rift' the newspaper reported: 'The former Taoiseach Jack Lynch has called on the GAA to clear up the confusion over the attitude to subversive organisations, which has led to a blazing row with gardaí. Mr Lynch, who won six All-Ireland medals with his native Cork, said he was deeply sorry that a rift between the gardaí and the GAA had erupted, as he had always been satisfied that the GAA had consistently and unequivocally condemned violence. Lynch went on to say: "I hope that gardaí will not withdraw their support for the

GAA as the links between the gardaí and Gaelic games are very close, with at least one member of the force on every county team."

The newspaper also quoted Jack Marrinan: 'As a 32-county organisation it does seem that among the GAA membership there are some who give moral, and even material support to sinister and outrageous causes. The playing of some ballads at GAA matches can give offence and can be divisive. It would be a notable tribute to John Morley, Henry Byrne and Seamus Quaid if it took care not to do so again until times changed and the old innocence returned.' That was published on 2 November 1980.

The following day the officer board of the GRA met the GAA leadership who came out with their hands up. The GAA issued a statement which included a specific assurance that president Paddy McFlynn condemned the murders and the people who carried them out.

This was a surgical operation to neutralise the 'snakin' regarders' among the GAA membership. Commissioner McLaughlin could not shut the GAA down on this ambivalence, nor could the Minister for Justice Collins. Jack Marrinan, with Jack Lynch and Mick O'Connell on his side, could play McFlynn and his supporters off the field, and together they did. It was a shame that it took the deaths of Seamus Quaid, John Morley and Henry Byrne to achieve this.

# 11

---

# Failings in kidnap investigation lead to deaths

Three decades encompassed the career of Jack Marrinan. In the quiet decade of the 1950s he was a diligent member at a south Dublin station, attending university in his spare time and generally impressing those whose path he crossed. The internal garda ferment of the 1960s saw him thrust into a leadership role, articulating the aspirations of a new generation of members of the force. The 1970s began with the Conroy report and far-reaching changes in the operational structure of the Garda Síochána and ended with a catalogue of dreadful deaths of members, which would continue into the following decade. In response to the Northern conflict garda recruitment had been stepped up, and as the 1980s began there were 5,000 members, or about half the total strength, with less than 10 years of service. At the same time Marrinan was aware that his own retirement was now firmly on the horizon. He could have gone in 1983, with 30 years under his belt, but had the option of continuing until he was 57 in 1989. That was his preferred option. He needed to tie up some very dangerous loose ends, given the pressure from terrorism. The new GRA structure was more representative than the GRB had been, that was clear enough, but he also needed to wean

his members off the 'all roads lead to Marrinan' approach. Members
and senior ranks alike could not forever rely on having him as Mr
Fixit for all problems large and small.

In the wake of two oil price shocks in the 1970s, inflation was
running at 18% in 1980. Within the GRA pressure was building on
pay. Unions were entitled to 'cost of living' increases under national
pay agreements. Further increases– above the cost of living – had to
be funded by productivity, more work for more pay, meaning that
they would be 'cost-neutral ' to the taxpayer. But gardaí risking their
lives against terrorists insisted that they were a special case.

Squaring this circle wasn't going to be easy. In December 1980,
Jack Marrinan set out the position to his members.

'About a year and a half ago our pay rates were fixed by Louden
Ryan. Improved pay increases were accepted by a slim majority.
The belief was that there was no alternative, even though they gave
no increase to young members, even if one overlooks the rent allowance increase. Since then teachers and nurses have had better
settlements and many of our members believe that we should have
used industrial pressure to force an increase in the Ryan rates.

'The fact is that the law prevents us from pursuing such a course.
And our association still believes that we have a totally justifiable
case for better pay, and that it can be achieved. We have negotiated
a £2 increase for Saturday allowance and extended night duty payment from 8pm to 6am to 8pm to 8am.'

In February 1981 he told members that a crucial vote on pay
was due the following month. The result of a secret ballot would
be known around 23 March. They would ballot on an increase of
eight per cent from 1 October 1980, plus a special increase of £1
per week. If accepted, it would also attract a seven per cent pay
increase in the second phase of the national pay round.

'A garda would reach maximum pay after eight years and benefit in total to a salary increase of almost £800 per annum on

appointment and to almost twice that amount with 15 years' service', he told members. Concessions required included carrying of guns in specified circumstances, centralised clerical facilities, civilian replacement of some gardaí, attendance at in-service training and changes in rural policing.

The scene was set for a turbulent GRA annual conference in 1981. 'Conferences are peculiar affairs', Jack said. 'The Oxford dictionary defines them as the act of consulting together, but in practice they can assume a variety of shapes from cosy chats to running battles, with some items getting lost in the manoeuvres, or buried in the mayhem'. This conference, held in Blarney, Co. Cork, went close to the mayhem billing. The government had made a pay offer, based on the national pay agreement with the trade unions. GRA members had just voted by a large majority to reject this offer.

Marrinan spelt out the consequences to the assembly:

'We will not be rash, but we will be firm. The reasons the pay claim was rejected was it did not satisfy the overall pay scales, with specific weaknesses at upper and lower increments. Also, there was no retrospection, and this was doubly damaging because of the high expectancy. Finally, the productivity elements, including special tours of duty, brought down the deal in Dublin. Moving forward there are only two real alternatives. To strike is outside the law, and mass sickness would be cowardly. What we propose is a two-pronged plan; firstly, a ban on all overtime except for state and border security, followed by the ultimate sanction- mass resignation.'

The meeting agreed that an overtime ban would begin on 1 May 1981 and if there was no progress, resignations would begin on 15 May. A prolonged discussion took place on forming a trade union. The conference narrowly rejected a motion to have the question of the constitutionality of the gardaí joining or forming a trade union tested in court.

The conference ended with a formal dinner with the Minister for Justice Gerry Collins and Assistant Garda Commissioner Laurence Wren as guests. Collins replied to GRA president Jim O'Shea's appeal to him to break the deadlock saying that gardaí had done better out of recent pay rounds than others in the public service. Then he went on:

'At the moment we are in the midst of a recession, and the number of jobs being provided is not sufficient to offset those being lost. Mr President, you say you are satisfied that I and the government can grant the improvements needed to secure the present settlement. I'm afraid that it is my responsibility to let you know that the realities are that I and my colleagues in government will have to consider this situation not only against the background I have mentioned, but against that of the present economic and social situation.'

So the stage was set for conflict. The only question now was this– how many members would resign on 15 May? None, as it happened. A short news report in *The Irish Times* on 1 May 1981 said the overtime ban had been deferred following eight hours of talks. The government had withdrawn their proposed new duty rosters, among other concessions, the newspaper said.

Brian McCabe, one of the newer members of the GRA executive committee, was able to fill in some of the missing pieces. 'The plan of action was that on 15 May if a pay settlement had not been reached members would fill out a resignation form. These would then be delivered in bulk to the association office in Phibsboro where they would be retained until all members had decided.' This was a very dangerous tactic - what if the official side refused to budge, and the resignation forms had to be submitted? Those who resigned in this way would be either be so few that the management could let them go, or if more numerous they would be blackballed for promotion or otherwise victimised and their careers would be blighted. There was also a suspicion that those who shouted loudest at conferences for action would be smart enough not to write letters of resignation.

McCabe said that the executive committee had met at the end of the annual conference to consider the next steps.

'Intimations from Jack were that Gerry Collins was adamant that the pay award was sacrosanct, but he wanted the matter settled, and a few extra bob was available if we could think up some additional claim. Eventually Michael Conway suggested a claim for uniform maintenance allowance, and when it was immediately accepted by the official side and the membership, the dispute was over.'

That had been a very close call. There had been no going back for a higher pay increase. To keep the younger members on his side, Jack had been forced to roll the dice on winning eventual acceptance away from the heated atmosphere of the conference hall. It had worked, but once used that tactic would not work again. Interestingly, Gerry Collins had read the situation correctly. Had the resignations gone ahead, the GRA might not have survived. The unrest had been sidestepped – it had not gone away.

The IRA hunger strike in northern prisons was about to reach its dreadful climax, putting police forces in Ireland under unprecedented pressure. On 5 May 1981, IRA leader Bobby Sands died on the 66th day of his hunger strike. The RUC bore the brunt of it, but gardaí were affected too, as public reaction veered from outrage, horror and anger to deep sadness, and voices were heard calling for revenge. Masked men with black flags openly stopped traffic on the streets of towns and villages throughout Ireland, as one by one fasting prisoners reached their end. A dreadful sequence of deaths continued until October, when the hunger strike was called off, but 10 men had died while the world looked on in horror.

At the election of GRA central executive officers in September 1981 Jim O'Shea stepped down and Frank Mullen was elected president in his place. Galway's Michael Halpin became vice president and Tim Hurley became treasurer.[43]

Hurley, from west Cork, had joined the force in 1964 and had served in several Munster stations, before settling at Watercourse Road in Cork city. He began to get involved in representation in 1970. Since childhood, maths had interested him; an evening course at Hamilton High School in Bandon perfected his knowledge base, and he became a director of St Paul's Credit Union in Cork, which largely owed its existence to energetic chief superintendent Paddy Power from Marino, Dublin. When Tim Hurley was elected to the executive of the new GRA in 1978, he was an obvious choice for treasurer, and he became a committee member of the Garda Benevolent Society and represented gardaí at the legal and finance conciliation committee.

A Cork-based contemporary of Tim Hurley, Charles McCarthy, displayed an unusual range of talents and qualifications. He had degrees in arts and law and a diploma in education, and lectured in law at Cork Regional Technical College. From Naas, Co. Kildare, his father and grandfather had been gardaí. His first station was Shandon Street, Cork city. When the GRA elections took place in 1978, Charles was elected to the district and divisional committees; positions he held until his promotion in 1989. An erudite and polished speaker, his contributions at GRA annual general meetings were a highlight and his expertise on the Panel of Friends was valued. Sadly he died too young in 1990.

43 Other members of the incoming executive in which new faces were making their presence felt among the older hands were: Donal O Gallachoir, Mayo; Noel Kevane, Bandon, Cork; Tony Hand, Carlow-Kildare; Sean Brennan, Limerick; Pascal Feeney, Tipperary; PJ Davey, Donegal; P J Coll, Clare; Joe Marshall, Laois-Offaly; Pat Maloney, Waterford-Kilkenny; Pat Mahon, Cavan-Monaghan; Brian McCabe, Louth-Meath; John Ferry, Sligo-Leitrim; Bernard Keating, Templemore; John O'Sullivan, Kerry; Michael Guerin, Wicklow-Wexford; Liam Cunnane, Longford-Westmeath; Bill Dunne, Roscommon-Galway East; Frank Lavin, Aiden Woods. Donald Mc Dermott, Pat Fox and Christy Lonergan represented the DMA (Dublin), John Hartigan and Henry A Murphy, SDU and CDU, Garda Headquarters.

In December 1981 journalist Conor Brady posed the question: why is garda morale so perennially low? He answered himself by stating:

'The answer is that the basic structural reforms which Conroy called for in 1970 have not been implemented or attempted. They have been funked. The force's role, purpose and organisation needed fundamental re-appraisal. This never took place.'

Brady argued that successive governments wanted the force kept in a state of semi-intimidation.

'There were several reasons for this; first a docile and unimaginative garda force did not pose any threat to the Department of Justice's omniscience, nor would it question any directives, even if they were in breach of statutory responsibility.

'Secondly, it was cheap; if garda standards were kept low the rate of remuneration did not have to be high. Finally, there was a feeling that if the garda force became too smart, competent, or capable it might exercise a bad influence on a tranquil and predominantly rural society. So, it was a case of retaining an unsophisticated garda force for an unsophisticated people', Brady concluded.

These depressing sentiments were published in the *Garda Review* of December 1981.

A left of centre Limerick TD Jim Kemmy had made accusations about gardaí doing 'nixers', selling videos, building bungalows, and acting as security men, and accused some of 'shopping with the helmet' (buying goods in uniform but not paying for them). Marrinan forcefully rejected the accusations and defended the right of guards to do what they wished in their spare time. 'Double-jobbing was endemic in Irish society', he said. Commissioner McLaughlin's response was more nuanced: he called for a report on the matter and warned that guards whose work was impaired by private activities would be transferred.

A Fine Gael-Labour coalition took power in mid-1981, with Garret FitzGerald as Taoiseach. FitzGerald appointed Jim Mitchell as

Minister for Justice. Representing a Dublin working class constituency, his tenure was brief, and mainly confined to containing the fall-out from the hunger strikes. Soon after being appointed he locked horns with the GRA over his intention to abolish the death penalty. An editorial in the *Garda Review* of July 1981 took aim at his proposal and those who supported it, including an old friend from Macushla days.

'Last month the National Conference of Priests of Ireland passed a motion for the abolition of the death penalty, and its replacement with, "an adequate alternative measure to safeguard the lives of citizens". The same conference was split in support for the work of the gardaí, supporting us on a vote of 29 to 19. Monsignor Tom Fehily said they wanted the motion deleted on the ground that they had reservations about garda conduct in some areas. How come priests cannot recognise good from bad, order from chaos and rectitude from gangsterism?'[44]

The Fine Gael-Labour government fell in 1982 over an ill-judged tax on children's shoes. Charles Haughey returned as Taoiseach and appointed former garda Sean Doherty as Minister for Justice. Doherty, a personable man, was a political lightweight, and when the Haughey government fell before the end of 1982, Doherty's term of office ended- but not before he had interfered in garda operational matters. First, he tried to get a sergeant transferred who had been prosecuting after-hours drinkers in Doherty's local pub. Then Doherty arranged to have the RUC arrest a witness in an assault case and hold him in custody so he could not give evidence against Doherty's brother-in-law on an assault charge in Co. Cavan. This incident was known as the Dowra affair and damaged relations with the RUC for some years.

Garret FitzGerald, now Taoiseach again, appointed Michael Noonan, a 39-year-old teacher from Limerick, to replace Doherty.

---

44 Capital punishment was abolished by law in 1990, and confirmed by referendum in 2001.

Noonan barely had a few days to get the hang of the job before he found himself at the centre of momentous events. During the November election campaign just ended, rumours of telephone tapping had circulated. Also it transpired that Assistant Commissioner Joe Ainsworth had provided a garda recording device to then Tánaiste Ray MacSharry at the request of Sean Doherty. MacSharry recorded himself discussing with another Minister, Martin O'Donoghue, how to replace Charles Haughey as Fianna Fáil party leader. There was another troubling matter. Commissioner McLaughlin and Deputy Commissioner Ainsworth had met RUC Chief Constable Jack Hermon on 18 December 1982 without advising the government, as they were required to do.

FitzGerald and Noonan then got together with Dick Spring, Labour Party leader and Tánaiste and attorney general Peter Sutherland of Fine Gael. All agreed that McLaughlin and Ainsworth had to go. On 19 January 1983, the two men were summoned to meet Noonan and Andrew Ward, secretary of the Department of Justice. They were given 24 hours to resign or be dismissed. The following day the government announced that McLaughlin and Ainsworth had resigned. A separate announcement confirmed that the telephones of two political journalists, Bruce Arnold and Geraldine Kennedy, had been tapped. The secret recording of the MacSharry-O'Donoghue conversation was also confirmed. It was an unfortunate end to the careers of two hard-working and talented officers. Marrinan felt that McLaughlin deserved better and regretted the loss of a Commissioner with whom he worked well.

Before he left office, Seán Doherty had made a commitment to an 'aerial wing' for the force. A helicopter, in other words. That commitment was not then honoured, with tragic results as we shall see.

When Garret FitzGerald had appointed Michael Noonan as Minister for Justice in 1982, he was an unknown entity. Marrinan called an executive meeting and asked if anybody knew this guy or anything about him. Limerick-based executive member Seán Brennan said he lived near Noonan and he could set up a 'getting to know you' meeting. No civil servants present, no favours sought or granted, pints and yarns the only items on the agenda. Noonan turned out be good company, nobody's fool, and he and Jack Marrinan were no longer strangers to each other.

A constantly recurring problem was the state of garda stations around the country. It had been raised during the Macushla episode in 1961, and members of the Fehily committee had said they were shocked at the state of public offices and what were supposed to be living quarters for unmarried gardaí. This fuse was reignited in December 1980 when, according to the *Garda Review*, 'The patience of members gave up, and the station party quit the old leaky, draughty, decrepit building [in Oughterard, Co. Galway] of which we are ashamed.' A year earlier a replacement building had been bought. Plans were drawn up to adapt it but the Office of Public Works dragged their heels on making a start. The walk out– and the publicity it attracted– had the desired effect, as temporary premises were quickly obtained and work began on permanent quarters.

In October 1982 Wicklow [town] garda station was the scene of a second walk-out. GRA and AGSI members walked out of the damp, rat-infested, and dilapidated old station, and undeterred by the teeming rain, carried out their duties from the car park across the road. Members of the 27-strong station party not on duty that Friday morning turned out to support their colleagues. As in Oughterard, members were protesting at the sub-standard station accommodation and the lack of progress at securing a contract for its replacement. Det Garda Joe Comiskey, then the longest-serving member at Wicklow, took up the story. 'Two hours after the walk-out sanction of finance for a new Wicklow station was given. Our protest worked where negotiations failed.'

There were more serious matters, matters of life and death: Abolition of the death penalty was back on the agenda. Since 1964 it had been removed from all crimes except the murder of a policeman on duty. Nobody had been hanged since 1954. In his brief period in office as Minister for Justice, Jim Mitchell had introduced the Criminal Justice Bill in the Senate:

'For my part— and I believe I speak for the great majority of people— I am completely opposed to the taking of life, whether by the state or by anyone else, and I believe that the time has now come for this country to finish the job that was begun in 1964 and to remove completely from the statute book the right of the state to inflict death on any person for whatever reason in the future.'

Coming as it did after seven garda murders, the GRA executive committee passed a motion recommending that capital punishment be retained for the murder of gardaí acting in the course of duty. Marrinan insisted strongly that a largely unarmed force needed the protection of the death penalty as a deterrent to the murder of members.

The death of Garda Patrick Reynolds, shot in the back at Avonbeg Gardens, Tallaght, when he and three other gardaí disturbed a gang counting the proceeds of a bank raid, came a few short months after the capital punishment debate began. Jack's angry 'no time for bleeding hearts' editorial was published in the *Garda Review* in February 1982. It gives a good account of the frustrations felt by members of the force, and also of what the author could be like when the gloves came off.

'Patrick Reynolds was an unarmed garda in uniform duty when he was shot in the back, a few hours after midnight on February 20, 1982. As a garda he expected a certain amount of danger in his work, but he never had a chance. Neither did [his colleagues] Tom Quinn, Leo Kenny, Michael McMahon, or Paddy O'Brien, when they went to a simple disturbance call.

'Patrick was the first garda murdered in 1982.

'The rest of us are left with a horrible question. Would stronger penalties or longer sentences have prevented these deaths; perhaps that is the weakness in evaluating capital punishment? Hanging the murderer of Garda Reynolds will not bring him back, but it might save his fellow members.

'We had no garda murders between 1943 and 1970. Since then we've had eight fatalities: four over the past 20 months. Something must be done immediately to demonstrate once and for all that the government will not tolerate this level of criminality. They must act with absolute determination to end this violence. All talk of abolishing capital punishment must stop, and the strongest signals sent out that the ultimate punishment will be retained on the statute books. This is no time for bleeding hearts.

'The single most effective deterrent to the activities of criminals is the sight of a garda on duty. Given the personnel we can do the job. Without them we can't. Today most of our provincial towns are bereft of gardaí. We do not have sufficient gardaí to keep our patrol cars on the road, and when they are, they are manned by half crews. Our rural districts cannot provide round the clock service. Patrol cars lie idle in station backyards, and beats have not heard a member's footfall from one end of the week to the other.

'Last month our Commissioner spelled out the case for urgent reform to our legal system. Let us, in simple language, repeat it again. We need authority to detain suspects for questioning. Every police service that we know of except us has such authority.

'A person suspected of having committed an indictable offence should be required to give his fingerprints, allow himself to be photographed, and should be compelled to yield possession of their clothing and footwear for forensic testing.

'Suspects should be obliged to surrender swabs, samples of hair, clothing, urine, fingernail scrapings, or any other samples considered essential for the procurement of best evidence.

'An accused person should be obliged to give evidence, and be subject to cross-examination where a *prima-facie* case has been established.

'In the interests of establishing the truth, material evidence should not be automatically refused on the grounds of a technicality. Clear evidence that an accused committed a murder or rape should not be discounted, and the suspect set free, simply because a garda procuring this evidence was in technical breach of the rules. An example would be having detained a suspect for a short period when there was no right in law to do so.

'The names of civilian witnesses should not be supplied in copies of a book of evidence. Currently a suspect is entitled to submit an alibi after he has read the evidence against him. We urge that such alibis must be offered at the first opportunity before the book is served.

'There should be a new offence of withholding information, and consecutive sentences should be applied in respect of crimes committed while on bail. It should be an offence to falsely allege ill treatment while in garda custody.

'If the foregoing proposals were conceded by the legislature, our ability to deal with criminality would be greatly improved. In the week of Pat Reynolds's murder, a garda was taken at gunpoint in Limerick and locked in a bank safe, while another who came on an armed robbery in Dublin city centre was forced at gunpoint to lie on the ground.'

Jack Marrinan knew that many items on this list were politically undeliverable. His outburst was published almost verbatim in the Dublin *Evening Herald* a few days later. Notice in particular his reference to powers of arrest. Gardaí had been criticised for making arrests under the Offences Against the State Act of 1939, intended for use in wartime, and their pleas for updated powers of arrest had fallen on deaf ears. Also noteworthy is that his argument falls in a direct line from Commissioner Eoin O'Duffy's 1923 instruction that in the hierarchy of priorities, prevention trumps detection of crimes.

There's something else that was also becoming clear. Ireland was in a state of flux in a way it had never seen before. The strains caused by the IRA campaign in the North were spilling over into domestic politics. Three elections took place in two years, Haughey's leadership of Fianna Fáil came under sustained challenge, the Fine Gael-Labour coalition under FitzGerald would eventually collapse over public spending. All this uncertainty caused a vacuum of leadership and the police were not immune. The brief terms of office of commissioners Garvey 1975-78, McLaughlin 1978-83, then Wren from February 1983, and ever-changing Ministers for Justice, Collins, Mitchell, Doherty and Noonan - four in all between 1977 and 1982 - only served to emphasise the leadership hiatus. The only consistent authority who could speak on the measures needed to meet public order challenges facing society was Jack Marrinan, and this would remain so until Fine Gael's inexperienced Minister for Justice Michael Noonan found his feet.

Around this time, a young reporter contacted the Garda Depot seeking the Commissioner's views on a recent spate of crimes. Seán Flynn was working for the *Sunday Press*. An unidentified garda told Flynn that the Commissioner was loath to make public statements, and it would be best to contact Jack Marrinan. On policing matters, as opposed to industrial relations, the Commissioner and the general secretary of the GRA were of the same mind, he was told. The simple fact was that Jack Marrinan had become the public face of the force. Within garda ranks there would be a price for this. Some younger members, concerned by increased risks they ran daily and also the effects of inflation on their wages, began to mutter about their general secretary being preoccupied with matters other than pay and conditions of work. And that critical undercurrent would continue until Jack's retirement.

Before he left office Seán Doherty had told the GRA that he accepted that a commission should examine the working of the force and asked for ideas about terms of reference. The GRA response took the form of a lengthy submission in which Jack Marrinan confronted contradictions prevalent in Irish society, almost as if he were a preacher conducting a retreat for very recalcitrant offenders.[45] Many of these sentiments had been aired in a speech he gave to a GRA conference in 1982 attended by Doherty as Minister for Justice.

In it, Jack put some searching questions to the Irish public. There's more than a whiff of the old-time preacher about his passionate words.

'You want unarmed policing, and I believe in unarmed policing, yet what can we say to the unarmed garda faced with a sawn-off-shotgun wielder, or the unarmed garda in a family car trying to keep up with the bandit in a high-powered vehicle? My association has always contended that guns would come between our members and those we serve, and that our communities are safer when police are unarmed. We must look again in terms of the times we live in. The fact that we ourselves prefer not to carry arms is not really the central point. I believe that the answer to the armed criminal can be found in stiffer laws and penalties, but if it transpires that there is no other way to reduce the sense of helplessness in the face of armed crime it may be necessary to give the gardaí more access to arms.

'Unemployment is rising yet we have no outlets for the energies of those without work. Is it any wonder that some are attracted into criminal gangs? Don't think you can isolate policing from the daily lives of people, their behaviour and attitudes, their needs and obligations, their jobs and the lack of them.'

---

45 An account of the submission appeared in the December 1982 *Garda Review*. The account above is a brief summary.

He instanced a range of social crime, vandalism, petty thieving, shoplifting, traffic offences, drug taking and trafficking, all feeding into a general picture of lawlessness.

'Simple enforcement systems have lost their effectiveness across a whole spectrum of national life. Rules are there to be broken, ignored or got around. Persistent and flagrant violation has added to the creation of a climate of disrespect for all law and regulation; thousands of drivers and car owners avoid paying motor tax and insurance.

'Parking regulations are flouted. Bus lanes, clearways, taxi ranks, loading bays mean nothing to many Irish people who want to park. Social welfare and insurance schemes are being 'milked' through widespread dishonesty. Planning laws are frequently held in disregard. Houses and developments are put up in flagrant violation of the law, and then allowed to remain since they constitute a *fait accompli*.

'Regulations on public safety, fire and so on are not universally enforced, as witnessed by well-publicised disasters[46] and by anyone who cared to check on safety procedures in clubs, factories and even government offices. TV licence evasion is widespread, and after 21 years of national television services a simple system to register all TV owners and renters has still not been implemented.

'Our community cannot be selective about the rules that it supports. Can a businessman who advertises over a pirate radio be too outraged about the public's approach to parking regulations when he finds his distribution or delivery held up by an illegally parked vehicle in his loading bay?

'It is vitally important that the sense of lawlessness be tackled, and if this is not done the task of An Garda Síochána in the years ahead will not only be difficult but impossible.'

---

46  The Stardust nightclub fire in north Dublin had occurred earlier in the year, killing 48 and injuring more than 200.

Here Marrinan has moved beyond representing his members. He is challenging society to confront the consequences of its 'ah sure there's no great harm in it' attitude to breaches of the rule of law.

In a March 1983 *Garda Review* editorial Jack Marrinan wrote:

'We welcome the appointment of Commissioner Laurence Wren. He is experienced in administrative and operational police matters and has had an exacting and thorough apprenticeship during the four decades of his garda vocation.'

In April 1983 the Garda Representative Association conference was held in the Talbot hotel, Wexford town. Two motions attracted particular attention.

Danny Smith, a Raheny delegate, proposed a motion for extra pay for Dublin members. 'The nature of their workload is heavier. The motion may be defeated at arbitration, but let it be so, and not here at our conference'. Christy Lonergan seconded it.

Cork delegate Tim Hurley opposed what he called a divisive motion. 'Remember more garda lives have been lost in the country than in the city'. Another delegate Greg Burke supported him. 'I have to cover 7,000 acres on a bicycle, and the members in the DMA make extra money on overtime.'

Pat Sullivan, who had been stationed in the DMA south central for a decade, posed the question, 'How many members outside the DMA have been followed home, and received annoying phone calls? I cannot go shopping with my wife without being abused.'

Jack Marrinan responded, 'Doubtlessly urban areas impose severe pressure, but we are a national garda force.' The motion was carried and the division in the ranks would prove costly.

More was to come. Patrick Fox, a Dublin delegate, proposed a motion of no confidence in the general secretary of the GRA: Jack Marrinan. Colleague Oliver Egan from the same division seconded the motion. When garda Fox was invited to speak on the motion he declined.

Brian McCabe, secretary of the conference arranging committee, said, 'It is too much to cast these aspersions, and pass over the motion. I ask the proposer to have the guts to follow it through.' Other speakers supported him.

Jack Marrinan rose and said, 'This motion was supposed to be a critical issue at the conference. We had been threatened with it, and that there was a case against us. It is not fair not to follow it through. I would like to know the reasons for this motion, and to respond to them. I came prepared to answer any claims. Anyone who puts such a motion on the agenda should not leave it in the air. It is just not good enough.'

Patrick Fox said, 'I am here to represent my district. I have done. I have nothing further to add.' The motion was defeated with two for, nine abstentions and the rest against, but the divisions in the GRA were now public, clear for everyone to see.

Marrinan's push for structural reform picked up a gear in 1983. On 19 May the Minister for Justice Michael Noonan opened a high level GRA conference in Dublin on policing reform. Speakers included Proffessor Mary McAleese, a legal academic who would later serve two terms as president of Ireland, Prof John Kelly TD, another legal academic and Bill Taylor, secretary of the Northern Ireland's police authority.

At the outset Michael Noonan commended the GRA for assembling people of such eminence. 'There has been a growing number of allegations in the recent years, and particularly in recent times, of outside interference in garda affairs. A significant number of them were true, and there is no doubt that they gave rise to considerable questioning, not alone within the force, but also members of the public', Noonan said.

The Minister said the government accepted the need for a Garda Authority.

'We have therefore decided to introduce an independent element to ensure that there is no interference; and I use the words with the connotation of "undue interference" in the proper administration of the force.

'This does not mean there will be any lessening of responsibilities of the Justice Minister to the government. The Minister will continue to be as accountable, answerable for An Garda Síochána to the Dáil and the government, and in a democratic society this is essential and proper. What is needed is a balance between that accountability and the need for the force to get on with its work without undue interference.'

Here Noonan was saying that it is all very well to seek a police authority, but the shaping of it and defining the limits of its powers is a complex matter that will not be easily resolved. His speech was almost certainly written for him in the Department of Justice and one can almost hear the gritting of teeth that accompanied its composition. In organising a high-level seminar like this in a university and getting a Minister to open it and commit to a police authority, Marrinan and the GRA had taken the ball off the pitch of internal negotiations and gone for a wider, more influential audience.

Superintendent Patrick Culligan[47] asked, 'Who should investigate complaints of criminal activity against the gardaí?' Prof Kelly replied, 'This would be a separate function from investigating complaints which might not be of a criminal nature, such as bad manners, or other matters which might be considered as bad policeman-ship.'

Sergeant William Keaveney, vice chair of the AGSI, voiced his concern for the autonomy of the force with less control. Kelly replied that unless there is political will to create and maintain a buffer between the gardaí and the public things are not going to get better but worse.

---

47   Garda Commissioner 1991-6.

Jack Marrinan asked the speakers if they were asked to write down the terms of reference of such an authority, what aspects would they be most careful of?

Surrey's Chief Constable Sir Peter Matthews stressed the danger of political interference. Bill Taylor said 'that whatever body is created it should be representative of the whole community. It must be acceptable, and the appointees must be people that the community trust.'

Sir Peter in his address said, 'Your force is only as good as its staff. You must go out and sell yourselves; talk to the people, encourage them to approach the police and help them to get on with each other. There has been ample evidence of how thoroughly gardaí investigate complaints against themselves, but this does not always come across to the public. The gardaí would do well to help the community to get on with itself,'

A significant contributor was John Kelly, a former Fine Gael Minister and professor of law at University College Dublin. Disappointingly Kelly, whose views carried weight across the political spectrum, would prove lukewarm on a police authority and Noonan would leave the Department of Justice with that task unfinished.

John Kelly was important politically. But so also was Mary McAleese, Reid professor of law at Trinity College Dublin. She was from Belfast and had lived in Northern Ireland until a few years earlier and was close to Fianna Fáil. McAleese did not pull any punches. She is quoted here at length because she articulated many of the problems facing the force at the time, problems which Jack Marrinan was trying to confront in his final years at the GRA.

'Since first coming to live in the Republic my work has often brought me into contact with the gardaí, and my respect for them is immense. I value very dearly the privilege of living in a society where I can and do have confidence in the forces of law and order.

But that trust and confidence has taken many severe blows over the past years, and particularly last year.

'We live with a certain amount of abuse – everyone knows that some people can get parking fines fixed, drunk driving charges dropped, we know that politicians use influence to get friends and relations into the gardaí, and that there was political influence in the promotions of high ranks in the gardaí. Few approved, but equally few realised how insidious they were and how dangerous it was to regard them as a pragmatic reality.

'Recent experience has shown how far the rot has set in – it even moved one commentator to suggest that it was naïve to expect anything better from our police since the general level of honesty in our community is so low. If it is naïve then I make no apologies for being naïve. We are entitled to expect better, and we are entitled to be shocked.

'A garda or minister of government who abuses the power they have by virtue of their uniform or office is more odious than every species of thieves or armed criminals put together. Both debase the right of a community to penalise deviants, it makes a mockery of the law-abiding, and institutionalises double-standards which seriously erode the community's belief that the law is there to protect them, and that the gardaí are the force to enforce it without fear or favour.

'The recent phone tapping and bugging scandal highlighted that the relationship between the Minister and the gardaí is anti-democratic, and it must be a priority to dissociate the Garda [force] from the government. Whatever else this Garda Authority does, it must as a matter of priority disassociate itself and the government from the gardaí in a number of respects. The Commissioner must be allowed to run the operational side of policing without having to look over his shoulder for the approval of the Minister, and whatever structure is envisaged, it must put the two at arm's length from each other.

'Despite the Minister's reservations about an independent Garda Authority I see no sound reason why such an authority could not be entrusted with the job of organising and controlling the gardaí, referring to the government only in matters relating to legislation and finance.'

Prof McAleese did not spare Fianna Fáil, a party to which she was closely aligned. The Doherty, McLaughlin and Ainsworth goings-on would not have come to light without a change in government', she said.

'Men of considerable influence seriously destabilised and demoralised the gardaí and damaged public confidence in both the gardaí and the government; yet the public are expected to be satisfied with resignations.

'The power currently vested in the government which permits it to promote members to the higher echelons of the gardaí is a major source of anxiety to gardaí and the public alike. We can no longer rely on the government's integrity or self-discipline to ensure that promotions relate solely to merit – this is a job clearly for the authority, and it calls for an open and overtly fair structure. I see no valid reason why all senior vacancies, including Garda Commissioner, should not be advertised and open to competition.

'We have at last admitted that abuses and corruption exist within the gardaí – of course they do because the temptations and pressure they face are greater by far than those of the rest of us. This is precisely the reason that extraordinary safeguards are called for. Most of us realise that our courts are not an adequate safeguard against such excesses; indeed the experience of most common law countries is that they have been exasperatingly reluctant to take to task members of the police, and their reticence is shared by those responsible for the investigation of complaints and initiating proceedings against our gardaí. In the present climate who would trust the gardaí to investigate complaints against themselves any more than one can get one solicitor to sue another, or one doctor to accuse another of negligence?

'Gardaí have for some time demanded a number of changes in the law which would have the effect of increasing their powers. I would be the first to accept that some such changes are justified, but if they are legalised without the prior establishment of institutions designed to strengthen confidence in the gardaí they may well be another nail in the coffin of police-public relations.'

Here Mary McAleese previews the 'deal' which will deliver more effective garda powers in exchange for agreeing to a mechanism for processing complaints of garda misbehaviour.

It was a challenging speech and made uncomfortable listening for many present. Jack Marrinan's verdict was that the debate had started. He was pleased that Noonan was taking garda matters seriously. He wanted his members to know what was being said, and a full report appeared in the *Garda Review* in June 1983.

The push for reform continued into 1984. On 16 March, the *Irish Independent* devoted almost a full page to 'Keeping the long arm of the law straight', by reporter Jim Farrelly. This had Jack Marrinan's fingerprints all over it. The reporter began by interviewing Edmund Garvey, sacked as Garda Commissioner in 1978, getting him to spill the beans on his experiences of political interference on the police. [48]Garvey first said that he was proud that his political impartiality was clear, insofar as he was promoted to Assistant Commissioner by Fianna Fáil in 1973 and made Commissioner in 1975 by Fine Gael. As Commissioner he had always wanted to promote the best people in the force. Interview boards consisted of two civil servants and just one garda and that did not help. For promotions to detective, sergeant, and station

---

48   In the meantime Garvey won exemplary damages of £500 for the manner of his sacking, as he had not been given a chance to answer the complaints against him, just told to go.

sergeant he was accustomed to being lobbied by politicians who wanted jobs, promotions and sometimes transfers for their constituents. But when it came to senior officers, the situation was much worse. The Commissioner did not have the final say on who was to be promoted. The government, via the Department of Justice, did. The Commissioner drew up lists of guards whom he wanted to promote and submitted them to the Minister for Justice for approval. Garvey confirmed to Farrelly that, 'since the inception of the force there were two promotion lists he knew of that were not acted on by one Minister, while another Minister queried three names on a promotion list before sanctioning them.' Garvey also instanced a Commissioner who had put on record his strong objection to the promotion of a person he had previously turned down for promotion.

In Garvey's personal experience, he said he had been over-ruled when he reacted to 'very serious circumstances indeed' by standing down a patrol car and putting two members back on the beat; political interference had caused him to backtrack. 'Pressure from politicians and indeed from the Minister's own office wore him down and eventually he restored the car and the status quo at the station.'

Garvey went on to complain about political interference in disciplinary matters. As Commissioner he had fined a member for allowing his garda overcoat and identity to be stolen by the IRA. Politicians had made representations to him to reverse this. Also as Commissioner he had issued a circular forbidding members from acting as greyhound 'slippers' at dog racing meetings in their spare time. He said he was asked by politicians, including one Minister, to withdraw this and he refused. After he left office his circular was withdrawn, leaving gardaí free to take the job.

There was more. Garvey said he had a very tough attitude to the 'fixing' of summonses. He was aware of it going on and indeed it was practised widely by one or two of his most senior officers.

However it was difficult to get evidence on 'fixers' – there was little he could do beyond trying to give a good example and encouraging his senior officers to do likewise.

In talking openly to Farrelly, Garvey had lifted the lid on the politicisation of the garda force, confirming what had been long suspected. Politics came into play in recruitment, transfers, appointment to senior positions and discipline. An ever-present danger was that the garda who obtained advancement or was spared disciplinary sanction following representations by a politician might henceforth feel compromised. The politician might later 'call in the favour' by way of fixing a drunken driving charge, for example, or forestalling a valid garda objection to a public house licence application.

The article concluded with approving mention of Jack Marrinan's call for 'a system of training in management, leadership and police science on a professional basis'. Such a system would release 'the talent within the force and produce men and women who would be apparent to their peers as the obvious men to take over the vacant slots [in garda management].'

Larry Wren's commissionership had started badly. Sergeant Patrick McLoughlin was shot dead at his bedroom window in Dunboyne by a young man whom he had previously cautioned for smoking cannabis. McLoughlin was a highly regarded member of the force, both in the neighbourhood and among his colleagues. He was 42 years old, married to Dolores and they had three children.

A series of kidnappings took place, following the IRA's financial success in the Ben Dunne kidnapping two years previously. There were six kidnappings or attempted kidnappings in 1983. Fear of kidnapping was rife. The children of wealthy families were ferried to and from school in cars which sat very low on their springs, due to doors and windows being reinforced. Popular entertainers had burly bodyguards in their retinue. Jack and Mary Marrinan's children were given garda covert protection. A newspaper columnist who criticised the IRA received calls warning him off, naming the school attended by his children. And a senior officer in the Prison Service, Brian Stack, who worked in Portlaoise prison, was murdered on his way to a boxing match in Dublin. This was an attempt to intimidate the staff in Portlaoise prison where republican prisoners were being held.

In August gardaí successfully foiled an attempt to kidnap Canadian supermarket tycoon Galen Weston at his Roundwood, Co. Wicklow home where he lived with his wife Hilary Frayne, a former fashion model.

On 24 November 1983, the IRA made another attempt to get money from Weston. The manager of his Irish businesses, Don Tidey, an Englishman, was seized at a bogus garda checkpoint near his home in south Dublin. In December, garda intelligence picked up unusual activity around Ballinamore, Co. Leitrim, a known IRA hotspot. A search party of army and gardaí located Tidey and his captors hiding in a dugout in Derrada Wood. Shots were fired and a young garda recruit and a soldier were shot dead as the kidnappers escaped. A detachment of 50 recruit gardaí from Templemore had been sent to help in the search. Tidey was rescued but at the cost of two lives. Here's an account of that day's events from one of Gary Sheehan's fellow recruits who was with him in Derrada Wood.

'We had about half of our training completed and halfway through December we were looking forward to a long weekend off. One evening after supper we were all summoned together, marched to the barrack master's office, and supplied with wellingtons and long waterproof coats. When we asked what it was all about we got no answer, but were told to go to bed early and not tell our families.

'The next morning, we were called at 3am and directed to the square where a fleet of buses were lined up. It was such a black dark winter's night; we could hardly see each other. I fell asleep till daylight and having awoke, someone mentioned we were in lovely

Leitrim. I thought of the first few words of the famous song. "Last night I had a pleasant dream. I woke up with a smile".

'There were no smiles as we huddled together on an early morning of icy sleet and bits of snow. The army were present, armed and properly uniformed for the weather conditions. They also knew more than we did. I overheard snippets. The name Tidey was mentioned.

'We were lined up by an officer and told that we would be searching rough terrain, and the operation was code-named Santa Claus. About a dozen units were lined up, Rudolf 1 to 12. I remember thinking of Dasher and Dancer and Prancer. I can't remember which group I was in but there was about 20 of us. We had an inspector, a few sergeants, about a dozen recruits, a few local gardaí, about six detectives and a good gang of very professional looking army men with guns. I think one of our top ranks had a radio. We were strung out in a line, with an armed member of the army or gardaí between the uniformed unarmed members. It was hard going in heavy constant rain. I was drenched from head to foot in minutes.

'Derrada Wood was a barren ridge of terrain planted with Sitka spruce trees. Due to the undergrowth our line was walking-cum-crawling. Suddenly, I heard a rat-a-tat sound. I thought it was icicles crackling on the trees, until someone mentioned a machine gun. The order came along the line to take cover. I sensed danger, heard bodies crashing through the undergrowth, then a deadly silence. All I could do was keep my head down and pray. The drip and the crackle of the trees was the only sound until, suddenly, more shots echoed, very close, then deathly silence. Word came that we had a man down and so had the army. The line had become a broken straggle of prone bodies. I spotted the training insignia on a shoulder; his face looked into mine, a look of unrecognisable terror. Later we met, and I knew him well. I had been in so much shock that I didn't recognise him.

'None of our class were allowed attend Gary Sheehan's funeral. The reason given was that we had no clean uniforms. Members of the July class turned out and formed a guard of honour.'

Another member of the Templemore staff who was with the recruits in Derrada Wood, also recalled those events.

'It was pitch black when we left the Training Centre. There were rumours about Don Tidey, we had been warned not to tell the recruits. After a long journey we arrived in close proximity to a wood in Ballinamore, Co. Leitrim. I was allocated 10 recruits, all half-trained. Underfoot the terrain was very uneven. The army lads were much better equipped.

'A deathly pale garda recruit whispered to me: "There's men with guns in here". Before I could react, gunshots came. I shouted a warning, pushed the young lads nearby on to the horizontal and looked for a path to get them to safety. I counted my complement but could only reach nine. Just then an inspector arrived. "Take over", he said. "I have to go. Gary Sheehan has been shot dead."

'A piece of me died with those words. I was in a daze. More than shock. Some officer wanted to question me. I could hardly speak. He said it could wait till morning. I said get it over. Thoughts uppermost were what should I have done differently? I was bursting with emotion, especially anger. What were the young innocent lads doing here? Who made that crazy decision? Who in the name of God planned this escapade that led us into a death trap?

'Later after the funeral there was a de-briefing and Commissioner Larry Wren had the floor. Marrinan tore into him and his cocooned retinue. I never felt so proud of Jack when, in his strong Clare accent, he unleashed himself on our authorities. It was a complete and utter disaster, he said. Advantage was taken of young, innocent, impressionable, untrained recruits, who because of their natural exuberance and enthusiasm were placed in mortal danger.

'Wren replied: 'Jack if it happened tomorrow, I'd put them in again.'

This search was a job for a helicopter, not half-trained recruits. Marrinan had complained repeatedly to senior officers and the Department of Justice about using recruits in dangerous situations. He held back from doing so in public or putting his thoughts in writing for fear of alerting terrorists to a weak spot in garda defences. Wren knew why Marrinan was angry and knew he had just cause.

Gary Sheehan, aged 27 and single, was from Carrickmacross, Co. Monaghan. His father was a garda. Jack Marrinan said that going to see the Sheehan family had been very difficult, the very worst moment in his working life. He had been completely lost for words. He also mourned the loss of soldier Patrick Kelly, aged 35 from Westmeath. The army private was married with four sons, the youngest of whom was 11 weeks old. Many years later during a lengthy interview about his career, Jack had to stop and compose himself when recalling those two deaths in Derrada Wood.

In his January 1984 address to members Jack Marrinan wrote:

'The new year opened with the realisation of the sacrifice associated with a garda career. The expectation, optimism and excitement that accompanied an alert, highly motivated and intelligent recruit Garda, Gary Sheehan, to follow his forefathers and become a guardian of the Irish people's peace was ended in a moment of uncompromising viciousness when he fell to a bullet of murderous terrorists at the edge of a desolate Leitrim wood on a bleak December afternoon. Beside him fell Patrick Kelly; a loyal and honourable member of our army.

'In releasing Don Tidey both young men saved a valuable life and deprived the unscrupulous kidnappers of a ransom that would be undoubtedly used to finance and promote further murders and destruction.'

Around this time, heroin was taking hold of the cities and towns of Ireland. In Dublin the Dunne family, originally street traders in the Camden Street area, held sway. While the introduction of heroin generated considerable public alarm, good police work put the Dunnes away.

Larry Dunne being jailed left an opening into which a resourceful career criminal, Martin Cahill, also from Dublin's southside, stepped. As a younger man he had been part of the Dunne gang. His target was the closely guarded Thomas O'Connor and Sons manufacturing jewellers in Harold's Cross, near where he grew up. The IRA had considered the factory beside the greyhound track as a source for funds for the struggle, but finding that the security was near impregnable, abandoned the idea. The factory's alarms had a direct line to the garda control room at Dublin Castle, and the Special Detective Unit patrols were an ever-present factor. Nonetheless, on the morning of 27 July 1983, Martin Cahill and eight others, armed to the teeth, gained access to the O'Connor factory and safes and left with gold and jewels valued at £2 million. Though it was clear who had done it, no successful prosecutions followed, and there was a great deal of egg on the face of Commissioner Larry Wren.

## 12

# Murders and kidnapping - Final showdown between Jack and the Doc

Mick Dowd was with Frank Hand when he died. Both were detectives, members of a specialised armed escort unit. Early on the morning of August 10, 1984, both men kitted up and requisitioned official transport in Garda Headquarters in Dublin's Harcourt Square. Mick was armed with a cased Uzi sub machine gun and a holstered 38 calibre Smith and Wesson revolver. Frank, the driver, also carried a holstered revolver. They went to the GPO where, following an inspection by senior officer Fachtna Murphy, they were told to escort an armoured van delivering cash to rural post offices in Co. Meath.

Mick Dowd recalled their first stop.

'We had a delivery for Drumree post office and as the familiar green An Post sign came into sight the cash transport vehicle moved from the brow of the road and halted. Frank pulled in a little way behind. As the staff in front began to alight, I sensed movement in my rear. Checking my side-mirror I saw two masked figures carrying guns moving towards my car door.

'Instantly, my senses froze. I sensed that my life was in the most deadly peril. A hesitant half-breath before the gunman was at my door and the black circular gun-barrel was pointed directly at me. The deadly click, and time was a blur as the terrific blasts almost lifted my side of the car. Somehow the insulated padding on the inside of my door prevented the bullets from penetrating and definitely saved my life.'

Frank Hand had jumped from the driver's seat. He was shot dead on the spot. Mick Dowd was also shot and suffered facial injuries, from which he recovered. Many years later Dowd told me: 'Frank had boundless enthusiasm and energy for life. I think of him every day.'

Frank Hand joined the force in 1977 and became a detective in 1981. One of seven children from a Co. Roscommon family, he worked in Donnybrook and Irishtown stations, and the Drugs Squad, and was assigned to the Central Detective Unit early in 1984. Shortly afterwards in July he married Garda Breda Hogan. They were just back from honeymoon when the Provisional IRA raided Drumree post office. The IRA gang got away with almost a quarter of a million pounds. The day's cash delivery began at the most remote point of its round– a vulnerability which a garda sergeant had alerted his superiors to the previous year, but nothing had been done to counter it. They were sent out with a quarter of a million pounds, in a remote village, sitting ducks for the IRA.

Jack Marrinan spoke for the anger of his members in the *Irish Press*[49] a couple of days later. 'Last Friday's murder and robbery were all the more serious because everything points to the fact that those who carried them out deliberately intended to gun down the garda escort before they robbed the post office van. Obviously, they saw this as the quickest, safest and most efficient way of getting their hands on the money. Life did not matter. Gardaí were expendable. This marks the point where we must say "stop" and mean it.' His article went on to deplore the failure to pass into law the Criminal Justice Bill intended to equip gardaí with adequate powers of arrest.

49    13 July 1984.

They were bitter heartfelt words. Breda Hogan had just five weeks of married life with her handsome garda husband. The following April she gave birth to a baby girl who would never know her father.

Jack Marrinan was now entering the last lap of his service as general secretary of the GRA. He had completed 30 years in 1983 and might have gone then. For his own sake, perhaps he should have. Mary and his children wanted him to retire – they hadn't seen enough of him at home for years. He had already had a serious warning about his health. Under regulations then prevailing he had the option of serving until he was 57, and he took it. Many of those who had joined with him – the second generation – had their time done and had moved on. However the juggling act must continue: his members were under fire and needed representation, the battle against terrorism was continuing, the force was not yet fit for purpose operationally, nor would it be until the legal framework was reformed. The Criminal Justice Act of 1984 brought with it welcome improvements in powers of detention of suspects, but some important provisions of it would not be activated until the Garda Complaints Bill was enacted. The trade-off between stronger legal powers for gardaí and co-operation with new complaints structures needed very careful handling, and the headstrong tendency among the GRA showed little appetite for the compromises necessary to deliver much-needed change.

On 27 January 1985 a break appeared in the clouds. Commissioner Larry Wren announced a garda training advisory committee to include experienced personnel from the private sector and the academic field, along with representatives from his own staff as well as from the Department of Justice. This new committee, 'will make recommendations on training from recruiting intake stage, including the courses provided in the Garda College', according to his statement. Wren's announcement went on to say that it would consult fully with garda representative associations.

Marrinan welcomed the choice of chairman. An independent and respected public figure, Dr Tom Walsh was an agricultural scientist with a fine record in the public service. Most of the other people nominated could be relied upon to deliver a sound evidence-based appraisal and Jack had no worries on that score. But he also spotted the 'weasel words' in the announcement– 'consult fully'. To one versed in the ways of the Department of Justice this could only mean one thing – no GRA representation. The only garda included on the 10-strong committee was Deputy Commissioner Eamonn Doherty, representing management. Marrinan found himself back in the never-never-land of the SKC reports, reports so secret that no person of garda rank could read them.[50]

And now this. 'For several years past we have pointed out the need for improved and more up to date training of all ranks', Marrinan complained. 'At every opportunity we have pleaded that all members should be better prepared for the increasingly sensitive and complex job that we do. Could anyone envisage a similar committee being set up to enquire, review and make recommendations on the training of teachers, solicitors, civil servants, or electricians, without representation of the relevant professions being directly involved? Is our banishment an indication that gardaí have nothing to offer on their own training?' Jack Marrinan asked wearily.[51]

Also in February, the *Garda Review* marked the retirement of one of Jack's contemporaries, Brian Sheehan, who had given stout service to the GRA as an executive member and to the public as a

---

50  Along with Dr Walsh and Deputy Commissioner Doherty the members were: Dr J F Lucey, UCC, member of the Higher Education Authority, Dr Eunice McCarty, Director of Social and Organisational Phycology UCD, Paddy McDermott, Director of the National Council of Educational Awards, WJ Arundel, Chief Executive Officer City of Dublin VEC, Robert Buckley, Chief Executive Officer Cork VEC, Brian A Gillespie, Managing Director Unidare Engineering, Dublin, Dermot Egan, Group Personnel Director Allied Irish Bank and Desmond Mathews of the Department of Justice.

51  *Garda Review* editorial January 1985.

detective in Dublin. 'Due to his powerful physique and his amiable personality he was admirably suitable for the special rigours of the capital city', Michael Conway wrote. He reminded readers of the big Limerickman's work for his colleagues as chairman of the GRB, his work for Garda Medical Aid, St Paul's Benefit Society and St Raphael's Garda Credit Union.

In March, District Justice Brian Kirby heard a case where a motor cyclist was prosecuted for dangerous driving. In summing up the judge said: 'Gardaí should not waste the court's time by bringing dangerous driving charges against drivers who merely make a mistake. They are at most guilty of a momentary aberration. All you are doing is making nice fees for members of the legal profession.' Jack Marrinan responded pointedly in the *Garda Review*. 'I doubt if it could be accepted that there is any harshness when dealing with [erring motorists]. The evidence would seem to point the other way. A momentary aberration could result in someone's death.'

Motoring offences were already high on the GRA agenda. On 17 April 1985, at the AGM in Bundoran, Jack Marrinan said that stolen high-powered cars were being used to ram patrol cars and he had raised the matter with Michael Noonan and Larry Wren. He submitted a plan involving 50 specially trained gardaí supplied with fast-moving heavy-duty vehicles and spiked chains for use in controlled situations. The plan was rejected.

GRA president Michael Halpin, in his address to the delegates, spoke directly to Minister for Justice Michael Noonan who was present. 'New measures to tighten security of large cash shipments, following the murder of Det Garda Frank Hand, had never been implemented. You agreed to take certain steps. Nothing has happened. Minister, I ask you will the Garda Band have to play the *Dead March from Saul* again?'

The Minister denied that no action had been taken. 'Following the raid in Drumree post office, the garda authorities carried out a review and introduced new security measures', he replied. 'These were aimed at reducing risks to the personnel involved, while all aspects of the cash shipment problem for social welfare and other payments are still being examined.' Noonan said that an £11 million radio communications system would be in operation shortly.

Noonan also said that the Garda Complaints Bill would shortly be published. 'This will pave the way for the introduction of the remaining provisions of the Criminal Justice Act. As you are aware a number of very important provisions of the latter act are already in force, and when it is complete it will serve as an effective instrument in the effort to curb crime', Mr Noonan said. The 'carrot' of reform making prosecutions easier to obtain would not be implemented until the 'stick', the complaints procedure, was in place. Nobody openly challenged the morality of delaying measures which could have saved garda lives.

Jack Marrinan proposed that the GRA support video recordings of interviews of suspects. They would be a great advantage to the gardaí, he said, and the GRA had nothing to fear from the practice. That motion too was carried.

In June there was another tragic death. Sergeant Patrick Morrissey was shot dead by two INLA members after a robbery at Collon, Co. Louth. That tragedy bit deep and the cumulative effect of eight garda deaths in five years was frightening on every level. A closer look at the man who died might help in understanding some of what was lost on that summer day in Co. Louth in 1985.

Morrissey understood where good police work begins as one colleague discovered some years earlier when they went on foot patrol along the streets leading to Dublin airport. A young garda was anxious to show the lie of the land to a more experienced colleague new to the station. He wasn't expecting a memorable lesson on what going on patrol was about.[52]

---

52   This account is taken from my memoir *Get Up Them Steps*.

The two men left Whitehall station on foot together. The younger man –myself - takes up the story.

'With Paddy in tow, at my usual gait, I moved ahead pointing out the Crofton Airport Hotel, Dr. Eustace's estate, and High Park convent. At each landmark Paddy stood, facing them from the edge of the footpath. He moved slowly, almost ponderously, limiting my progress.

'At the shops at the brow of the hill Paddy was dawdling a dozen yards to my rear. Just as he joined me, a young cyclist sped by on the footpath. Paddy quickly moved across his path causing him to back-pedal to a halt. Having planted one foot on either side of his front wheel, Paddy's big hands squeezed both brake levers, checking they worked, rocking the bike back and forward. A few onlookers stood with their ears cocked. Paddy leaned forward; there was no notebook, or words, only a barely audible whisper. "In the dark, being seen and having the brake blocks to control your speed are vital for your safety and that of other road users."

'The youngster gave his name, address and age. Paddy was so cool and gentle as he emphasised his caution with repeated taps of his forefinger on the handlebars beside the vacant front light holder.

'As we resumed patrol my comrade dictated the pace. At the next junction he stood facing the traffic. Without taking his eyes from the road he spoke quietly from the near side of his mouth. "You're travelling and thinking too fast. Slow down. Our duty is to observe people's behaviour and movement."

'He turned to face his young colleague. "Never let a breach of the law go unchecked. You have to programme yourself to react to the minor breaches before you become capable of tackling more serious confrontations. The first commandment is to get to know your public."

'He whipped out his notebook and opened a clean page. "Day, date, time and place. Name and address." He wrote the cyclist's details in his notebook. "The next time we meet he'll remember me, and if he doesn't, I'll be able to call him by his Christian name.'"

On 27 June 1985, Sergeant Patrick Morrissey, age 49, father of four children, was callously murdered by two men who had just stolen £25,000 from Ardee labour exchange in Co. Louth. Morrissey chased after the fleeing robbers. They fired back at him. One shot hit him in the leg, bringing him to the ground. A second shot to the head killed him instantly. He had seen the robbers– hence he had to be murdered. That was the brutal logic of the time. From Cavan, he was a pioneer of the Garda Sub Aqua unit and had led many searches following maritime accidents. This was reflected by the attendance of fishermen from many ports at his funeral.

The reputation of the force had been taking a battering and this came to a head in October 1985 with the publication of a judicial tribunal of inquiry report. In April 1984 an infant had been found dead at White Strand in Co. Kerry. The infant had been stabbed 28 times. Where was the mother? Attention turned to a Kerry woman, Joanne Hayes (25) of Abbeydorney near Tralee who had been pregnant but had no baby to show for it.

The subsequent investigation – 'the Kerry Babies case' – attracted headlines all over the world. It became a massive embarrassment for Ireland. That story has been told elsewhere. The problem for Jack Marrinan and the GRA was that it caused reputational damage to the force when it was under very heavy pressure from terrorism and needed extra powers to control it. A judge-led inquiry was intended to resolve this sad episode but had the opposite effect. Politicians, mindful that public opinion was unsettled by this case and that of the Sallins train robbery, were in no hurry to act on greater powers of arrest for the garda force.

None of it made policing with consent in the face of a murderous onslaught by armed terrorists any easier. Morale was at a low ebb. The pay increases of the Ryan report of 1979 were now history, eroded by inflation and high personal taxes. Cutbacks in public spending had bitten. Overtime was cut in 1982 and again in 1986, accompanied by a virtual embargo on recruitment and a freeze on many promotions. Being a guard was not a sinecure, it never had been, but members were now feeling exposed and stressed on too many fronts. This was no time for the general secretary of the GRA to walk away.

In July 1985, the *Irish Independent* reported that Marrinan was in dispute with Commissioner Wren over gardaí in Dublin refusing to operate a new incident logging system. The newspaper suggested that the problem was lack of consultation. Prickly as ever, Wren did not reply to Jack Marrinan's submissions on that point. Eventually a meeting between the GRA and senior officers brokered by the AGSI sorted the matter out.

On 28 January 1986 in Strasbourg, France, Jack Marrinan as vice chairman of the Eurofedop Council on Policing called for the setting up of a central police authority to deal with cross border crime: Europol. It was essential to introduce agreed criteria in all states for dealing with crimes such as trafficking in drugs, arms, explosives, white collar crime, environmental protection, and terrorism. It seems obvious now, but Jack Marrinan was one of the few who foresaw the effect on crime and policing that the erosion of national borders, then just beginning, would bring. He would repeat this message at GRA conferences up to his retirement.

Back home from Strasbourg he knew that the Walsh inquiry had completed its work and a preliminary report had been with the Department of Justice since Christmas. In February 1986 the *Garda Review* published a summary of the GRA's lengthy submission on training. Headlines would focus on the two year training period and the Leaving Certificate as the entry level qualifications, but the GRA's detailed submission was much more complex than the headlines suggested. The heart of the GRA position on recruitment and training was contained in this part of the submission:

'Those having most discretion in enforcement of the law are the lower ranking garda members. Therefore, it is essential that their training equips them for this unique work in the community, in that it may involve the legitimate use of force, or coercive action. The personnel selected for appointment to the garda service should have the basic education, the physical and psychological qualities, and be of a character and temperament to be able to meet the objectives of this radically new training programme.'

The garda was the first responder and he or she must be equipped to cope– often alone – with all manners of crime, petty and serious, disturbances, tragic deaths, minor incidents and catastrophes in a level-headed and constructive way. Everything else in the GRA submission built on that – a two-year foundation training programme leading to a diploma in policing with provision for further qualifications. Skills deficits needed to be addressed, specifically in coping strategies and stress management, and training modules developed to involve new recruits in a wide range of experience as well as a programme of continuous development for all ranks.[53] Marrinan never tired of telling anyone who would listen that a police force was like an upside-down army. The most important member held the lowest rank. And the only valid measure of garda success was not to be found in itemising deployments but on the invisible list of crimes prevented.

The Garda Complaints Bill 1985 was published on 13 June 1986. While accepting the principle of accountability, the GRA immediately sought changes to allow members to defend themselves against malicious complaints. The executive nominated Jack Marrinan and John Ferry, who would succeed him as general secretary, to a working party consisting of Department of Justice officials and members of the representative associations– except the

---

53  Summarised from a lengthy piece in *Garda Review*, February and March 1986, and statements by Marrinan.

AGSI which did not take part. Two sections of the proposed measure were problematic. Marrinan wrote:

'Under Section 7 of this legislation members are being held responsible for every aspect of their being, and at the whim of anybody who wishes to invoke the procedures for reasons however silly, spurious or even malicious. Those who complain will now have absolute and legal access to all members' private and personal information. Also, Section 4 would seem to give the Garda Commissioner *carte blanche* when taking measures to obtain and preserve evidence.'

Noonan agreed to amend section 7 to apply to gardaí on duty only and promised to re-draft section 4 (5) to remove the impression that the Commissioner would have a free hand in such investigations. Progress was also made on issues of double jeopardy; the malicious or libellous use of the measure, and payment of defence costs. Eventually a GRA proposal that the time limit for lodging a complaint should be reduced from six to three months was conceded. The GRA would avail of conciliation machinery to address other problems it had with the measure. It is a measure of how divisive the subject was that the anti-Marrinan faction within the GRA insisted that Ferry be included in the working party along with the general secretary. It met on 21 occasions, and Marrinan and Ferry reported back to the executive on each occasion.

Observing these matters from a distance, having left the garda rank on promotion in the meantime, Pat Tierney recalled a conversation with Jack in the Garda Depot in aftermath of the Macushla revolt.

'One day a group of us were crossing the Depot Square and we met some of the pre-GRB representatives. After exchanging a few words, we moved on. I said to Jack, "How would you feel having them oul greyhairs representing you?" He didn't miss a step but responded, "You know what Pat? In a few years the young members will be saying the same about us."'

Jack's hair was now as white as snow.

If 1985 had been bad, 1986 would not be much better. Detectives had a long simmering grievance about promotions, and it found its way into the courts. The draft Garda Complaints Bill continued to worry members. The GRA awaited a response to its lengthy submission to the Walsh committee, and the background suggested that there would be fireworks at the GRA annual conference. On 14 February Alan Dukes, previously Minister for Finance, succeeded Michael Noonan as Justice Minister. Noonan left unfinished business in the form of the regulations applying to complaints and the much discussed but unrealised garda authority. On 10 March Marrinan called on Dukes to publish the Walsh report, which had been laying on Noonan's desk since Christmas.

When the delegates gathered for the GRA annual general meeting in Limerick on 22 April 1986, the mood was not good, despite pay increases of £10 to £15 per week being agreed. Marrinan began by spelling out the details of the 25th pay round.

'It will provide a 3% pay increase in May [next month], a further 2% in January 1987 and another 2% in May 1987. Salaries will increase from £7, 397 to £7,907 per annum for recruits in training and for a garda with 12 years' service to £12,689 from its present level of £11,841.'

GRA president Michael Halpin welcomed Alan Dukes to his first GRA conference. Halpin reminded the Minister about Sergeant Pat McLoughlin who had been shot dead as he opened his bedroom window, as his living quarters adjoined the station. The public display of sympathy by the Minister and his department was contrasted with the subsequent reduction in the award offered to his widow when they claimed he was not on duty at the time of his death.

He also called on the Minister to do more about protecting gardaí from Aids (a major problem for homosexuals and drug users and cause of much anxiety among the general public) than merely sending out a circular and a supply of plastic gloves. Nor had anything meaningful been done about the dangers in escorting large amounts of cash, following the death of Garda Frank Hand, he said. And he raised again the exclusion of the GRA from the inquiry on training and called on the Minister to publish the Walsh report.

In his May 1986 *Garda Review* editorial Marrinan reflected on the meeting in Limerick.

'There was a stridency about our recent AGM, which distinguished it from others. Delegates were tougher, even militant. Given that most conferences have their colourful speakers, the 1986 event stood out as one with a strong tinge of frustration in the way delegates perceived their force. Particularly evident was their apparent inability to rectify the chronic mismatch between the policing demands of modern Ireland and the ability of An Garda Síochána to meet those demands. In his address the Minister did not give grounds for optimism. His uncompromising responses to our president Michael Halpin's well-constructed motions held little joy for the force. Compensation for personal injuries, including drivers, remain unresolved, though he did promise movement in the provision of legal aid state funds for actions against our members.'

What Jack didn't spell out was that relations between the GRA general secretary and the Garda Commissioner were now in freefall. Wren took serious exception to Marrinan's Limerick speech. Jack's first draft had included an observation that 'at present the sole activity of senior officers is marching into graveyards in the wake of slain colleagues.' Prior to the conference Jack had asked Brian McCabe to have a hard look at it as he felt it might be a bit strong. McCabe agreed and the phrase was dropped. However, the *Evening Herald* had seen the original version and published it.

Wren was hopping mad. At the monthly meeting following the Limerick conference, Jack made himself unavailable. Commissioner Wren was sitting at the table with his fists clenched. He was steaming.

He demanded an apology. Two GRA executive members, Michael Brennan and Brian McCabe, defended Marrinan. McCabe insisted that no apology was needed as the words were not said. The GRA delegation produced a recording of Jack's address so Wren could hear that the offending words were not in the final version of the speech. The accusation was withdrawn through gritted teeth.

Regular meetings between the GRA executive and Larry Wren were then suspended. The GRA said no progress was being made and the May and June 1986 meetings had become over-heated.

'Our association has become frustrated and disenchanted by the Commissioner's attitude towards us, and continued interaction does not seem to be in the best interest of the membership of the GRA or the Garda Síochána as a whole.'

In June 1986 Wren published the crime report for year ending December 1985. In it he cited a 40% increase in armed robberies, from 440 in 1984 to 616 in 1985, one of which had taken the life of Paddy Morrissey. Wren also focused on the launch of the Neighbourhood Watch scheme, allowing the public a role in local policing. Jack Marrinan supported this. He had seen this working on a recent trip to the USA and championed its use at home to bring gardaí closer to the communities they served. Now it– and its rural counterpart the Community Alert scheme– was coming into use in Ireland. Marrinan lobbied hard for it as 'a structured way of getting the community involved with the gardaí without the risk of vigilantes.' Neighbourhood Watch clearly had some criminals worried as leaflets opposing it were circulated in working class areas of Dublin prior to its introduction.

On 24 October 1986 a half-yearly GRA meeting was held in the Ardilaun Hotel, Galway. Jack Marrinan updated the gathering on recent developments.

'The unsatisfactory situation whereby matters which would normally be dealt with directly through Commissioner Laurence Wren are being dealt with through other senior officers is a cause for concern. Issues are being taken to the conciliation council which might be more appropriately dealt with between the GRA and the Commissioner', he said. [54]

Stresses on many fronts, political, administrative and human resources, were spilling over into heated confrontations between the two sides at conciliation level. Those stresses were also becoming obvious internally within the GRA, as the inability to resolve disputes, large or small, heightened tensions within the association. Obduracy breeds reaction. Marrinan and the GRA executive were in danger of being roasted on the spit of management intransigence fuelled by unhappy and fearful members.

On two major issues, the Garda Complaints Bill and the Walsh training report, no difference so great separated the two sides that could not be resolved with patience and goodwill. The yet-to-be published Walsh report, Marrinan already knew from his own sources, contained much of what the GRA had sought. Delaying tactics looked like bloody-minded obstinacy.

Scott gold medals were awarded to Frank Hand and Paddy Morrissey by Nuala Fennell, Minister of State at the Department of Justice, at a ceremony in Templemore on 4 December. Her father had been a garda, and her presence as Minister was seen as an encouragement to the growing number of women in the force.

Early in 1987 Jack Marrinan had suggested that an armed garda section be set up to move large sums of money from place to place. 'Robberies of large amounts of money has concentrated the public mind on the uncomfortable thought that unscrupulous armed raiders would think nothing of taking a life and hold the country to ransom. It should be possible to set up a specially trained unit, in uniform, clearly identifiable as armed gardaí.' The banks could pay for this service, he suggested.

---

54   *Garda Review*, November 1986.

The 1987 annual conference of the GRA, held at Rosslare, Co. Wexford, heard the GRA president appeal to the Minister for Justice not to let senior officers spoil the move to a common uniform by wearing white shirts to distinguish them from the blue shirts worn by the lower ranks. 'We are not like the Chinese army of the 1960s, where insignia of rank was not worn. We accept that each rank should have its appropriate insignia, and that they should be prominent and identifiable', Christy Lonergan told Gerry Collins, back in office for his second term as Minister for Justice, though he made little secret of having hoped for a more senior post.

The Minister neatly ducked the uniform issue, relying on his own fashion sense. 'The white shirts of the higher ranks are not a pretty sight', Collins replied with a straight face. 'They do not combine very well with the new uniform and the blue shirts are much more suited to the new tunics. However, my department will not become involved in the shirt conflict.'

Although the 1987 AGM was attended by 26 divisional committees consisting of 145 delegates, and there were 60 motions on the agenda, it lacked the passion of previous assemblies. The battle over the training report had been won. Dr Tom Walsh was invited as an honoured guest and received a ceremonial plaque. An attempt to endorse the wholesale arming of members was debated and defeated, a motion on compensation for injuries on duty was passed, the Garda Complaints Act attracted further criticism, and there were protests about burglar alarms taking up too much garda time- as they were. A debate on cutbacks attracted most interest. Marrinan took the opportunity to tell members that the GRA had made confidential objections to the deployment of recruits at the Tidey kidnap, when garda recruit Gary Sheehan lost his life. Recruits had also been deployed in Dublin the previous Christmas. All in all, the conference was muted and some observers detected a lack of appetite for conflict given all that had happened.

Nobody would have accused Larry Wren of being overly diplomatic, but he kept his tone unconfrontational in his address, even when he said that the cap on overtime would have to be observed – 'I repeat under no circumstance will I allow our £10 million overtime allowance for this year to be exceeded'– and Jack Marrinan and GRA president Christy Lonergan, for their part, chose not to raise the temperature. It was Wren's final GRA conference as Commissioner and he paid tribute to his adversary Marrinan, saying it was difficult to imagine a GRA conference without Jack as general secretary.

Wren then made a joke when he said that Jack might sometimes have been too successful in representing members. Recently, Wren said, he saw a member quoted in a newspaper saying that he could not afford to apply for promotion to sergeant, as he would lose £2,000 in overtime. Disincentives to promotion were not good for the force, he said. Marrinan knew well what Wren was driving at. Pay for overtime worked was a right, but expecting regular overtime as part of one's pay packet was damaging to the force. On this, both men were firmly agreed. True to form, Wren's joke had a serious edge.

Jack Marrinan gave the 1987 conference a stark warning about cutbacks affecting future crime detection and prevention. He noted that the figures for 1986 showed a drop in overall crime, 'making our country a safer place to live for the third year in a row.' However, a major problem was the 55% increase in armed crimes with a 31% detection rate and 8.7% of the near £45 million stolen recovered. 'It would be better if the annual crime report included what adjustments are being made to deal with the problem areas', he wrote.[55]

'There was a time when gardaí would pursue offenders for as long as there was any hope of catching them. Now, except in the most serious cases, the clock and the possibility of incurring extra expense play a major role in such investigations. This is reflected in

---

55    *Garda Review* September 1987.

results. Already, the force is under-financed; it has suffered parings and cutbacks to the point where some of these essential functions are often cut short or left undone.'

He continued on a subject close to his heart:

'Almost 20 years ago Conroy recommended a welfare service for our force. Six years later they gave us one welfare officer. Over a decade later we still have one welfare officer although the strength of the force has swelled from 8,424 in 1976 to 11,118 in 1987, and the number of problems confronting gardaí has mushroomed.'

He cited the ESB. The electricity company had a similar number of workers to the gardaí. In 1983 it had 19 welfare officers compared to one for gardaí. 'How long more can members who have been confronted by armed attackers or been involved in close calls, continue to be expected to deal with trauma and stress by themselves?' A workforce under threat from armed terrorists would inevitably contain some quiet casualties, many of them rescuable. Apart from crime-related trauma, to whom could a member in financial or marital difficulties turn for advice, or when a family member was sick, or was being bullied at work? For this neglect senior officers and the Department of Justice stood condemned. As Marrinan concluded: 'It does seem that nobody really cares about the problem cases.'[56]

The immediate genesis of the Walsh inquiry lay in Eamonn Doherty (the Doc) persuading Wren that the current system of training recruits was 'broken' and he needed to act. With Wren's support, Doherty, in tandem with PJ Moran, director of the Garda College (as Templemore became known), wrote the final report and drove a process which replaced 18 weeks of basic training plus a four week refresher with an ambitious two-year programme. Much of what was proposed first surfaced in GRA submissions; some had been established GRB-GRA policy for years. At the core of the

56   *Garda Review*, October 1987.

final Walsh report was the concept of the policeman and woman as 'specialised aiders, working in partnership with other agencies in helping the community to maintain law and order.' No longer a police force, more a police service- this was music to Jack's ears.

In November 1987 Jack told members that Gerry Collins would shortly implement some Walsh recommendations.

'Mr. Collins has said that at present the force could not wait up to three years for the next big recruit class, because around 350 members are lost annually through retirement.' New members were needed urgently, as the GRA had been insisting. 'In the meantime up to 30 from the 2,000 strong panel of five years ago would be called up in January (1988). This will be the final class to get 22-week training.'

The first student gardaí to undergo two years of training were enrolled in 1989. In 1992 the Garda College was recognised as a third level institution by the National Council for Education Awards. Marrinan had always kept his finger pressed on the training button, and he must have taken quiet satisfaction when the University of Limerick and the Garda College developed a degree course in police management for senior officers in 1992.

All this lay in the future.

Larry Wren's retirement in November 1987 was marked by a farewell message in the *Garda Review* which wished him 'peace and contentment at the end of a busy dedicated and successful career'. But the editorial, written by Jack Marrinan, went on to criticise the handling of the recent kidnapping of a Dublin dentist and the shooting of Det Garda Martin O'Connor as he was being freed. 'This means that he [Wren] leaves the force in some disarray.'

Marrinan had gone public with his criticisms of the search for O'Grady and his kidnappers – telling the media that there 'was not the same level of activity' as in previous kidnap searches.[57] O'Grady

---

57    Public Accounts Committee, 16 May 1991.

was a son-in-law of Dr Austin Darragh, a medical entrepreneur whose company had floated on the New York stock exchange the previous year, yielding $8 million for a 20% stake. The kidnapper, Dessie O'Hare from south Armagh, known as the Border Fox, had recently been released from Portlaoise Prison having served six years for a firearms offence.

John O'Grady was abducted from his home in an exclusive part of south Dublin on 14 October 1987. Twelve days later he was located in a transport container parked behind a cottage near Midleton, Co. Cork. Armed Special Branch officers and other members surrounded the premises, but the kidnappers shot their way out and got away with their captive in handcuffs. Then O'Hare, angered by the unpaid ransom, raised the stakes by cutting off two of the dentist's fingers and leaving them where they would be found.

Two gardaí were detailed to check on a house in Cabra, a Dublin suburb. Martin O'Connor was one of them. Here's his account of what happened:

'Friday 5 November 1987 is one of the dates I will always remember. Sgt Henry Spring and I went to a house in Carnlough Road, Cabra, on a routine inquiry into the kidnapping of dentist John O'Grady. We had no idea that in the space of three or four minutes our lives would change forever. On entry to the house we were confronted by four unshaven men with guns– two shotguns, a rifle and a revolver. My mind went into overdrive– how do we get out of this situation alive? I looked at Henry and I knew we were thinking similarly. He was unarmed, I had a revolver. This was every policeman and woman's worst nightmare. Henry was speaking calmly to the men as he was hit on the side of the head by the butt of a shotgun. Two of the men started shooting. I returned fire from my revolver and got outside the door. John O Grady escaped in the turmoil and confusion. I got shot three times and it was all over. I feel lucky to have survived and I put this down to two things. First,

I was near a hospital and the medical staff were able to stop the loss of blood which is the main cause of death from shooting. Secondly the fact that Henry and myself remained calm gave me the opportunity to get outside, otherwise we would have been shot in the house and the saga would have been similar to the Cork escape and would have gone on longer. I subsequently spent nearly six weeks in hospital and after five operations I ended up with about 150 shotgun pellets in my abdomen which never really cause any problems.

'I remember Jack Marrinan coming to see me with a cheque for *£2,000 from the GRA*. That was like winning the lotto in 1987. And Michael Conway reassured me that the Garda Medical Aid scheme would cover my medical expenses. It is only when you survive a life and death situation that you realise the benefit of family and comrades. The men and women of the garda family rallied around me, and my wife Rosaleen and our two children, giving enormous support which made us feel secure and valued. The only people I wanted to talk to after the incident were gardaí. I felt they understood me better and could empathise with me more. 'I sometimes think good overcomes evil eventually. The timing of the shooting in Cabra was 12.10pm. Intermediary Fr Brian Darcy was on his way to a hotel in Cork with a ransom of £2.5 million[58] to hand over at 12.30pm. Imagine the cruelty and destruction that would have ensued if Dessie O'Hare had got his hands on that amount of cash?'

Eventually O'Hare was taken into custody. He put up a fight, and when finally arrested he had eight bullet wounds; another member of his gang was shot dead resisting arrest. Inasmuch as the kidnap victim O'Grady was freed, it was a success- but one for which the Garda Síochána paid a high price in having its

---

58  Fr Brian Darcy confirms that he was asked to act as intermediary and says the sum he was carrying was £1.5 million. While driving to a hotel in Cork to hand over the ransom, he learned that John O'Grady had been released.

organisational weaknesses exposed, and the personal price paid by Martin O'Connor could have been much worse.

According to Conor Brady, serious weaknesses were exposed by this case. Cutbacks had been a factor but not the only one. Operational failings had compounded difficulties. Information-sharing within the force had not worked properly, cordons and checkpoints had not been co-ordinated effectively, and intelligence on O'Hare's group was deficient. Within existing resources and firepower the force should have been able to deal with O'Hare more effectively, Brady argued.[59]

Wren must have hoped for a more auspicious exit. Unlike his two immediate predecessors who had been told to go, he was re-tiring on age grounds, his record unblemished. He had served as Commissioner through four difficult turbulent years. He had held the line and he was due honour for that. Larry Wren was a conscien-tious man whose off-duty hours were devoted to his family, his faith and his work for the poor. He told senior officers to spend more time at their desks and less on the golf course. Though conscientious, he lacked the vision to see through the fog of antiquated regulations he had inherited to the purpose they were intended to serve– providing an efficient modern police service accepted by a public which had already moved on from the simple certainties of his youth. Marrinan and Wren acted from principle: both cared deeply about their call-ing, both were coming to the end of their careers, but they inhabited different worlds. Marrinan was a visionary who could chivvy and charm and inspire people to see things his way. Wren was an austere and doughty practitioner of an outdated era of harsh discipline. The outcome was predictable – a stalemate which sadly did neither man nor the force they both loyally served any favours.

His successor Eamonn Doherty would fare no better. He took up office as a more popular officer than Wren had been. His stint in

---

59  TGoI, p.219.

Templemore meant he was personally known to many of them, and his approachable manner was enhanced by an uncanny memory. On meeting a member he hadn't seen for 15 or 20 years the Doc was likely to immediately recite the astonished garda's name and number. In training, the young recruits found him tough but open-minded. 'If you wanted to challenge the Doc over anything', one said, 'you would need to have your homework done. He'd listen to you, probe you for details, then if you'd got your point across, he'd become enthusiastic about it and want to know all you could tell him.' John Smith had spotted that 20 years earlier. Bluffing was no use so far as dealings with the Doc were concerned, recruits soon found.

However as Commissioner he inherited a poisoned chalice in the shape of public expenditure cuts, and this brought him almost immediately into conflict with Marrinan and the GRA. It had long been clear there was no bitterness over the fact that 28 years ago, it had fallen to Doherty as the superintendent in charge in Rathfarnham to dismiss the young Clare guard over his part in the Macushla affair. In the meantime both men had established themselves and respected the other's achievements. Marrinan valued Doherty's input into the Walsh reform of garda training, and the implicit acceptance of the GRA submission it contained, and hoped the two men could work well together.

That didn't happen. The Doc would only serve as Commissioner for a bare 13 months from November 1987 to December 1988. As he took up office, Jack Marrinan in the *Garda Review* wished Doherty well, but added a warning:

'Never before has the force been in such need of a Commissioner who can lead from the front. The garda service he inherits is dedicated and willing, as its individual members undoubtedly have proved recently.

'Unfortunately, we are weak organisationally. We have lots of brave, conscientious members who will display heroism far beyond what anybody could demand, and where it is within the means and direction of superintendents to have gardaí provide a service, it is provided expeditiously and well. Our capacity to deliver diminishes rapidly as the scale of an operation increases. The weaknesses in our structure have been exacerbated by the stringent economies which deprive superintendents of any real discretion to employ off duty members where extra help or backup is needed.

'We in An Garda Síochána must not take that part of the blame that rightly belongs to [Ministers who have failed to provide resources], but by our Commissioner's public silence we have done so. Mr Doherty must realise that as Commissioner he will be left holding the buck when things go wrong, and rightly so if they go wrong, because of any weakness or fault on his part. But when he is not given the means to do what is demanded he should say so loud and clear.'

When the *The Irish Times* reported this at some length, the reporter added that Doherty appeared stung by the forthright nature of these remarks, as both men had worked well together in the past.[60]

Had Jack Marrinan got wind on the grapevine that the Doc was about to take a bite out of members' pay packets, or was he just reading the signs and knew something nasty was about to happen? Taoiseach Charles Haughey had recently warned every Minister that no expenditure should be regarded as sacrosanct or immune to elimination or reduction. Haughey had returned to power after the FitzGerald-led Fine Gael-Labour coalition collapsed over its inability to control public expenditure. Ray MacSharry's brief stint as Minister for Finance was to eliminate the imbalance between income and expenditure, and nothing- health, education, welfare, security- was sacrosanct. Not for nothing was he called Mac the Knife.

The scene was set for a confrontation of epic proportions. Doherty had his orders from the Department of Finance. For his

60    *The Irish Times*, 12 November 1987.

part Marrinan's members had made it clear that he was to fight cuts with every weapon at his disposal.

The shape of those cuts was about to be revealed. Within weeks of taking office Doherty announced in December 1987 that parading time payment was being withdrawn. This threw the force into a ferment. Parading time was a 15-minute period for briefing members about to go on duty in busy city stations. Annual garda expenditure amounted to £260 million, and the Department of Finance wanted to save £2 million by abolishing the parading time payment. *The Irish Times* report also warned that further cutbacks were imminent.

As Jack's last full year in office approached, he came out with all guns blazing. 'The volume of up to-the-minute information which a garda needs when taking up duty is on the increase, with the use of computers and new communication systems, as well as increasing crime figures. These create an essential need for a rapid turnover of critical information on which a garda going on duty needs to be briefed.' City stations provided round the clock service of eight hours duration, he argued. The 15-minute overlap was important in ensuring that the streets are not left policed. From the point of view of the individual garda, it meant losing 15 minutes guaranteed overtime a day, a loss of about £10 per week from the average pay packet.

Gardaí would go to law to challenge these cuts, he warned. On Sunday 12 December 1987 Judge Blayney, at a special sitting of the High Court held in his home, granted a temporary injunction against the withdrawal of parading time. Gardaí were not alone in being incensed by another decision– to curtail the juvenile liaison service at weekends. Many people were angered that young offenders could be jailed as if they were as adults– something the scheme was intended to avoid. 'JLO officers are most active at weekends when they normally call on young persons in the privacy of their homes', Marrinan said.

The January 1988 *Garda Review* defended the system of conciliation and arbitration which had served the force well. That was where management should have raised the parading and juvenile liaison issues, not acted without consultation, Jack's editorial argued. That was the ground on which the temporary injunction had been obtained. The GRA and the AGSI, representing sergeants and inspectors, had taken legal action to defend the conciliation and arbitration scheme, the editorial said.

Marrinan also drew attention to recruitment which had paused. 'Last month alone one chief superintendent, seven superintendents, three inspectors, 28 sergeants and 24 gardaí left the force on retirement or resignation.' It was all to no avail. The amount saved through this round of cuts appeared petty and bad-minded from a garda perspective, and only made a kind of sense later in the context of cuts to health and other essential services.

A less serious matter was the garda golf course at Stackstown in the Dublin mountains, close to Marrinan's home. After the raid on O'Connor's jewellers in Harold's Cross in 1983, 24-hour surveillance had been imposed on Martin Cahill. In retaliation Cahill's gang dug up the greens at the garda golf club and slashed the tyres of cars parked near the Garda Club in Harrington Street. 'These are attacks on society on whose behalf the gardaí are employed, and it would be a serious matter if it were not seen as such', Marrinan declared, but he must have seen the humour in it. He enjoyed going out on the course with his sons at Stackstown at weekends.

Despite the unresolved problem about payments for parading, some progress was made. A Garda Advisory Board was established, led by the chief executive of the ESB, Patrick Moriarty.[61] A Kerryman with an accountancy background and an approachable manner, in the ESB he had slain two dragons: the domination of

---

61  Other members were Brian Dennis, managing director of HB Dennis Motors, Dermot Egan, director of group marketing AIB, Desmond Mathews, secretary Department of Justice, Eamonn Doherty, Maurice O'Grady, director general Irish Management Institute, Commissioner Con Power, Director of Economic Policy Confederation of Irish Industry, Sean Scanlan, professor of Electronic Engineering University College Cork.

the higher ranks of the company by graduate engineers, and wildcat strikes by shift workers in power stations. Moriarty had faced them both down. How much influence he could bring to bear on the Garda Síochána remained to be seen, but Marrinan knew he was a good man to have in your corner and welcomed his appointment in the *Garda Review* of March 1988. He also welcomed the news of three new Assistant Commissioners, known as the three wise men, and the formal acceptance of the Walsh report.

Nonetheless the GRA and AGSI were in the High Court defending the conciliation and arbitration scheme, trying to stop the removal of the parading payments. That ended in failure on 19 April 1988 when at the full hearing Judge Murphy ruled that while the lack of consultation was regrettable, it did not affect the legal rights of the parties.

'Public Support Means Garda Success' was the slogan for the 10th GRA annual conference, which began in Killarney on 3 May 1988. Among the 151 delegates attending was Anna O'Doherty, a first-time female delegate representing the Central Detective Unit.

In the presence of the Minister for Justice Gerry Collins and Commissioner Eamonn Doherty, GRA president Christy Lonergan opened the conference forcefully. After a few remarks about claims for members injured on duty and other matters, Lonergan went straight for the ministerial jugular accusing the authorities of putting lives at risk during the O'Grady kidnap.

'Since you, Minister, were with us last, we had the O'Grady kidnapping which put the force to another severe test. During the affair we wrote to you outlining certain misgivings and criticisms about the way things were going. We refrained from public comment, even though these issues caused our members a lot of concern. When the affair was over, we carried out an extensive review of how it was conducted. This established that we were not mistaken in our original representations. There was a difference of opinion between you and us about the availability of resources during the kidnap operation. You are probably still of the view that constraints on the employment of resources did not apply at the time. We believe the search would have been safer and more effectively carried out if available off duty members were employed to help out.

'You have clearly given the impression that they could be employed if needed. Let me emphasise yet again that these searches were not carried out as thoroughly or with the same regard for safety of the unarmed garda searchers as local superintendents would have wished, because these superintendents did not feel free to employ off-duty personnel for the task. That is a simple matter of fact.'

Lonergan went on to complain about the removal of the parading payment.

'Minister you told us last May that you would consult with us prior to any cutbacks. I am afraid this guarantee did not amount to much when the axe fell. We feel very let down.'

Collins responded with his usual aplomb and the occasional flash of steel.

'I understand that my reputation based on previous appearances before you built up a high level of expectation that I will again arrive bearing good news. Ladies and gentlemen – times are tough; tough for us all.'

Collins then came to Lonergan's main point.

'I do not intend to say very much on the O'Grady [kidnap] case. You expressed your view on resources and I have also done so. My view is that the resources required must be decided by garda management. It is my responsibility to ensure that the Commissioner has the resources he needs for every police task entrusted to him. During every phase of that kidnapping I was assured by Commissioner Wren – in response to several enquiries I made that he had all the resources necessary.'

Collins thanked the force for helping out during a recent strike by prison officers – it was much appreciated, he said.

On the parading payment, he challenged what the GRA president had said. 'When a garda Commissioner finds himself prohibited by a court injunction secured by staff associations from putting his instructions into effect it is hard to see this as anything but a challenge.' Then it was back to affability. Collins concluded by saying that gardaí knew him well enough to know that, 'as Minister for Justice I will do my best for An Garda Síochána.'

Jack Marrinan in his address to the conference welcomed proposals to make chief superintendents more accountable for specific management of their divisions as a welcome step towards decentralisation.

'Hopefully it will no longer be necessary for a chief or a superintendent to wait for approval from the Phoenix Park before they can assign extra resources.

'Also, to be welcomed is the new emphasis on our personnel branch. The GRA has frequently made the point that in a personnel-intensive service like ours, not enough attention is given to welfare.'

He said the recent High Court defeat came as a great disappointment. The GRA was awaiting counsel's opinion on the viability of appealing Judge Murphy's ruling to the Supreme Court, he said. Marrinan then turned to another court case and it was clear that he was addressing a section of the GRA membership, rather than the Minister or the Commissioner.

'The Supreme Court decision in the detectives' case will be a disappointment to those who brought it. It arose because of detectives' dissatisfaction with the new promotion system, which requires that all who are newly-promoted, except those in technical posts, must pass examinations before being eligible for promotion; and that those promoted, except those in technical areas, should spend the first year of their new rank in uniform.

'Detectives claimed that theirs was a special rank, and that they were entitled to vertical promotion in detective branch. They also claimed that regulations which prohibited them from forming their own association were unconstitutional. The court ruling has settled the issue.'

Marrinan then issued a forthright warning. 'Detectives have always had a major influence in the running of the GRA– providing four of the last five presidents. Their interests have always been looked after.' Marrinan urged detectives to accept the decision and move on. That should have been that, but detectives were unhappy, which would simmer and come to the boil again after Jack Marrinan's retirement.

Two court challenges, both lost. In his heart of hearts Marrinan was probably not sorry. Injunctions are a poor means of solving industrial relations problems. You can negotiate a deal with a senior officer or the Department of Justice, but not with a high court judge. If gardaí now understood that courts were not the places to settle differences with their employer, they might be more invested in the negotiating process, with all its flaws. These were difficult concepts to get across to someone who has just lost £10 a week out of a pay packet under constant attack from rising prices.

There was another outcome to that conference, and to understand its significance we have to go back to events in Dingle in late 1985. On the morning of 27 November, Sergeant Mossy O'Donnell, accompanied by two colleagues, went to the home of an individual who lived alone west of Dingle. He held a bench warrant for the arrest of the man, Berthold Maas, a German, whose recent arrival to the area, along with eccentric and threatening behaviour, had come to the notice of gardaí many times. He frequently proclaimed that he was the last descendant of the Celtic chieftains, gifted with special magical powers and he had come to reclaim his throne.

The guards knocked on his door but got no response. They were sure that someone was hiding within. Having knocked repeatedly they identified themselves and stated on several occasions that they would force entry unless admitted; they eventually forced the door.

The dwelling had a high arched roof and the wanted man had blockaded himself in the attic. They shouted to him to come down, but he refused to comply. Suddenly the attic door flew open and a shower of bricks fell on top of the guards below. Sergeant O'Donnell recalled what happened next: 'It was black dark up there with swirling dust and shouts and roars descending on our bodies. Suddenly, I felt Garda Joe Curran collapse beside me. Tim Collins shouted "Joe's been hit. He's been struck with an arrow." Joe was on the ground with an arrow protruding from his chest. Tim and myself lifted him outside and radioed Dingle for an ambulance.' He was taken to hospital where the arrow was removed. He was treated for chest injuries and was unable to return to work for a fortnight.

Meanwhile, Superintendent Ginty, Inspector O'Neill, and Det Sergeant Tim O'Callaghan arrived at the scene. Gardaí began removing slates from the roof to gain access and the wanted man surrendered. Sergeant O'Donnell found a crossbow in the attic and the man in custody admittied to firing the arrow that injured the garda. A judge committed him to the Central Mental Hospital in Dundrum, Co. Dublin.

When someone is attacked by an armed person, the assailant is usually prosecuted under the Firearms Acts, but they didn't mention bows and arrows. Time passed and nothing was being done. At the 1988 GRA annual conference executive member Seán Brennan decided to intervene. He dramatically produced a crossbow and showed it to his fellow delegates. He said that the weapon was believed to be of Chinese extraction and that in medieval times it was regarded as the foot soldier's ultimate weapon. He stated. 'Today with the advent of technology its range and accuracy has improved dramatically, which has rendered it as an even more dangerous weapon. Arrowheads are mainly metal, shaped like a spear with some having barbs, and can leave the bow at up to 80 miles hour. These deadly weapons are advertised as suitable for large and dangerous games as well as survival situations', he said. He proposed a resolution calling for them to be banned, and this was passed with the addition of stun guns, then beginning to make an appearance. This intervention featured prominently in media reports of the conference.

Early in February 1989 the Minister for Justice, Gerry Collins, circulated the new Firearms and Offensive Weapons Bill. The new measure would amend the Firearms Acts 1925-70 and designate crossbows and stun guns as firearms, he said. Thus a motion proposed by Seán Brennan at a GRA conference in 1988 became law the following year. It was a timely reminder of how far Marrinan had brought the association in terms of influence and effectiveness.

In May 1988 Marrinan had complained to the Garda Press office about newspaper articles regarding security in prisons during the recent prison officers strike. His main target was the *Irish Independent*. It was alleged that gardaí who had been called-on to provide for the safety and security of inmates, and who had been detailed for duty in the Aids section of Mountjoy Prison, had reported sick.

'This allegation is entirely false, as is the allegation that gardaí detailed for duty in the prison were ordered not to speak to striking prison officers, as well as the report that of 18 April which stated that prisoners in Portlaoise Prison refused their dinners and threw them out in the landing. This contrasts strangely with reports in some newspapers that the meals had improved during the strike.'

In July 1988 Jack Marrinan told the central executive council of the GRA that he would be retiring on age grounds not later than July 1989. His time was up. The garda retirement age was about to be extended to 60 following a joint approach by the GRA and AGSI at conciliation, but 'the extension' as it was called came too late for Jack.

In September Jack Marrinan attended the International Association of Civilian Oversight of Law Enforcement in Montreal. Present were ombudsmen, police complaints commissioners and police unions from 37 countries as well as numerous police chiefs. On his return he said that 'the system we have is reasonably satisfactory for dealing with complaints compared to what obtains elsewhere' and he told members that international links were valuable and should be maintained.

In November the *Garda Review* considered the first annual report of the Garda Complaints Board. Marrinan noted that an age-old police problem had been updated.

'The citizen wants law enforcement as he sees it on television-impartial and strict– but not when it applies to him. He wants to be able to complain if he is the subject of strict law enforcement. Businessmen would like gardaí to keep undesirable elements out of their town, others would like gardaí to break up cider parties or to prevent crowds from congregating at street corners.

'Not so long ago gardaí felt that when, in their judgement, such steps were called for, they could take them. Any garda now does it at his/her peril. Society wants people to do what they want to do with minimum interference. Any garda who prevents a citizen from exercising his rights is liable to punishment– he may be the subject of legal action or a complaint to the Garda Complaints Board. Sometimes the line between the exercise of one's rights as a citizen and depriving another citizen of their rights can be very thin, but woe betide the garda who misjudges where it lies and acts on that misjudgement.'

No sooner had Eamonn Doherty become Commissioner, he was retiring, or so it seemed. In December 1988 Marrinan's farewell tribute to the Donegal man praised his appointment of the 'three wise men', Culligan, Moran and O'Reilly, as assistant Commissioners, so-called because they had university qualifications. Their report following the O'Grady kidnapping had brought about a sound structure for the future, he said. Marrinan also praised Doherty for Operation Mallard, a nationwide search which netted large quantities of arms and ammunition, and regretted the effects on the conciliation and arbitration machinery of the unilateral cuts in parading time and the Juvenile Liaison scheme.

He wished incoming Commissioner Eugene Crowley well, reminding him that 'he has a diligent, responsive and responsible team of over 10,500 members who are engaged, as he is, in the pursuit of excellence in policing.' He was pleased that Cork-born Crowley was on record as saying that the most important thing for new guards was this: 'All young gardaí must make the first approach to members of their communities. They must build up trust and greater contact with local people which will benefit the force and will become invaluable in preventing crime.'

The final year of Jack Marrinan's service as general secretary of the Garda Representative Association was one of change on many fronts. In January it was announced that gardaí were to become police monitors in the troubled African state of Namibia. Recently promoted Assistant Commissioner Patrick Culligan was promoted to Deputy Commissioner in charge of operations, and former Special Branch head Ned O'Dea became Assistant Commissioner in charge of crime and security. A new £1.6 million station was opened in Naas. Tallaght's new garda station had 12 new members assigned to it, and trucks with cranes became available to remove illegally parked cars in Dublin city. The Single European Act was coming down the tracks and with it came increased immigration responsibilities for the force as borders between member countries were relaxed and, in some cases, became invisible.

In March Jack Marrinan announced that all ranks up to chief superintendent would receive a six per cent phased pay increase from July 1989. But he wasn't finished scanning the horizon yet. In April in south Yorkshire, a crowd control problem got out of hand as football fans gathered for a match at Hillsborough stadium in Sheffield, between Liverpool and Nottingham Forest. Despite 800 police being present some 96 people died, and hundreds were injured.

Marrinan saw the danger. Something similar could happen in Ireland, and the Garda Síochána could get the blame. 'Any crowd can be swayed by excitement, sentiment or panic, and a person who undergoes these sensations can often do things which they themselves would never normally dream of doing. In a crowd nothing is more dangerous than panic. In confined spaces it can spread like wildfire.' In the April issue of the *Garda Review*, he cited the 1987 Munster hurling final at Thurles as a near miss. Supporters had tried to gain access through the town terrace-end stiles which were closed. They were told by a garda inspector to enter via another stile, but they were adamant they wanted to get in through the stile they usually used. The crowd then pushed their way to the gate and rocked it with bodily pressure, putting strain on the adjoining wall. If entry had been gained it would have started a stampede, leading to possible loss of life. A quick-thinking plain clothes Detective P J O Rourke produced his gun and the crowd took fright and backed off before loss of life occurred. The gun was not fired. Marrinan was anticipating developments in the way that one might have hoped that senior officers or the Department of Justice would have been doing.

'Armed only with the law and public support' was the theme of the 11th annual conference of the GRA, which opened in May 1989 in Bundoran, a windswept resort on Donegal's Atlantic coast. This was Jack's swansong.

In his opening presidential address, Christy Lonergan welcomed the six per cent pay increase which the GRA had just won, changes to the electoral register which had previously identified members and a new social welfare measure which improved the lot of injured members. 'We have also secured a satisfactory outcome to rent allowance claims and discussions with authorities are nearing completion on the establishment of a new consultative council.' He called for special armed units to escort cash-in-transit and condemned the removal of the Divisional Task Force in the light of recent arms shipments. He also criticised the lack of weapons training for members obliged to carry arms. Even specialised units were not undergoing regular firearms courses and lives were being put at serious risk, the GRA president said.

Gerry Collins, who would shortly be replaced as Justice Minister by Ray Burke, answered Lonergan rather sharply: 'Commissioner Crowley is examining proposals to reform the task forces, and is awaiting a written submission from the GRA.' There was another pointed exchange over members who had been infected with Hepatitis B on duty. Lonergan raised the grudging way in which a vaccine was being made available to gardaí, and he expressed shame that a guard taking it must sign a waiver removing liability from the state for side effects. Collins replied that the disclaimer was there on legal advice and that any garda who made a genuine case for being vaccinated would be reimbursed.

Commissioner Eugene Crowley told the conference: 'I am studying proposals to revive the Divisional Task Force in an effort to pinpoint IRA arms dumps across the country. And I am urging all our staff to step up the hunt for an estimated 1,000 Kalashnikov rifles and four tonnes of Semtex explosives. We need to be on "red alert" to detect the storage and movement of arms and munitions by subversives, and I must pay a heartfelt "congratulations" to our members in Donegal and Monaghan on their weekend seizures.' He went on to issue a special warning. 'The IRA will not hesitate to murder us as they have done in the past.' He said the increase in the number of assaults on members was also a matter of most serious concern. 'The statistics now show a yearly average of 1,378 cases of assault against on-duty gardaí – an increase of about 300% on the first recorded figures of 1972.'

Jack Marrinan spoke of preparation needed in advance of the opening of European borders in 1992. 'The force will take on many new responsibilities, including the replacement of custom checks at entry points on land and sea. Gardaí will need training and new skills including language skills', he said. 'It is well known that there are international links between terrorist groups, some of which have come together over the past few years and may have established an international strategy. In the past the IRA is known to have had contacts with other European terrorist groups and the Garda Síochána must be prepared to deal with this international dimension.'

On a lighter note Garda Jerome Twomey of Dublin's Pearse Street wanted uniformed members to be allowed to wear beards. As a bearded member he said other officers in Europe wore them. 'I don't think they encounter any problem in this regard', he said. He was supported by PJ Stone from Waterford, another bearded member who would later become the third general secretary of the GRA. A motion to that effect was passed.

It fell to an outsider, Gerry Collins, to make the speech marking Jack Marrinan's retirement.

'Jack is your friend, your colleague, and your principal representative and spokesman in looking after your interests, and you don't need me to spell out what he has achieved for you, the GRA, and indeed the Garda Síochána.

'There is no comparison between the conditions which obtained in the 1950 and 1960s and what you as present-day gardaí now enjoy. Believe me it was all down to this man – Jack Marrinan. Not all of the younger members here tonight fully appreciate that, but the older members will.' He said that many groups of workers had obtained improved pay and conditions in the recent past, but gardaí under Jack Marrinan had done way better than most.

'I know from my own discussions and meetings with Jack, and from what I have heard from those who had the task of facing him across the table at meetings, that Jack was one of the ablest and shrewdest negotiators around. Every claim he ever put forward– and he put forward a few in his time– he fought for with vigour, with tenacity, and if the occasion demanded it, with quite a bit of passion.

'He was a very formidable force when in full flight. But if he fought hard, he fought fair and honourably. He never lost sight of integrity or reason or logic, and his word was his bond. When you reached an agreement with Jack you had an agreement which would be honoured as far as he was concerned– there was no question of reneging or sidestepping anything that had been agreed.'

Collins, who would shortly become Minister for Foreign Affairs, acknowledged Mary Marrinan's support for her husband's heavy workload. There would be many tributes for the retiring GRA general secretary, but Collins, from Abbeyfeale, Co. Limerick, hit the right note when speaking about a neighbour's child, Jack Marrinan from Lisdoonvarna, Co. Clare.

Commissioner Eugene Crowley also spoke warmly of Jack. One sentence covered a great deal of ground. 'During his many years as your leader he made an outstanding contribution to the Garda Representative Association, in particular, and the Garda Síochána in general, and it will be difficult to imagine your association without him.' On all three counts Crowley was on the nail: representing members' interests, developing the force to make better use of its members' talents, and questioning how a post-Marrinan GRA would fare.

An editorial in the July 1989 issue of the *Garda Review* noted Jack's service to members and wished him well in retirement.

'On 2 July 1989 Garda Jack Marrinan retired as general secretary of the Garda Representative Association and as a member of An Garda Síochána. His retirement marks the end of an illustrious career in our force, during which he served for 27 years as General Secretary of our association.

'In 1961 he played a prominent role in the Macushla affair, which gave rise to the new Representative Body for Gardaí which provided new and improved negotiating rights in relation to welfare and conditions of service. In response to another crisis in the mid 70s he once again embarked on another reorganisation, which in 1978 gave birth to the present Garda Representative Association. This association provided representative committees in every district.

'In his 27 years of stewardship he formulated and introduced clearly identifiable improvements in pay, conditions of service and welfare. He stamped his professional and indelible mark on An Garda Síochána at home, and on many occasions represented us and our country abroad with great distinction.'

The GRA tribute might have mentioned the three major landmarks of his career, the Conroy, Ryan and Walsh inquiries. Taken together they put the force on a professional basis, rewarding members for their unique service and delivering considerable benefits to the public they served.

The man who became very annoyed on hearing a colleague described as 'just an ordinary country garda' – insisting that 'there's no such thing as an ordinary garda'– died on 12 May 2015 in Tallaght Hospital in Dublin.

An obituary in *The Irish Times* described him as 'the transformational figure in the modernising of the Garda Síochána at a time of great social and economic change. Jack Marrinan's role in driving change was much more significant than that of any of the ten Commissioners with whom he served', the newspaper said.

# TRIBUTES TO
# JACK MARRINAN

# Tribute to Jack Marrinan

## BY CONOR BRADY

This is the text of Conor Brady's tribute to Jack Marrinan, given at a retirement party on 19 October 1989 in Malahide, Co. Dublin. Brady was editor of *The Irish Times* between 1986 and 2002 and a founding member of the Garda Síochána Ombudsman Commission 2005-2011. He is the author of two books about the force and a series of crime fiction novels featuring a detective in the Dublin Metropolitan Police.

\* \* \*

The legacy of Jack Marrinan has been well chronicled. It is difficult to say who should be most grateful to Jack Marrinan for the fact of his existence in public life for the greater part of 30 years.

Perhaps it should be the gardaí of all ranks whose living standards and conditions of employment were transformed out of recognition by his remarkable skills. Or perhaps it should be the public service as a whole whose lot was directly improved in ratio with the successive awards made to An Garda Síochána.

Perhaps it has been some among the senior management of the force over years who were saved, time and again, from their own folly and short-sightedness by the harsh good sense that Jack Marrinan doled out in private to so many officers.

Perhaps it should be some of the civil servants whose insensitivity towards the force had so often had to be countered by his moderating intervention.

Perhaps it should be the public at large which now benefits from the operation of a police service which, for all its faults, is professionalised and streamlined to a degree that would have appeared impossible in the early 1960s when Jack Marrinan was in the process of building up the then Representative Body for Gardaí.

I first met Jack Marrinan in 1968 when researching a series of articles for *The Irish Times* which sought to look at an emerging story, garda grievances and the setting up of a commission under the late Judge Conroy to enquire into these. The series was called; 'The policeman's lot', and I had a head start on the subject as my father had been a garda superintendent, and although he died when I was quite young, I thought I had some knowledge of the social and political culture of the organisation.

Jack Marrinan opened my eyes. This was an organisation which was trapped in a time warp. The prevailing dogma was the 19th century code of conduct of the Royal Irish Constabulary. Pay was poor, discipline was harsh and morale low. Leadership in some instances at certain levels was jaded and the dead hand of the Department of Justice lay on everything.

In fact, Jack Marrinan had already won his first major victory– arguably his greatest– in getting the Conroy Commission. He gambled rightly that any group of clear-thinking outsiders, once they saw the internal reality of An Garda Síochána as it was, could not do other than recommend far reaching and radical reform.

Later, when I left *The Irish Times* to help relaunch the *Garda Review*, I had the opportunity to watch his modus operandi at first hand. I learned there was no single key to his extraordinary performance. Rather, if I may extend an analogy, he had a bunch of keys.

The first of these was professionalism. Whatever had to be done would be undertaken at the highest level of performance. If the organisation required the services of a consultant, a barrister or an accountant, it had the very best.

Jack had realised at an early stage how traditional assumptions were challenged, how new precedents were set, how old practices were broken down, how power was brokered, and how real change could be achieved. The garda case would no longer be stated, cap in hand, with muted appeals to the state not to forget its faithful servants in blue.

The second was sheer, unabating, back-breaking effort. He frequently broke the 100-hour week in the early 1970s, when I knew him in Phibsboro Tower. The day might start in the Garda Depot, move on to the Department of Justice, then to the office, and it could end anywhere and anytime: at midnight at Store Street, 4am on the Border or with a group of TDs in the Dáil bar at a time and at a hour best left unspecified.

And then there was the personal qualities. Razor sharp in debate, an instinctive and profound grasp of human psychology, a deep sense of humanity; never, ever forgetting the essential humanity of those with whom he had contact – the young garda with a problem, the distraught wife or parent of a member in difficulties, the over-wrought supervisor, or the hapless civil servant whose responsibilities have suddenly become a nightmare.

Above all the other qualities that I encountered in Jack Marrinan I will place those of integrity, loyalty and an unwavering sense of honour. I never knew him to be other than a straight dealer. I never knew him to break his word.

I never knew him to be disloyal to a friend, through fair circumstances or foul. I never knew him to yield an inch in defending the integrity of his members, the force as a whole and the state which it served, and I have never known him to relent in affirming the dignity and the honoured place which attach to the calling of a police officer in a free society.

As a newsman, there was aspects to Jack Marrinan's persona which infuriated me, although I have no doubt they will be regarded by others as virtues. In our 20 years of friendship I have gained many valuable insights; but I have never got a news story! Never once did I have a tip-off or a lead. He sat through lunch with me the day of the Crinnion-Wyman swoop in Dublin and never as much as winked- though he knew precisely the dramatic events which were unfolding.

I have recollections of the dark gloomy years when one operational embarrassment followed another and Jack met the media, putting a brave face on, saving officialdom from itself; often, in effect, defending the scarcely defensible. His principles were to defend the organisation, to reassure the often doubting public, to make his protest and to express his criticism in private.

What, if anything, can be counted on the negative side over these dramatic and successful years of Jack Marrinan's leadership? I believe the only significant target not reached was the re-definition of the force's role and function which was called for in the concluding paragraph of the Conroy Report in 1970. The exercise called for by Conroy remains as yet to be undertaken: a stripping down to fundamentals of what the force is about, a modern definition of is targets, objects and needs.

If the political will and vision to complete this exercise can ever be mobilised, the powers that be at that time will be short-sighted in the extreme if they do not accord Jack Marrinan a significant role in the process.

Finally, in running one's mind back over this exciting period one recalls the extraordinarily supportive structure of people who worked and lived around Jack. To attempt a complete list would be impossible. But two people in particular must be identified with his contribution. Jack Marrinan had the great support of his beloved wife, Mary (née Dempsey) through all his years as general secretary and indeed before. She was a tower of strength to him, right through the tough years, sharing the ups and downs. Ladylike and charming, she could also be steely, strong and direct when circumstances required it.

His other great support was Michael Conway, always at his right hand and always courteous and stalwart. Michael combined the roles of assistant general secretary and manager of the Garda Medical Aid scheme. Wise, generous, kind, conscientious and energetic, he was both a good friend and a vital colleague."

Conor Brady
Dublin, November 1989.

# My Dad

## BY CLARE MARRINAN

My father's job underlay our lives as kids. We knew that he was a garda. A lot of people thought he was Commissioner. He didn't have regular working hours like our friends' fathers had. He would often come home late or be interrupted with work at the weekends. I have memories of him bringing me into his office at weekends. While he worked away, I had fun running up and down the corridors playing with the photocopier and testing out the stationery.

He never talked about the seriousness of his job or details of what went on. He didn't have to; we knew he was an important man because of his appearances on the news and in the newspapers. We knew by the way he was stared at when out and about and by a kind of reverence shown to him by people when they interacted with him. Our unusual surname generally led to a 'Oh are you related to Jack Marrinan?' Of course we'd roll our eyes to heaven and tell them yes.

There were times when we weren't allowed to walk to or from school with our friends. I did walk home one day after being told I'd be collected, and I couldn't understand why my mother was so upset. It was in later years that I found out that the family had been advised to be vigilant because of threats to our lives. As I understand it there were times when my father had to check under his car for incendiary devices before travelling. I later found out that the IRA had a dossier on us and contained details such as where we went to school and what we looked like.

On a night out with friends in my early 20s I suffered a minor assault. At the garda station afterwards, a garda told me that he couldn't believe how much I had changed since he was assigned to keep an eye out for me when I was a kid. Something I was completely unaware of.

Once my father was contacted by an anonymous but very credible source, warning him that my boyfriend at the time was a senior member of the IRA and that they suspected that he was going out with me to get access to him. That was a difficult time for me.

Dad was very loving and affectionate, I adored him. He was very protective of us; I only ever remember him getting very cross with me once. We weren't allowed out as late as our friends. My brother once argued with him that at 16 years old he was the legal age to get married, but why was he not allowed to go the disco. As teenagers, we had a one-storey extension at the back of our house: it jutted out under my bedroom and it came in very handy for creeping out at night when our parents thought we were tucked up in bed.

Dad was very intelligent, insightful and wise. He had this amazing talent of being able to understand a situation or problem holistically. He looked beneath the details that were provided and seemed to recognise a depth to a situation that perhaps no one else could recognise. Watching the news he'd express a different angle to a story that wasn't being told. As his daughter, he was the perfect person to go to if there was a problem, never judgemental and always had the right solution. Over the years many people would come to him for advice and take him into their confidence.

He loved people calling to the house, and a bit like Mrs. Doyle in Father Ted, he'd always make sure they were fed.

He had natural leadership qualities: at a very young age he was made principal of a national school in Co. Clare. Dad told me the story about how he became the manager of a tea shop at 16 years old. He went to England (Manchester perhaps) during a summer to earn a few quid, and got a job washing dishes in a tea shop. When a customer ordered their tea at the till, they were asked to leave a small deposit on the teapot. Their deposit would be refunded once they returned the teapot when they were finished. Mostly the customers just left the teapot on the table and didn't collect the deposit. The manager of the shop at the time was out for a while and Dad was asked to clean tables. The owner noticed that the takings had increased during this time. It turned out that the manager had been pocketing the deposits from the customers who left the teapots on the table. Dad was promoted to manager. Many years later, he was awarded the 'Freedom of Boston' in Massachusetts. He said it was for 'helping them out with policing matters'. He was also invited to address the United Nations.

My father came from a humble and loving family. He really loved his parents and siblings. He was very proud of being a member of the family and being from Lisdoonvarna and being a Clareman. His siblings were successful. The women were independent, strong and successful, running their own businesses and having careers in teaching and nursing. Perhaps these were some of the qualities he admired in my mother- she owned her own hairdressers, ran a small catering company and a clothes boutique. I believe that people thought Dad was paid a lot more than he actually was for the position he held, when in fact our mother's earnings supplemented his income.

He was a kind man and made time for people from all walks of life. I can remember multiple instances when he'd make time for strangers and unfortunate people; he always seemed to lift their spirits. When travellers used to call to the door he would stay and chat with them for a while, and of course give them something to eat. I remember he brought some traveller kids off the street into my birthday party one year; a couple of guests left. I didn't notice– we were having fun.

Another memory I have is of one Christmas day in the early 1980s, Dad was told of some homeless people living on the railway tracks in Dun Laoghaire. He asked me to accompany him to pay them a visit. I remember I was dressed in a lovely warm pink woollen jumper, a new pair of jeans and gold-coloured shoes embellished with pearlized beading. We walked through the brambles along the tracks and came across something truly tragic. A young couple were wrapped in blankets inside a small dark tent. The woman had a dead baby swathed in her arms rocking to and fro. The man had a look of bewilderment and grief on his face. The baby had been born in the tent earlier. Dad bought them food and cigarettes. On the way home Dad stopped at a garda station to report the incident and get help for the couple. Dad couldn't have anticipated exactly what we were going to come across that day. He wanted to teach me how other people lived and to realise how fortunate we were. I often think about how there was no room in the inn for that couple and while instead of celebrating the birth of Jesus each Christmas, they mourned the loss of their child.

Dad was a republican and active member of Fianna Fáil. He was the chairperson of the local *cumann* for many years. He turned down a promise of a senior Dáil position if he ran for Fine Gael in an election.

After representing An Garda Síochána at an official cross border event in Northern Ireland he was summoned by one of his superiors. There had been a complaint about him. He was reprimanded for insulting the hosts by refusing to toast the Queen at the end of the speeches. He was told not to let it happen again. Being a republican, this did not sit well with him. He was stuck between a rock and a hard place. The other people at the event who didn't toast the Queen were Sinn Féin, and he did not want to be associated with them. Being in a dilemma as what to do at the next event, he got advice – from (nationalist politician) Austin Currie, I think. The next time he stood up and smiled at everyone making sure not to take a sip from the glass. Another situation negotiated successfully.

He was very fond of his GRA staff at Phibsboro Tower. Many of them were like family to him and stayed in touch after he left. A friend and I worked there for a few weeks on placement during transition year. It was a busy and pleasant workplace. I got the impression that the staff had a great deal of admiration and fondness for Dad.

# Childhood memories

## BY DAVID MARRINAN

My earliest memories are not of my father but of my mother and the business she ran with her sister in Crumlin. This is most likely because Dad was away a lot and when he was at home, he worked very hard and very late. This may have influenced me in parenting decisions taken for my own family, where I took a back seat financially to my wife and mainly stayed at home with the boys, undertaking part-time and charity work over career.

Early memories of Dad involve driving to Lisdoonvarna to spend several weeks of the summer staying with my grandfather, grandmother, and uncles. I was always amazed that he could remember all the directions to get us to his hometown. I also remember Dad telling me that his father had died in 1969 but I don't remember making the journey to Co. Clare for the funeral, so I don't believe I did.

I do not recall Dad being big into sport, but I found out later he did play in goal as a youth for his parish and he was an 'alickadoo' (chairman I think) of Trinity CLG. He brought me to three sporting events growing up, just three but all major. In 1977 he brought me to Lansdowne Road to watch Ireland narrowly lose to England. Later that year we drove to Semple Stadium for the Munster hurling final featuring Clare, and finally in the autumn of that same year, the All-Ireland football final where Dublin defeated Armagh. The football final would have been the biggest thrill for me then as I knew all the names and expected the Dubs to bring the Sam Maguire cup to every school and housing estate in the county.

Things would change as I was sent to a rugby school, and this became my major sporting interest. We did attend the 1995 hurling final to watch his home county Clare lift the Liam McCarthy cup, but even though he got me a ticket we were not together. He once came to see me play rugby in a match against a garda team. I presume he was supporting me. I brought him up to the club after the game and introduced him to the coach, former Ireland and Lions captain Ciaran Fitzgerald. Ciaran shook his hand and said "Ah, David's dad". After a lifetime of being "Jack Marrinan's son" that was a first for me, though Fitzy may have had his tongue firmly in his cheek.

Afterwards we were having a drink with Ireland out half Paul Dean and his now wife Lorraine, and I still can see the utter shock on my father's face when she went up to buy a round of drinks. Women didn't buy drinks! He left early and I stayed on for the disco, and when I returned my Mam gave out to me for "sending your father home in that state". He was giggling as she scolded me. He seemed perfectly ok, and to be honest I can't remember ever seeing him negatively affected by alcohol.

He played golf, and I remember caddying for him. To me he looked awkward, and the ball never flew high, but the main thing was it was always straight, and I reckon that's how he collected his fair share of prizes.

He enjoyed music, but strangely for a Clareman he was more into jazz and classical music than traditional Irish music. You would be more likely to find records by Oscar Peterson or Ella Fitzgerald in his collection than the Tulla Ceili Band. His father played the trombone and I think he got a kick when I ended up playing that instrument in the school band.

The nine o'clock news bulletin was very important in our house, not so much for us kids but for Dad. It was never missed. If he wasn't home to watch the news, it probably meant he was on the news and we had to hold a tape recorder up to the telly to tape him so he could listen to how he sounded later. The Irish news always clashed with the latest BBC comedy and so I would have to get all the jokes second hand the next day in school.

Another thing I remember is the phone never stopped ringing unless he left it off the hook. Press, TV and whoever else wanted to talk. Our number was in the phone directory, so we got the odd airing of grievances, too. Once I listened through a rant from a member of the public lambasting the guards. I never passed on the message as I thought it may upset him. Now I have no idea why I thought he would be that soft.

He was a strict parent, and I was told I could not go to discos until I was 16. But by the time I was 16 the Stardust fire had happened and that got pushed out to 18. I felt very hard done by, as all my friends would be talking of the *craic* and I was missing out. I remember being very angry at the time.

He did allow me to go 'wild camping' with a few friends when I was in 2nd or 3rd year in school, to Manor Kilbride on the Liffey. On the second day he drove the whole family up to visit. I don't know if he found it funny, I must say I do now, but I was mortified at the time. Thankfully they didn't stay for long. Years later I locked my car keys and infant son in the car at the same place and rang Dad to come and help—giving the directions 'remember that place I was camping, well...'

He travelled a lot by plane, and this used to upset his mother, as she was terrified of flying, and she had me terrified of flying. I didn't do a lot of flying but I ended up being terrified for him. My

Granny had instilled a dread that his plane would crash, and I was always worried until he returned home. My other memory of his travels was driving to the airport to see him off, at times watching as he ran out to the plane to be last to board just before the doors of the plane were closed: always running late.

Sometimes he would take me into his office in Phibsboro. I even have vague memories of an earlier time when he was based in the Phoenix Park. I got to know some people there. Part of the routine was a Knickerbocker Glory in the diner below the towers in Phibsboro. He was always having a laugh; being his son I didn't find him all that funny, but my friends used to think he was hilarious.

I think it is fair to say he was a bit of a snob– certainly with regard to education. He did try to get me to move schools to Roscrea from Templeogue College, but I was having none of it as their rugby team was well below ours and I had a great group of friends in school. Also, when I chose a science course at the Dublin Institute of Technology in Kevin Street, he wasn't pleased until he found out the course led to an honours degree from Trinity College, his alma mater. Though science was not his chosen path he must have instilled something scientific in my brother John and I. We never missed science and nature TV programmes. I remember watching *The World Around Us*, *Life on Earth*, *The Ascent of Man* and others like that with him. I don't remember him being much of a reader of fiction– another trait I have inherited from him.

When I moved to London after college, he and Mam came over to visit once. Then before I left for Australia, Dad came over again to visit me in London. His health wasn't great. He had been scheduled to receive a quadruple bypass– he never told me about it. He had the operation and was recovered by the time I got the news over in Australia. Later I realised he wanted to see me before he went in for surgery just in case but didn't want to burden me with the worry.

At home he had never been much involved in domestic chores, but in retirement he did try his hand at preparing dinners. I wasn't around much then, but he certainly got by. In later years, when I would drop by with our boys the first thing he would do was take out a pan and start cooking them sausages. That's their strongest memory of him. When I was a child he worked late and was away a lot but when he was there– he was there for us.

# Tributes to Jack Marrinan

I was 'present and correct' at the Macushla. I had witnessed many street protests but there was nothing compared to the police frenzy that evening. There were several agendas with the usual mouths and slags of the job taking over with extraordinary outbursts. In truth I thought that some should have been arrested. There was also a political angle to it until Jack Marrinan took charge. He had a cut about him and a special aura. He put forward reasoned argument, was cool under pressure and used vocabulary and phrases which were a lot more coherent and plausible than the ranting of those spouting diatribes. Even the most outspoken members calmed down and listened. '

*John Collins, GRA member and Jack's friend*

\* \* \*

John Hynes was a Roscommon youngster in the 1970s. He recalls watching television with his postman father as Jack Marrinan was being interviewed by Brian Farrell about the Conroy Commission. His father remarked that Jack Marrinan was the greatest man that ever joined the force. John Hynes went on to become an acclaimed crime detective in Dublin and the Division of Roscommon-Galway.

*Conversation with Sergeant John Hynes 2014.*

The Conroy Commission turned the job on its head. It was such a metamorphosis that almost a half century later retired members consider it a defining moment in their careers. Doubtless there will be other major developments in garda industrial relations, but it is unlikely that anything to equal the scope and scale of Conroy will ever again be achieved. I also believe Jack Marrinan's overall contribution to the betterment of the force was significant, even memorable. He proved himself to be a man of more than ordinary capacity. Cool under pressure, he made the art of negotiation his forte. His skill at handling large open meetings was unmatched.

*Eddie O'Donovan, GRA Executive 1980s.*

\*    \*    \*

I was elected to the Central Executive Committee from 1983 to 1990. In the mid 1980s, along with Jack and Matt Givens, I was a guest of the Berlin police force. In 1990, following Jack's retirement and in company of Jack and Donal O Gallachóir, we went back. The Berlin Wall had just gone, and it was an amazing sight. The Germans were mad about Jack. They sought his advice when they were starting their own police association. I was amazed at the ease in which he integrated with police from various jurisdictions. He seemed to be on first name terms with many. His openness and genuine charm were unbelievable.

*Tony Fagan, GRA Representative, Wexford.*

\*    \*    \*

In my opinion Jack was the best negotiator any organisation ever had. My recollection is that he raised garda pay by the equivalent of two civil service grades. He had pride in the force and would never support any unsavoury behaviour by any of his members. He was respected– almost admired– by everyone of the opposition; notwithstanding that he was a thorn in their side most of the time.

*Paddy Terry was a senior civil servant negotiating with*
*Jack Marrinan on behalf of the Department of Justice,*

\* \* \*

Jack Marrinan had a close working relationship with Adrian Hardiman who was involved during the Ryan Commission. Hardiman possessed one of the most insightful legal minds of his generation. Privately I recall them having great verbal battles firing words and arguments from all angles. Eventually, Adrian would shrug and say 'You might be right there Jack".

*John Durcan, President of the Association of*
*Garda Sergeants and Inspectors, 1986 - 1990.*

\* \* \*

I first encountered Jack in 1981, when as a young sergeant I was attending my first AGSI annual conference. As the years rolled on, I became increasingly involved and ended up working closely with him from 1987. For the next two years, there was hardly a day that we did not talk on some matter or other. He always gave great advice and never misled. He was very astute, always played the long game, and was widely connected. He loved a good story, could debate any topic, prepared assiduously, and had the stamina of a marathon runner, and staying up late burning the midnight oil was never a problem.

The words of Henry Longfellow in his poem "Toiling upward in the Night".[62] come to mind when reflecting on the many attributes of Jack.

*The heights by great men reached*
*and kept were not attained by sudden flight,*
*But they, while their companions slept,*
*were toiling upward in the night.*

*We have not wings, we cannot soar;*
*but we have feet to scale and climb,*
*By slow degrees, by more and more,*
*the cloudy summit of our time.*

Jack reached the summit in his time, left a fantastic legacy and I am proud to call him my friend.

*George Maybury, former AGSI General Secretary*

\* \* \*

Jack Marrinan has retired from An Garda Síochána, and from his position as General Secretary of the Garda Representative Association. Thousands of members have also retired over the years, but it is fair to say that very few, if indeed anyone, will have left such an indelible mark on the Force.

---

62 Henry Wadsworth Longfellow (1807–1882) was an American poet and educator.

I worked closely with Jack for over twenty years, and I know what he has done for all gardai and their families. When I joined him in 1965, the fledgling Garda Representative Body had only got off the ground. At the time, there was so much work to be done that it took a man of unconquerable courage, unlimited energy and undiminished vision to make inroads into the hugely powerful organisation that was An Garda Síochána.

I often think it's a pity that the members who joined in the 70 and 80s never experienced the conditions under which the previous generations survived.

Unlimited hours with no compensation, time off at the whim of authority, very poor accommodation that had to be occupied and widows and children of members who died were abandoned and left in very poor circumstances.

Jack had no equal in preparing submissions on any subject and in following them up across a table at conciliation. His submissions to the Conroy and Ryan Commissions as well as the Walsh Committee are monuments to him. His time was given so generously, so much that if you were looking for him, the last place you would look was his home.

I believe that no association or trade union looked after his members as well as the GRB and GRA under Jack's guidance.

When pension and insurance schemes became available to us, he negotiated from the front and went around the country meeting members and encouraging them to join up. As a result, the majority did become involved which in itself is a great tribute to him.

Finally, on behalf of all members, I wish Jack and his beloved Mary and family many happy years in retirement.

*Michael Conway, GRA Assistant General Secretary and*
*Secretary of the Garda Medical Aid*

# Acknowledgements

I am indebted to the Garda Representative Association (GRA) and Retired Garda Members Association (GSRMA), for support along with Saint Raphael's and Saint Paul's Garda credit unions. Sincere thanks also to John Greene, Conor Brady and the indispensable Kieran Fagan whose expertise was invaluable.

The friendship and support of Mary Marrinan and her family has been central to my efforts. I hope they will find a fair account of Jack's life and achievements in these pages.

My thanks are due also to innumerable garda colleagues, who gave their time and thought without reservation, as well as those who provided photographs and other memorabilia. I thank them all for helping me to record the good times and the bad times we saw together.

A fair wind brought me to Currach Books where Garry, Alba and their staff steered me safely through my four-decade voyage. Approaching the centenary year of An Garda Síochána, it is noteworthy that Garry's grandfather, Tim, was a first-time joiner, and his father, Michael, continued the family tradition until the end of the last century.

# Sources consulted

Allen, Gregory. *The Garda Síochána*. (Dublin: Gill and Macmillan, 1999).

Beresford, David. *Ten Men Dead*. (London: Harper Collins ,1987).

Bew, Paul and Gillespie, Gordon. *Northern Ireland: Chronology of the Troubles 1968-1993*. (Dublin: Gill and Macmillan, 1993).

Brady, Conor. *Guardians of the Peace* (Dublin: Gill and Macmillan, 1974).

Brady, Conor. *The Guarding of Ireland* (Dublin: Gill and Macmillan, 2014).

Carey, Tim. *Mountjoy: The Story of a Prison*. (Cork: Collins Press, 2005).

Doyle, Tim. *Get Up Them Steps* (Dublin: TJD Publications, 2001).

Gunn, Eamonn. *Sit Down Guard* (Louth: Choice Publishing, 2013).

FitzGerald, Garrett. *All In A Life* (Dublin: Gill and Macmillan, 1991).

Hanley, Brian and Millar, Scott. *The Lost Revolution* (Dublin: Penguin Books, 2009).

Heney, Michael. *The Arms Crisis of 1970* (London: Head of Zeus, 2020).

Hussey, Gemma. *At the Cutting Edge* (Dublin: Gill and Macmillan, 1990).

Kenny, Ivor. *Last Word* (Cork: Oak Tree Press, 2006).

Knatchbull, Timothy. *From A Clear Blue Sky* (London: Arrow Books, 2009).

McNiffe, Liam. *A History of the Garda Síochána*. (Dublin: Wolfhound Press, 1999).

O'Connor, Mary T. *On The Beat* (Dublin: Gill and Macmillan, 2005).

## ADDITIONAL RESOURCES

National Archives of Ireland, National Library of Ireland, *The Irish Times* on-line archive, Dublin City Library Service, Dun Laoghaire-Rathdown libraries, archive copies of Irish local and national newspapers, *Garda Review* and other garda publications, and Marrinan family papers.

# Want to keep reading?

Currach Books has a whole range of books to explore.
As an independent Irish publisher, dedicated to producing quality
Irish interest books, we publish a wide variety of titles including
history, poetry, biography, photography and lifestyle.

All our books are available through
**www.currachbooks.com**
and you can find us on Twitter, Facebook and Instagram to discover
more of our fantastic range of books. You can sign up to our
newsletter through the website for the latest news about events,
sales and to keep up to date with our new releases.

@currachbooks

@CurrachBooks

currach_books

CURRACH
BOOKS ·